MULTINATIONAL CORPORATIONS

MULTINATIONAL CORPORATIONS
and the
EMERGING WORLD ORDER

LEWIS D. SOLOMON

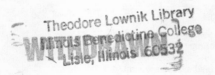
National University Publications
KENNIKAT PRESS // 1978
Port Washington, N. Y. // London

Manufactured in the United States of America

Published by
Kennikat Press Corp.
Port Washington, N.Y./London

Library of Congress Cataloging in Publication Data

Solomon, Lewis D
    Multinational corporations and the emerging world order.

    (National university publications)
    Includes bibliographical references and index.
    1. International business enterprises.
2. Underdeveloped areas—Investments, Foreign.
3. International economic relations. 4. Food
and Agriculture Organization of the United Nations.
Industry Cooperative Programme. I. Title.
HD2755.5S65   338.8'8   77-17904
ISBN 0-8046-9196-7

CONTENTS

PART THREE
THE IMPACT OF M N Cs ON DEVELOPING COUNTRIES

PART FOUR
INDUSTRY COOPERATIVE PROGRAMME OF THE F A O

ACKNOWLEDGMENTS

I gratefully acknowledge the financial assistance of the Travel and Maintenance Program of the Carnegie Endowment for International Peace and the University of Missouri-Kansas City Research Council in connection with my research activities on the Industry Cooperative Programme of the Food and Agriculture Organization of the United Nations. I also wish to thank Judith Sharp, my research assistant in the fall of 1976, for her help in preparing the footnotes. Portions of Charters 15 and 16 appeared in the summer 1977 issue of the *Texas Journal of International Law*.

MULTINATIONAL CORPORATIONS

ABOUT THE AUTHOR

Lewis D. Solomon is Professor of Law at George Washington University National Law Center. He received his law degree from Yale Law School in 1966 and has authored numerous articles in legal periodicals.

INTRODUCTION

The rise of the multinational corporation as a global force with implications for home and host nations and the international system ranks as one of the key features of the second half of the twentieth century. After World War II the United States established the political, economic and military framework for a world order. Under the hegemony of the United States, multinational corporations located in the industrialized world, first those headquartered in the United States and then those from Western Europe and Japan, created subsidiary entities in other nations. Giant firms came to rely on the seemingly limitless expansion of a world system characterized by relatively free flow of investment and goods among nations and an abundant supply of cheap energy. Corporate managers viewed the world as an open market for a burgeoning consumer society resting on a continuance of stable political arrangements that would permit corporate expansion.

In the 1970s, mention of the terms "multinational corporation" and "world capitalist system" usually evokes one of two responses: bountiful praise on the part of the executives and other representatives of giant firms, or condemnation of corporations for producing every ill befalling the globe. Although not detached from the problem of corporate power, this book strives for a more balanced approach and focuses on the impact of multinational firms on the economic, cultural and political processes of developed and developing nations. In addition to analyzing the national, regional and transnational means for controlling and regulating global private sector organizations, specific policy recommendations are formulated regarding the accountability of multinational corporations.

Apologists for multinational corporations point to the ability of such firms to transmit and allocate resources as part of a hierarchical global organization. The giant entities mobilize and combine capital with effective management. The efficiency advantages of multinational firms, that is, the use of resources to achieve economic growth, are stressed. Specific benefits derived from the multinational form of business organization allegedly include optimizing resources on worldwide levels, transferring modern technology and managerial skills, supplying capital to meet investment demands abroad, bringing products to satisfy consumer wants and training work forces in different nations. Global firms, it is maintained, provide benefits for both the home nation and the host countries in which the subsidiaries are located. By helping tie the world together, multinational enterprises may also lead to a reduction in conflicts among nations.

The influence multinational corporations have exerted and will exert on economic and social processes in various nation-states and in the entire world order demands that we understand the size of global giants, the concepts underlying big business strategy, the motivating forces behind foreign corporate expansion and the modes of financing this expansion. After first elucidating these elements, this study next analyzes problems that have arisen in industrialized nations as a result of the multinational system. Problem areas include economic challenges, namely, the obsolescence of significant portions of traditional economic theories regarding a competitive market and the Keynesian fiscal and monetary stabilizers; the possibility that foreign direct investment by multinational firms may have adversely affected the balance of payments position and created currency instability for various nation-states; and the rapid rise of transnational commercial banking and an unregulated Eurodollar market. Also analyzed are the specter of a technology gap, claims that global firms have reduced the number of jobs and redistributed income flows in home nations, and the involvement of multinational firms in the political processes of home and host nations. National and transnational remedies for these problem areas are considered, focusing on the need for, and the limited prospect of, transnational action.

The fiercest denunciations of global firms have emanated from developing nations. The Third World views the present international capitalist system based on multinational corporations as unacceptable. A sense of dependency, flowing from deep feelings of having been ignored and exploited in both the colonial and post-colonial periods, underlies the quest of Third World nations for a far-reaching redistribution of wealth, income, status and power. After considering specific economic, cultural and political indicia of dependency, this study will analyze the variety of means used by the Third World to redress the position enjoyed by multinational firms and the Western world. The means employed include improved bargaining techniques, national and regional political action, collective economic efforts and proposed transnational approaches.

The success of the Organization of Petroleum Exporting Countries altered the global balance of power by challenging the existing world capitalist system. The nuclear stalemate, the proliferation of nuclear weapons, and the efficacy of guerilla insurgency campaigns neutralized American military power and rendered political power less effective. Power on the international scene has, therefore, come to rest increasingly on the control of scarce resources and the ability to construct viable blocs of producer nations. How Third World nations will use their power is unclear.

As the Third World emerges from dependency, the shape of the future world order remains uncertain. Either the promise of a meaningful dialogue between industrialized nations and Third World countries or else the fearful threat of a confrontation overhangs an assessment of possible future changes in the world system. The means of facilitating the global transfer of wealth, income, status and power and the possibility of building a synergistic system that will yield benefits for developing nations, developed countries and multinational corporations are considered here. As an example of a synergic approach to transnational conflict resolution, the final part of this book critically analyzes the past efforts and the project possibilities for a catalytic organization, the Industry Cooperative Programme of the Food and Agriculture Organization of the United Nations, which attempts to bridge the gap between multinational agribusiness corporations and the food needs of developing nations. Efforts to transcend the polarity between corporate self-interest and the social needs of developing nations raise the hope that an ongoing dialogue in many forums may lead to new projects and institutional arrangements. However, a mismatch may exist between current corporate expertise and the economic and social needs of the Third World.

Implicit in a discussion of assessing and sharing the costs and benefits of multinational corporations and in structuring and implementing mechanisms to make decisions in these areas is the need to formulate the goals of the emerging world order. The present period of transition may provide an unparalleled opportunity for a fundamental reexamination of the economic, political and social institutions—multinational corporations, nation-states, regional political groupings, economic blocs and transnational arrangements—that produce, control and distribute wealth, income, status and power. The mechanisms for allocating and regulating economic and political power may undergo significant change. The possibility exists, however remote, that the new order may rest on the creation of organizations and institutions promoting an equitable distribution of the world's bounty, furthering human growth and enabling individuals to realize their potential. Others, it is hoped, may be led to rethink the present structural arrangements and investigate various alternatives, including the need for and the possibilities of achieving a new set of more self-contained economic, political and social institutions.

PART ONE

AN OVERVIEW OF M N Cs

1

THE ECONOMIC SIGNIFICANCE OF M N Cs

The key to the internationalization of business during the post-World War II period was not the traditional export or import of goods, but foreign direct investment. Direct investment, as opposed to portfolio investment (the purchase of stock or debt in a corporation), involves a more lasting commitment and a greater degree of control over the means of production and distribution. Although American firms took the lead in attempting to stake out a position of permanent influence in foreign markets, European and Japanese enterprises have increasingly undertaken foreign direct investment. Based on a continuation of the growth of international operations at twice the economic growth rates of industrialized nations, predictions abound that the foreign operations of worldwide multinational enterprises will reach enormous proportions by the end of the twentieth century. The specter exists that multinational corporations, if unchecked, may account for more than half of the world's industrial output and own an overwhelming proportion of all productive assets in non-Communist nations, with control concentrated in as few as two or three hundred giant enterprises.[1]

The importance of foreign direct investment for the economic posture of the world, nation-states in the West and the Third World, and multinational corporations may be gained by analyzing several statistics: (1) a comparison of the worldwide sales of multinational corporations with gross world product; (2) a comparison of the sales of leading multinational corporations with the gross national products of various countries; (3) an assessment of the growth in value of foreign direct investment and the geographical allocation of such investment by global firms; and (4) the significance of the profits from foreign operations for American multinational corporations and banks. Estimates indicate that in 1973 the international production, that is, production subject to foreign control, measured by sales of the foreign subsidiaries of multinational corporations totaled $450 billion out of a gross world product of $3 trillion.[2] American firms generated approximately one-half of the $450 billion total.

By the early 1970s the value added by all multinational corporations (including production in their home countries) had reached one-fifth of the world gross national product, excluding centrally planned economies.[3] The volume of international production by multinational corporations in non-Communist nations also exceeded the aggregate exports by companies in such countries. International production reached approximately $330 billion in 1971, as against total exports by all non-Communist nations of $310 billion.[4]

A comparison of the sales of the leading multinational corporations with the gross national products of various countries is equally impressive. In 1973 the sales of General Motors were bigger than the gross national product of Switzerland, Pakistan or South Africa; while the sales of Royal Dutch Shell surpassed the gross national products of Iran, Venezuela or Turkey.[5] Comparisons showing the annual sales by multinational corporations in excess of the gross national product of all but the most highly industrialized nations indicate the political and economic power of multinational enterprises. Apart from national, regional and transnational efforts to countervail the power of global firms, these comparisons are, in part, misleading. For example, most multinational firms achieve the bulk of their sales in their home nations; the sales figures include corporate sales of raw materials, parts and services; and the comparisons with various oil-rich nations are now outdated.

The aggregate worldwide book value of foreign direct investment in 1971 conservatively exceeded $165 billion. United States corporations accounted for more than one-half of this total, with nearly four-fifths of the aggregate owned by firms based in the United States, the United Kingdom, France and the Federal Republic of Germany. Out of the $165 billion figure, foreign direct investment by American corporations accounted for $96 billion, or 52% of the total, while firms based in the United Kingdom recorded $24 billion in foreign direct investment, or 14.5% of the aggregate. Corporations in France and the Federal Republic of Germany had foreign direct investments of, respectively, $9.5 billion (5.8% of the total) and $7.2 billion (4.4% of the total).[6]

In addition to the aggregate size of the book value of foreign direct investment by Western corporations, the post–World War II trend in foreign direct investment, as illustrated by statistics for American corporations, evidences an unmistakable growth pattern. The book value of all investments by United States firms abroad rose from $7.2 billion in 1946 to $11.79 billion in 1950, to $31.82 billion in 1960 and reached $78.18 billion in 1970. By the end of 1975, foreign direct investment by American firms had leaped to more than $133 billion, a 12.1% gain over the 1974 figures.[7] Beginning in 1929, investment by American firms shifted away from mining and smelting, trade, services and other categories to foreign direct investments in the petroleum and manufacturing fields. Within the manufacturing sector changes also occurred. Comparing the years 1964–1966 with 1970–1972, the share of overseas investments by the chemical industry dropped from 25 to 19% of the total for the manufacturing sector, and investments by the transportation industry declined from 25 to 15%. Gains were recorded by the electrical and nonelectrical machinery industries, which rose from 24 to 32% of the aggregate figure for manufacturing.[8]

The geographical allocation of foreign direct investments by multinational enterprises is important. By the late 1960s, two-thirds of the estimated book value of foreign direct investment by multinational corporations of all nations was located in areas of advanced economic levels with similar institutional and social structures. Only one-third of the estimated book value of foreign direct investment was in developing countries, with 18% of the total in the Western Hemisphere, 6% in Africa and 5% and 3%, respectively, in Asia and the Middle East.[9]

These aggregate figures for investment allocation fail to reveal the varying levels of investment by global companies from different nations in developing countries. By 1969 United States multinational corporations placed only approximately one-quarter to one-third of the book value of their foreign direct investment in developing countries and the balance in developed countries. Investments in developing countries comprised 38% and 60%, respectively, of the total foreign direct investment by United Kingdom and Japanese multinational firms in the late 1960s. Corporations developed different spheres of investment interest in the Third World. Japanese companies concentrated their investments among developing countries in Central and South America and Asia. For United Kingdom firms, 60% of their total investment in developing nations is equally divided between Asia and Africa, with 26% in the Western Hemisphere and 13% in the Middle East. Seventy percent of the foreign direct investment by American corporations in the Third World is funneled into Central and South America.[10]

The trend of investments overseas by American corporations can also be examined over a period of time. After World War II developing and developed countries shared American investments nearly equally. By the late 1960s the ratio tilted decisively in favor of investments in industrialized nations. American firms invested $25 billion (32%) in developing countries at the end of 1970, as compared with 42% of total book value in 1960. This shift is exemplified by investments in Latin America, which, while growing in absolute dollars, declined from one-third of the total in 1950 to 19% by 1970.[11] After 1950 investments by American firms increased in relative importance in Western Europe, particularly among the members of the European Common Market. This trend toward American investments in developed countries reflects the market orientation of multinational corporations, which seek outlets for their products in countries with larger markets and higher per capita income and consumption. Corporations perceived developing countries as lacking skilled labor and political stability and manifesting an "unfavorable" attitude toward the activities of global giants. Low-wage labor may not be low-cost labor because of productivity problems, which include the costs of training, high turnover and workers' inability to deal with a factory environment.[12]

Despite the difficulties in dealing with Third World governments and the arguments advanced in favor of expansion in industrialized countries, the importance of investments by United States firms in developing countries should not be minimized. Such investments generate critical raw materials for extractive industries and ultimately the entire society. The rate of return on investments, generally in extractive industries, in the Middle East, Asia and Africa exceeds, by a factor of three or four, investments in Canada and Europe.[13] Approximately 5 percent of total United States corporate profits are derived from Americans investments in developing nations.[14] Rising labor skill and income levels enhance the desirability of locating manufacturing plants in such countries to serve national and regional markets and for export purposes. Cost advantages, such as labor or raw materials, may continue to play an important role in the shift of manufacturing operations to developing countries. Increased labor costs and social troubles in Europe are lessening the allure of plants in Italy, France and Spain, as are demands by European governments that a subsidiary of a multinational enterprise must continue to provide jobs even in the face of slack demand. The devaluation of the dollar reduces the ability of expenditures by European subsidiaries to generate new capacity. Larger idle productive capacity in developed countries may, moreover, restrain the expansion of plant and equipment for manufacturing operations in such nations, even in the face of improving economic conditions.[15]

Despite gains averaging 10% per year in book value of foreign direct investments by American firms during the twentieth century, the accumulated book value of United States corporate direct investment abroad (including reinvested profits) bears a rather constant relationship to the gross national product of the United States. The accumulated book value of United States direct investment abroad (including reinvested profits) equalled 7.3% of the gross national product of the United States in 1914 and again in 1929. By 1946 the book value of American direct investments overseas had plummeted, only to rise in 1966 and 1970 to 7.3% and 8.0%, respectively, of the gross national product of the United States.[16] But the importance of foreign direct investment cannot be judged by aggregate figures comparing gross national product and accumulated book values. The gross national product figure may be misleading, as it includes soaring federal, state and local governmental expenditures and a variety of service endeavors.

The ability of foreign operations to generate profits for American corporations, particularly in comparison with more static domestic operations, may provide a better measure of the importance of foreign direct investment. The difficulty of accurately estimating profits from overseas operations must be recognized. Foreign earnings may be undervalued for tax and other purposes through a variety of mechanisms. Foreign operations of United States–based firms have generated at least 25% and more likely 30% to 40% of total net corporate profits.[17] For certain corporations, particularly firms in oligopolistic industries, profits generated by foreign direct investments are of considerable, if not overwhelming, importance. For example, corporations that regularly derive in excess of 50% of their net profits from foreign sources include Exxon, Mobil Oil, IBM, F. W. Woolworth, CPC International, National Cash Register, Uniroyal, Pfizer, Gillette and Black and Decker. Foreign operations generate more than 40% of the net profits of a number of companies, including Standard Oil of California, Dow Chemical, H. J. Heinz, and Chesebrough Ponds. Overseas activities also constitute a key profit center for leading commercial banks in the United States. Led by Citibank Corp. which derives over 60% of its net profits from foreign operations, foreign earnings for other major banks, including Chase Manhattan, Manufacturers Hanover, Morgan Guaranty and Bankers Trust, have approached or exceeded 50% of total annual earnings.[18]

In addition to American firms, Western European and Japanese corporations are actively involved in the direct foreign investment process. From 1965 to 1971 the growth of foreign direct investments by German and Japanese firms tripled that of overseas investments made by American corporations. West German companies increased their worldwide foreign direct investment stake tenfold, to $7.3 billion during the years 1960–1971, while Japanese foreign direct investments rose from $300 million in 1960 to over $4.5 billion in 1971.[19] Overseas investment by West German and Japanese firms, however, evidence a different pattern from the foreign activities of corporations based in the United States and the United Kingdom. Corporations in the latter two nations follow a similar investment pattern—approximately 40% devoted to manufacturing and 33.3% in extractive industries. Japanese firms, on the other hand, have concentrated investments in extractive industries as a means of securing raw material sources in an era of resource scarcities. Japanese activities in Brazil aimed at obtaining low-cost labor and raw materials are especially noteworthy. West German enterprises have emphasized the manufacturing and high technology fields, including chemicals, electrical products and transportation equipment.[20]

To round out the picture of foreign investment, Arab funds have flowed into Western Europe and the United States in the form of portfolio investments and investments for control. Public fears mounted in 1974 and 1975 regarding the possibility of massive Arab takeovers of American and Western European businesses. In the United States, for instance, Senator Harrison A. Williams, Jr. (D–New Jersey) introduced a bill, the Foreign Investment Act of 1975, which, among other aspects, would have authorized the president of the United States to screen and block investments creating a 50% or greater foreign ownership position in domestic companies with assets in excess of $1 billion.[21] A prominent American business executive floated a proposal to create a foreign investment review board designed to provide a prior review of all proposed foreign investments aggregating over 20% of the securities of any corporation with assets in excess of $10 million and the power to direct a court to "sterilize" such investments if an investor's actions became inimical to the laws or the interests of the United States.[22] The West German government also toyed with restrictive proposals. The Bonn government had under consideration a bill subjecting all foreign capital investments in excess of 10% of corporations with a specified turnover, or investments in excess of a specified size, to prior notification to the West German Economic Ministry and the German Federal Bank before the conclusion of the purchase, thus allowing the government to exercise moral pressure on the negotiations.[23]

Public pressure for enactment of these restrictive proposals abated as it became evident that Arabs were not taking control over Western businesses. Arabs found other outlets for their funds as the members of the Organization of Petroleum Exporting Countries embarked on extensive development programs. The recession-slackened demand for oil in 1974 and 1975 produced a decline in projected oil surpluses in OPEC hands. Funds from oil-rich nations that were available for investment purposes flowed into the American real estate market, not into corporate securities.

Confounding apologists for centrally planned economies, the multinational phenomena characterized by foreign direct investment spread to Communist nations, which increasingly began to engage in industrial and banking consortiums and joint ventures. The Soviet Union, Rumania and Poland now conduct banking ventures in Western Europe. Communist nations have also undertaken manufacturing activities in the West. Examples include the Soviet Union's auto assembly plant in Belgium, its oil refinery in Brazil and its participation in a steel complex in France. Poland has phosphate undertakings in Canada; Hungary owns a potash mine in Canada; while Yugoslavia owns a pharmaceutical company in Switzerland.[24] Multinational business, in short, is neither the province of American corporations nor that of enterprises from market-oriented economies.

The intrusion of Western European and Japanese firms into the United States illustrates how business has burst its national boundaries. Fueled by the growing size of corporations (a result of Western European efforts to merge firms and increase government subsidies for research and development), a broadening organizational and financial base, a lessening of governmental restrictions on the outflow of capital, and devaluations of the dollar, significant European investments in the United States began in the 1960s, especially in chemicals, aluminum and office equipment. A lowering of the relative cost of production in the United States reduced the gap in labor costs between the United States and other nations and made operations in the United States competitive. Diminished price-earnings ratios in the recession-punctured 1970s made American corporations attractive for foreign takeovers. Accordingly, British Petroleum acquired a controlling interest in Standard Oil of Ohio; the British tobacco firm of Brown and Williamson acquired Gimbel Brothers for $200 million; while North American Philips paid $168 million for Magnavox. The size and homogeneity of the more unified American market, coupled with access to the technologies of large-scale production and mass marketing, rendered facilities in the United States more attractive. These factors also propelled Japanese firms to undertake substantial investments in the United States and to account for an increasing proportion of foreign direct investment in the United States from the early 1970s. But the bulk of foreign investment in manufacturing operations in the United States continued to come from four nations—the United Kingdom, West Germany, the Netherlands, and Canada—that historically have invested most heavily in the United States.

By the mid-1970s, foreign direct investment in the United States, which had recorded an annual 15–20% upswing, reached significant proportions. At the end of 1975, foreign direct investment in the United States had grown to nearly $27 billion, up from $6.9 billion in 1960.[25] The deepening recession in many foreign nations in 1974–75 and a steep rise in the share prices of American corporations temporarily halted the surging rate of gain. But the upward trend continues unabated. Volkswagen has decided to undertake assembly operations in the United States, Michelin has invested in new tire plants in South Carolina, and the West German chemical giant BASF has built a petrochemical facility in Louisiana. Although investors from Western Europe and Japan have penetrated into the petroleum, manufacturing and service sectors in the United States, foreigners, to date, have not assumed a preponderant role in any American industry. The book value of direct investment by American corporations in other developed countries (except the Netherlands) remains several times higher than the book value of direct investments in American industry by firms based in those countries.

2

THE CONCEPT OF THE
MULTINATIONAL BUSINESS ENTERPRISE

Before analyzing in detail the internal need for firms to grow and expand their market shares and the external factors, such as the inducements offered by host nations, that propelled the expansion of American corporations abroad, it will be valuable to examine the multinational enterprise as an organizational concept.

The Industrial Revolution witnessed the creation of a hierarchical and authoritarian factory system based on a division of labor. In the mid-nineteenth century a single entrepreneur or family group controlled a business firm, which engaged in a single function in one industry. The last quarter of the nineteenth century and the early years of the twentieth century witnessed the rise of national corporations in the United States stemming from a domestic merger movement and a desire to better serve a rapidly growing economy. An administrative hierarchy ran a national firm and increased the extent of the vertical division of labor. Executives subdivided various business functions and created a horizontal division of labor. A nationwide vertically integrated production and marketing system required a head office group to coordinate and to plan for the growth of an entire organization. Emphasis turned from production to devising marketing strategies and continuous product innovation. This trend gave rise to decentralized multidivision firms composed of several divisions handling separate product lines and making the day-to-day business decisions. Each division had its own head office. A general office to coordinate the separate divisions and to plan overall strategy headed the new organizational structure.[1]

After World War II, American businessmen gradually came to view the world as a single economic unit. In the quest for optimal efficiency, multinational corporations attempted to create a world economic system through which coordination of the various business functions—production, finance and distribution—could take place without regard to the barriers, regulations or institutions of nation-states.[2] The global factory, it was felt by executives with a world view, could best achieve maximum efficiencies through the global coordination of production, marketing, pricing, planning and financing and by the mobilization of capital in combination with transfers of technological and managerial skills. The most efficient allocation of resources would require ever greater specialization based on the location of resources and economies of scale. The separate operations in different countries would serve the totality. As *Business Week* noted:

> The goal in the multinational corporation is the greatest good for the whole unit, even if the interests of a single part of the unit must suffer. One large U.S. manufacturer, for example, concedes that it penalizes some of its overseas subsidiaries for the good of the total corporation by forcing them to pay more than necessary for parts they import from the parent and from other subsidiaries. Says one of the company's executives: "We do this in countries where we either anticipate or already face restrictions on profit repatriation. We want some way to get our money out."[3]

As part of the global concept, managers perceived the world as an open market for an ever expanding consumer society. The single world market would culminate in linking Communist nations, particularly the Soviet Union and Eastern Europe, in various business ventures with Western firms and in the swapping of industrial products from centrally planned economies for consumer goods manufactured by Western corporations.

The multinational concept has generated benefits for corporations in the production, financing and marketing areas. Production on a worldwide basis can minimize production and transportation costs.[4] Each subsidiary can supply a range of parts or components, and subsidiaries can trade finished products with each other. For example, IBM assembles computers for its European markets from components manufactured in specialized plants in seven or eight different countries. Massey-Ferguson, a Canadian-based multinational manufacturer of farm equipment, combines a French-made transmission, a British-made engine and a Mexican-made axle with US-made sheet metal parts to produce in Detroit a tractor sold in Canada. Excess demand faced by a subsidiary in one nation can be redirected to another subsidiary with excess capacity, thus assuring high overall capacity utilization and minimizing unit costs. The Swedish ball bearing company SKF, for example, attempts to maintain a high level of capacity utilization by directing corporate orders to underutilized plants. Sharing the work load among subsidiaries keeps workers on the job, maintains a planned corporate rate of return and overcomes the business cycle in different countries. Specialization can be achieved by locating production facilities in a country possessing the most advantageous set of conditions. Although the alleged flexibility on the part of a global firm to shift production facilities is probably overstated,[5] the risk of nationalization theoretically can be reduced by dispersing subsidiary operations to different countries. Also, an operational capacity in, and inputs from, many different countries should minimize the external risks encountered by a firm.

From a financial standpoint a global operation should improve a corporation's access to the capital market. Funds generated in a nation where costs are the lowest can be used elsewhere where returns are higher. Financing institutions looking to the credit-worthiness of a multinational firm as a whole, including assets in many nations and its overall cash flow and competitive status, are likely to make loans on advantageous terms. A multinational firm may escape the capital transfer restrictions imposed by one or more of the countries in which it operates by making funds available on an intraorganizational basis from an advantageously situated subsidiary. Likewise, national interest rate restrictions can be detoured by multinational operations. Depending on the vagaries of international politics, the ever-shifting restrictions imposed on the transfer of capital can be detoured by a foreign subsidiary (or a consortium of affiliates) acting as "parent" for a financial transaction. Fluctuations in currency exchange rates can be hedged against by arbitrage and the flow of funds facilitated through short-term payments and transfers. The variety of currencies may further increase the options and extend the use of financial resources available to sophisticated managers. Repatriation of earnings can take a number of forms, including dividends, licensing fees, management contracts, fees for research and development expenses. Intra-entity transfers of goods and services permit another element of flexibility, namely, transfer pricing. Taxes can be minimized by reallocating revenues to nations with low tax rates.

However, in actuality the constraints of the organizational apparatus and impediments imposed by nation-states limit the advantages of financial flexibility. Although a multinational enterprise may borrow funds in countries with the lowest interest rates for use in nations with higher interest rates, the intrafirm linkages may not be optimalized because a nation's financial institutions may frown on intersubsidiary financings and because such transactions are extremely complex.[6]

The advantages of multinational operations for the marketing of goods and services include an ability to test products in different countries and to sequence the introduction of products. Products may also be specifically tailored to meet the needs of local markets. A variety of other pluses exist, including an easier opportunity to monitor technological developments in several countries and to create an informational network to facilitate entry into new markets and to learn about new products and processes. Conducting a multinational operation may also foster the hiring of the best technical specialists and managers and the maintenance of high levels of research and development in advanced technological areas. A world corporate system has emerged, as Raymond Vernon has noted, "[I] n which stimulation to the system could come from the exposure of any element in the system to its local environment, and response could come from any part of the system that was appropriate for the purpose."[7]

Conceptualization of corporate activities by the managers of multinational firms in terms of worldwide factors and demand patterns led to a global strategy based on the integration of subsidiaries with the parent entity and a centralized decision-making structure. The pyramidal hierarchy spread over the world. A decentralization ideology masked the reality of centralization, in which one corporate nerve center devised a common corporate strategy and made fundamental decisions regarding production, marketing, finance and research.[8] Discipline and continuity were maintained through common training and coordination.

That the size of multinational entities affects their control and financing patterns is evidenced by United States–based multinational corporations. One study concluded that only subsidiaries of "small" multinational firms lead independent lives. In medium-sized multinationals, i.e., those having foreign sales of from $50 to up to $200 million that comprise 29% of the firm's total sales, generally centralization prevails, with substantial direction from headquarters. Subsidiaries of such firms make more use of funds provided by the parent corporation when faced with the unavailability of long term funds or restrictions on local borrowing. Large multinational firms studied, i.e., those with over $1 billion in foreign sales and operating manufacturing subsidiaries in numerous countries, looked to detailed guidelines but left decision making to the management of each subsidiary. Thus independence in borrowing permits flexibility in financing through a variety of sources, including local nonbanking sources and Eurodollar and local bond markets. Although increased decentralization prevails in large firms, guidelines that serve a coordinating function are issued by headquarters. Financial personnel are attuned to a common set of policy guidelines and standardized procedures. Only "small" corporations, i.e., those with foreign sales of up to $50 million that comprise 18% of total sales and that operate manufacturing subsidiaries in fewer than eight nations, used a decentralized system viewing each subsidiary as an independent operation; at least with respect to financing decisions, decentralized operations with little direction from a headquarters prevail. The subsidiaries of these "smaller" entities rely on retained earnings and local borrowings, mainly from banks, and make comparatively little use of decision rules.[9]

A survey of the European subsidiaries and other units of 127 American corporations indicated that approximately 40% imposed "strict" control, 40% evidenced "loose" control and 20% had control that was intermediate, flexible, undeterminable or in the process of being changed. A trend toward stricter control was noted, stemming from three factors: the ease of communication and transportation; the development of the European Common Market, which resulted in the reorganization of distribution and marketing functions; and the growth and importance of the European subsidiaries as corporate profit centers.[10] Other expert observers view control by American firms as declining over time as foreign affiliates gain experience.[11]

In contrast to firms headquartered in the United States, American subsidiaries of Western European firms tend to achieve a greater degree of independence as the parent seeks to learn from the United States subsidiaries and to diffuse the information to other affiliates.[12] Generally, United Kingdom multinationals are characterized by looser organizational structure and decentralized resource allocation.[13]

3

THE RATIONALE FOR
FOREIGN DIRECT INVESTMENT

Despite the plausibility of the multinational enterprise organizational concept and the business advantages flowing from such a strategy, the motivation for direct foreign investment must be assessed and the sources of funds for overseas activities examined. In considering the reasons for overseas investment, this chapter focuses on American corporations since World War II. In most instances, domestic factors (factors operating in the United States), not external factors (factors originating in areas outside the United States), constituted the primary motivating influences.

Domestic factors include the existence of a few firms (oligopolies) that dominated their respective industries in the United States. These firms sought continual growth, in terms of both absolute size and share of the market, which could best be accomplished through expansion in foreign markets. The urge to expand took the form of investments to build production facilities rather than exportation of goods. Among other factors intrinsic to the American system, the desire to gain access to raw materials also played a significant role. Certain technological conditions, including advances in transportation, information systems and communications, facilitated the foreign investment process after 1945. With the advent of trans-Atlantic jet crossings in the late 1950s, firms could send technicians and managers abroad for short periods of time. The ability to monitor and control foreign operations was also facilitated by developments in communications, such as the telex, information systems and computers. These advances created a new interest in global opportunities and made corporate managers aware of the possibility of new competitive sources as a challenge to the prevailing oligopolistic structures in many American industries.

DOMESTIC MOTIVATING FACTORS

A special type of firm in the United States took the lead in investing abroad. As the International Labour Organization stated, "A tendency [exists] for foreign investments to gravitate to industries showing one or more of the following characteristics: (1) a high initial capital outlay; (2) a rapid growth rate; (3) a high level of technology; (4) a rapid replacement in the technologies used; and (5) a high degree of concentration in the home country."[1] Firms establishing foreign subsidiaries tended to be giant corporations, bearing out the fact that whether or not a corporation engages in foreign direct investment correlates with its size. A study of 528 multinational corporations among the *Fortune* 1000 largest industrials indicated that the odds that a corporation with gross sales in excess of $1 billion per year will engage in foreign operations are substantially greater than for a firm having annual sales under $60 million.[2] Beyond mere size, firms that invest overseas occupy a dominant position in the American market and operate in concentrated segments of American industry.[3]

With the exception of the aviation industry, companies that invest abroad are also clustered in research-oriented industries.[4] Such firms, for example, in the electrical, chemical, pharmaceutical, and computer fields, possess an advantage that they wish to exploit in foreign markets. The advantage over foreign competitors may stem from a variety of factors, including product differentiation, technological superiority, expertise in management or marketing, advantages in raising capital and various economies of scale, including vertical integration. Of particular importance is product differentiation, that is, minor physical differences, brand names, or distinctions created by advertising, which may be protected from imitation by patents or trademarks and/or the high cost of physical imitation. One study of United States–based corporations pointed to the high correlation existing between the extent of product differentiation and the proportion of firms in an industry having foreign subsidiaries.[5]

The decision to invest abroad may be viewed primarily in defensive terms. By establishing production facilities abroad firms may simply evidence a follow-the-leader behavior. The ability to control prices and profits rests on the paramount need to keep an oligopolist structure undisturbed. If the actions of another firm or firms is (or are) not imitated, the oligopolistic balance may be upset, thereby undercutting the ability of a corporation to plan and make decisions in anticipation of the response of other firms in an industry.

The defensive oligopolistic response may take the form of the cross-penetration of investment by firms in different nations. The "exchange-of-hostage" syndrome posits that an enterprise in country A establishes a plant in country B, whereupon a firm in nation B, fearing that the foreign intruder may disrupt the existing industry structure, sets up a facility in country A to take advantage of that market and to further cooperation in the industry. In short, cross investment enables firms to establish worldwide market positions and protect against challenges to an existing global oligopolist structure in an industry.[6]

A defensive response also led American firms in certain industries, for instance, commercial banking and advertising, to follow their customers abroad.[7] In 1960 eight United States banks had overseas branches with assets of $3.5 billion. By the end of 1972, more than one hundred United States banks had assets overseas in excess of $90 billion. This foreign asset figure exceeded $117 billion by early 1974.[8] Financing (and also service) organizations reasoned that they must follow the overseas growth patterns of their corporate clients to prevent a loss of business in the United States. Banks went overseas to serve the financial needs of expanding firms. Multinational corporations with coordinated international financial operations required coordinated banking support and an end to time-consuming and costly international banking procedures.

To meet the large-scale financing requirements of international industry, joint-venture and consortium banking flourished as European banks sought out American banking partners and vice versa.[9] These new modes of international banking enabled a financial institution to avoid the difficulties encountered by a newcomer to transnational banking and permitted banks with limited investments to engage in additional activities, including participation in multimillion-dollar loans, and to offer one-stop services to multinational corporations.

American banks also entered foreign markets through wholly owned subsidiaries—so-called Edge Act corporations—which could go beyond the usual range of domestic activities in order to enhance their competitve effectiveness in foreign markets where wider powers are customary. Wholly owned subsidiaries could engage in investment banking and make equity investments in nonfinancial companies in connection with a subsidiary's financing activities. As a result of these benefits, the number of Edge Act bank subsidiaries rose to 116 in 1975, with assets in excess of $7 billion.[10]

American banks also created foreign branches and subsidiaries to serve the growing Eurodollar and Eurocapital market and to place funds into the expanding inter-bank money market, which had become especially important by 1974. Banks sought to capture Eurodollar deposits, thereby providing funds to parent banking entities in periods of domestic credit stringency, such as 1966 and 1969-70. Financial organizations also attempted to avoid restrictive rules of the Federal Reserve System, particularly reserve requirements and interest rate ceilings on deposits that held down domestic deposits. Attempts by the federal government to limit the flow of funds outside the United States through the first voluntary and then mandatory foreign credit restraint programs also propelled banks abroad. In addition to attractive foreign profit possibilities, the relative stagnancy of domestic business opportunities led to the growth of overseas operations by American banks.[11]

Despite the continued success of multinational corporate activities, the financial difficulties encountered by banks in their international operations in 1974, marked by the collapse of Bankhaus I. D. Herstatt of West Germany, caused many institutions, particularly regional American banks, to become considerably more cautious and to retreat from their foreign involvement. Banks tightened their loan terms and imposed greater selectivity in making loans. More than fifty United States foreign bank branches were closed in 1974 and 1975.[12]

The oligopoly theory and the defensive variants, however, fail to explain why an industrial corporation would establish a foreign subsidiary rather than licensing or exporting a product. To fill this gap, Prof. Raymond Vernon developed the "product life cycle" model based on the sequential and predictable development of a product characterized by a transition from product differentiation to product standardization. Vernon succinctly described the product life cycle model as follows:

To begin with, U.S.-controlled enterprises generate new products and processes in response to the high per capita income and the relative availability of productive factors in the United States; they introduce these new products or processes abroad through exports; when their export position is threatened they establish overseas subsidiaries to exploit what remains of their advantage; they retain their oligopolistic advantage for a period of time, then lose it as the basis for the original lead is completely eroded.[13]

The product life cycle posits that American corporations have a significant advantage over foreign competitors in the development and production of new products because of the size of the American market and the resources available for research and development. Innovation is assumed to occur generally near a large market for a product. If innovation occurs elsewhere, commercialization of a product will probably still occur first in a large market. The location of plants in the United States, the world's largest market for new products, will minimize communication costs within the firm and with its customers and suppliers during the nonstandardized production phase, when production techniques are likely to change. During the introductory stages of product production and marketing, American companies therefore possess a variety of oligopolistic advantages.

Firms initially met an increasing foreign demand for a product by exporting to overseas markets with similar demand characteristics. This export strategy enabled companies to extend an initial oligopolistic advantage enjoyed in the United States. The diffusion to or imitation by potential foreign competitors of the technology involved in the manufacture of a product, the advantage of lower transportation costs enjoyed by foreign firms, and the existence of or the potential for government protective strategies then produced a change in American corporate strategy. To maintain a market position abroad in maturing products and to forestall the rise of lower cost foreign competitors who could imitate such products and bring pressure for protective governmental legislation, firms began to shift production to foreign nations. The threatened loss of export markets and the rise of foreign competitors induced American firms to establish foreign subsidiaries. A firm attempting to operate only from the United States might lose export markets to foreign companies, especially large European or Japanese enterprises. Factors affecting the time interval before foreign manufacturing commenced include economies of scale, tariffs, transportation cost, size of the foreign market and income levels in such market. Finally, as an item or component became sufficiently standardized and its skill content declined, American firms shifted activities to low-skill, low-wage countries. The product life cycle model, then, views foreign direct investment and the establishment of overseas subsidiaries primarily in defensive terms. Corporations go abroad in response to a perceived threat to established export markets.[14]

The product life cycle model contains several deficiencies. First, it fails to account for foreign direct investment by raw material or service firms (exports did not precede investment by enterprises engaged in the extraction of minerals or petroleum). Second, the model assumes that innovations originate only in developed nations. Third, not all products follow a cycle of production in the country of origination followed by exportation and the development of foreign manufacturing subsidiaries. Certain industries cannot follow the export route, e.g., food processing, because of perishability of products; likewise service firms. The theory, moreover, does not account for European or Japanese direct investments in the United States, which would seem not to stem from a desire to exploit or protect an oligopoly advantage. Also, investments by manufacturing firms in the United Kingdom and France may flow predominantly to former colonies rather than to countries with similar per capita income levels. Finally, the model appears irrelevant both to developing countries lacking a broadly based demand for consumer products and to the worldwide development of multinational enterprises comprising a series of specialized factories that produce one part of a product line that is then shipped elsewhere for final assembly. As a part of the latter trend, a plant in a developing country subject to centralized control by a parent company may produce a fairly sophisticated product as part of the enterprises's global activities.

The vast proliferation of foreign direct investment by American corporations may be better explained by the need for expansion and growth, both in absolute size and in share of the market, and the quest for raw materials. Sophisticated analysts have observed that continued growth, when coupled with an improving but not necessarily profit-maximizing trend, constitutes a prerequisite to the survivial of giant corporations. Such a policy serves both protective and aggressive purposes. A larger firm, especially one with a significant market share, is better able to stabilize its environment and achieve control over its prices and costs, thus preserving the autonomy of management from intrusions by shareholders, labor, customers or creditors. An expanding firm also provides more jobs and chances for promotion, together with higher pay and perquisites for those in the organizational hierarchy.[15] As Raymond Vernon concludes, "The management is concerned with maintaining loyalty, incentive, and initiative over the long run and, if necessary, is usually prepared to modify the classic return-on-investment calculations to keep the principal members of the team in play."[16] Naturally, the pressure to grow for the sake of expansion may also result in more profits and a higher price-earnings multiple for a firm's common stock and facilitate the attraction of top managers.

A pressure to expand for its own sake builds especially when coupled with the relative stagnancy of the United States market and the saturation of the domestic demand for a firm's existing products.[17] A corporation after reaching its domestic market share plateau, characterized by the attainment of a certain percentage of the domestic market, may foresee only marginal opportunities in the United States. Further investment at home in the firm's product line may only depress its overall rate of profit. Instead of diversifying into other product lines and meeting unmet needs, such as in the fields of energy and mass transit, United States corporate managers, in view of their sector-specific experience and reinforced by the difficulties encountered by the conglomerates built during the merger boom of the late 1960s, continued to look to foreign markets.

Firms with the requisite financial, managerial and technical resources sought to recreate themselves in other countries so as to grow faster than the American economy and to gain and hold a larger and more secure market share. Firms initially carried their oligopolistic advantages abroad to developed countries, where a consumer society and a sufficiently high level of disposable income existed. Penetration of developed nations, it was perceived, would also promote exports to other countries, including former colonies of European nations. Firms also invested directly in Third World countries to gain a foothold in a nascent consumer society of significant future proportions.

Marketing reasons, in large measure, account for the decision to expand by means of investment in foreign subsidiaries rather than exporting goods. Although a firm could achieve growth in size by tapping export markets, it would face the effects of market discontinuities, including differences in consumer demand, income levels, cultural values and technical conditions. To increase marketing capabilities, firms turned to foreign-based affiliates, which would also provide strategic flexibility. Operations with foreign affiliates may be adjusted to take advantage of new and different markets in terms of the segmentation of regions and countries stemming from different conditions. Production and distribution may be more closely attuned to local needs and preferences, including legal and safety standards, technical norms and better quality control. The supply and servicing of products are facilitated.

Other advantages enjoyed by investment over exportation include customers' anxiety about depending on a foreign source of supply and a firm's desire to assure steady supplies to customers; the ability to replenish inventories quickly; the quality and cost of ancillary services; the ability to tailor advertising and selling campaigns to a local market; improved distribution through the use of regional warehouses; the availability of local parts and technicians; the ability to package the product for local market; sales and service networks; and the chance to market test or introduce new products in one or several countries or in integrated regional markets. A defensive element, however, may also be present here: A firm failing to undertake foreign direct investment may be forced to concede to foreign firms not only its overseas markets but also its home base.[18]

A number of empirical studies highlight the importance of marketing factors. A study by the Chamber of Commerce of the United States of 160 American multinational corporations indicated that the leading reason for investing abroad was to better service an existing market, specifically, by developing a cluster of activities to make overseas operations more economical and expanding foreign operations to provide greater responsiveness to a local market.[19] A survey by the Emergency Committee for American Trade stated that 57% of corporations responding considered market demand factors, which vary depending on industry and include

ransportation costs, and a desire to tailor products to local needs and
stablish support operations, of prime importance in the foreign invest-
nent decision process.[20] This study minimized the importance of a variety
f government-imposed factors designed to influence trade flows or in-
luce foreign investment. In the context of a debate in the United States
egarding domestic governmental incentives to foreign direct investment
nd the impact of such investment on the American economy, particularly
n structural job losses, the value of such business-sponsored surveys must
e discounted. But the importance of marketing factors looms large.
A 1959 academic study of 533 foreign manufacturing affiliates of Ameri-
an corporations indicated that 62% of the subsidiaries were created
nitially to give access capabilities to overseas markets and to overcome
narket discontinuities at national borders.[21]

The push to secure sources of raw materials, especially by firms in
xtractive industries and by manufacturing entities dependent on natural
esources, constitutes another critical incentive for foreign direct invest-
nent. Corporations producing petroleum, aluminum, copper, steel and
ertilizer, among other goods, went abroad to meet their raw material
equirements.[22] In a study by the Emergency Committee for American
'rade, raw materials were cited by several industries, including chemical,
aper, nonferrous metal and food products, as the prime consideration for
he foreign investment decisions.[23]

The argument is both quantitative (as in the case of petroleum) and
ualitative (small amounts of manganese are critically important for the
roduction of steel). As Gabriel Kolko observed, "The ultimate signifi-
ance of the importation of certain critical raw materials is not their cost
o American business but rather the end value of the industries that *must*
mploy these materials, even in small quantities, or pass out of exist-
nce."[24] Critics of the essential raw materials explanation argue that the
Jnited States could dispense with a given raw material or find a substitute,
ither through discovery of the same raw material in other geographical
reas, the exploitation of low-yield domestic deposits, the creation of
enuine substitutes by means of technological innovation or by recovery
nd recycling techniques. However, while flexibility may exist in the
ong run, the short-run need for certain critical raw materials poses an in-
urmountable obstacle. It is difficult to make substitutions, to alter
roduction processes, or change consumption patterns. As Harry Magdoff
tates, "Any president of a big corporation who did not aggressively pur-
ue acquisition of foreign leases for raw materials because in the historical
ong run a domestic substitute will probably be found, would most prop-
rly be fired from his job."[25] In addition to the requirements of private
orporations, the present and future dependency[26] of industrial societies

on the importation of key raw materials from Third World nations, particularly petroleum, bauxite, chromite and manganese, has considerable significance for the formulation of the foreign economic and political policies of Western nations and for the role of corporate needs and societal requirements in the creation of such policies.

The oligopolistic organization of American industries, such as petroleum, provides another reason for overseas activity. Firms searched for raw materials in foreign countries to conduct vertically integrated operations —from mining to final processing and distribution.[27] Corporations sought to diffuse their risks by developing alternate sources of supply in different nations. A diversity of sources of supplies would also lessen the threat posed by actual or potential blockages of such deposits by competitors who might gain access to a new source of supply, thus tipping the stability of an oligopoly. The potential impact of nationalistic policies on the part of specified host countries generated an additional motive for foreign investment in other nations. Control over sources of supply made it easier to regulate the prices of an industry's end products by keeping production in line with demand and by ensuring that competitors would not gain access to cheap sources of raw materials. Vertical integration could also take the form of securing outlets for processed materials, thus further reducing risks.

A final domestic motivating factor is governmental encouragement. The United States government offered corporations going abroad a panoply of benefits, including investment guarantees, tax incentives, foreign aid programs first in Europe and then in developing countries, and a variety of financing institutions (such as the International Bank for Reconstruction and Development, International Finance Corporation, and Inter-American Development Bank, originally financed in large measure by the United States).[28] Foreign aid facilitated long-range corporate planning, minimized investment risks, passed on costs to the American taxpayer and kept nations in the world capitalist system. The importance of tax policy in encouraging domestic oligopolies and, in particular, encouraging corporations' pursuit of foreign investment opportunities, remains controversial. United States tax incentives and other governmental strategies to induce foreign direct investment probably played a less significant role in the decision-making process than other internal factors, particularly marketing and raw material requirements. As Richard M. Hammer, a partner in the accounting firm of Price Waterhouse, noted, for most firms United States tax considerations come into play only after the basic decision to manufacture abroad has been made and therefore constitute a minor causal factor.[29]

EXTERNAL MOTIVATING FACTORS

A variety of external factors also spurred investment abroad by United States firms. These external motivating factors include barriers to exports imposed by foreign governments as well as positive foreign incentives; corporations located plants abroad to take advantage of certain benefits, most notably low-cost labor, offered by foreign countries.

Foreign government restrictions on the importation of products from the United States constituted a significant inducement to the creation of foreign plants. A number of surveys, including studies by the Chamber of Commerce of the United States and the Emergency Committee for American Trade, indicate that tariff and other trade restrictions comprised the most importnat barriers.[30] Foreign nations also mandated local content standards, that is, a product to be sold in a country had to contain a certain percentage of components manufactured in that nation. Governments also imposed local content requirements as part of procurement and contract specifications for national purchases.[31] To surmount these nationalistic impediments to the expansion of the export sales, firms undertook foreign investments.

American corporations also responded to the creation of regional trading groups and a variety of foreign government incentive programs. The creation of a common external tariff regime among members of the European Common Market influenced corporate decisions to invest in Common Market countries. The implementation of a trading zone, however, probably was less important than the expectation of rapid economic growth in the European Economic Community and the prospect of potential cost savings derived from large-scale production as a result of the removal of trade barriers. Host countries have also offered tax incentives and subsidy programs to spur overseas investment, including low-interest loans, government capital contributions, accelerated depreciation, tax holidays, and exemptions from capital transfer restrictions, especially on the repatriation of profits. A number of Western European governments also used subsidies to direct such investment to economically "depressed" regions.[32]

Such incentives and subsidies were generally of only marginal importance in the foreign investment decision process, except for labor-intensive firms seeking low-wage labor. A study of twenty-nine United Kingdom firms revealed that only a few of the corporations considered inducements offered by Kenya and Jamaica to be of major importance in their decision to invest.[33] However, multinational corporations have repeatedly manifested intransigence when host countries have considered reducing tax incentives. As an example, global firms, *Business Week* reported, were upset when Belguim contemplated altering plans to phase out a modest 5% tax reduction on capital spending.[34] But one expert concluded that host governments realize that favorable tax treatment has little effect on the basic decision to invest abroad.[35]

Lower relative labor costs motivated firms in certain labor-intensive industries to set up plants in Third World countries. For example, in the late 1960s American, European and Japanese firms established subsidiaries in Southeast Asia, especially in the field of electronic equipment and instruments. Among the more noteworthy projects, through its National Frontier Program, Mexico sought to attract plants to that nation to assemble components produced in America in an industrial zone bordering the United States.[36] Corporations use such plants in Third World nations, so-called export platforms, to produce goods for export to other nations, including the United States. A further refinement involves complementary worldwide sourcing, with plants located to take advantage of cost differentials. For example, parts are manufactured in one nation and assembled in another, and the finished product is sold in still other countries.[37]

In certain industries, including consumer electronics (radio, television and phonograph), footwear, toys and apparel, the search for low-cost labor constituted a major decisional factor. As the cost of labor comprised a high percentage of the value of these products, corporations sought foreign plants to reduce labor costs.[38] Consumer acceptance in the United States of foreign-made goods meeting price and quality standards assisted this trend.

Except in labor-intensive industries, labor costs in most industries comprise a smaller percentage of total costs and are less important. Therefore, cost factors, particularly cheap foreign labor, generally assumed a position of secondary importance in the foreign investment decision process of American firms.[39] Donald M. Kendall, chairman of the Emergency Committee for American Trade, declared: "Mr. Chairman, there are always exceptions [e.g., the electronics field, radio and TV, textiles], but I know of no major multinational company that goes abroad to make investments because of low labor rates or because of tax advantages. They go abroad to make an investment to get a higher market share."[40] A more dispassionate academic expert concluded, "Usually, however, labor costs are but one of many factors considered in the decision-making process and the evidence accumulated by students of decision-making by multinational corporations seems to indicate overwhelmingly that the principal motive behind the great bulk of U. S. stakes abroad is not cheap labor."[41]

Whether the so-called export platforms will continue to grow in numbers and importance remains unclear.[42] Lower labor costs may be counterbalanced by relatively unsatisfactory productivity levels. After the two devaluations of the dollar in the 1970s, which made American operations more competitive, no definite answer can be given to the question whether the export platform concept will spread throughout American manufacturing. It may be possible for business to bring together low-cost labor and advanced technology. However, increased automation of industries may reduce the benefits of low-cost labor and reestablish the primacy of marketing advantages, particularly proximity to a market. Developing countries may also resist being confined to low-wage, low-technology plants. In any event, shifts in operations that have taken place and will occur have had and will continue to have a severe impact on the affected workers in the United States.

Still looking to the future, one may speculate that with the imposition of more stringent environmental standards in developed countries, Third World nations may attempt to lure industry with so-called pollution havens. However, except for a handful of industries, pollution control expenditures amount to less than a few cents for each dollar value of plant shipments. Also, advantages offered by host countries may be only temporary in nature, as the exportation of goods from plants in "pollution havens" may face the possibility of special tariffs imposed by industrial nations on such products. Finally, it seems likely that energy-intensive industries may relocate plants to nations offering an abundance of cheap power and raw materials.

To this point, the reader may conclude that the foreign investment decision entails a rational process by a corporation. Many times, however, such decisions have been unsophisticated and irrational. A firm's international outlook may stem from a drive launched by one high-ranking executive desiring corporate prestige. This manager may also have a desire to see the world and to contribute to foreign economic development. Or, pressure to invest may evolve from a commitment made while the firm was investigating a possible investment, stemming from an urge to persist, to overcome difficulties and make a go of the venture.[43]

SOURCES OF FUNDS

Contrary to the view of several analysts who maintain that under modern American capitalism, oligopolistically organized industries generate "surplus" profits that they cannot easily absorb domestically, the funds for foreign direct investment by American corporations during the past 25 years have come primarily from foreign sources. In his classic study *Imperialism: The Highest Stage of Capitalism,* Lenin stressed the export of capital and the need for business firms to seize control of key raw materials.[44] He viewed imperialism as a stage of monopoly capitalism in which banking and industrial capital merge and gain control of the state and the competition for capital outlets becomes a race between nations. The following features evidence the imperialistic stage: (1) the concentration of production and capital creates monopolies, which play a key role in economic life; (2) a financial oligarchy results from the fusion of banking and industrial capital; (3) the export of capital, as distinguished from the export of commodities, becomes very important; (4) international capitalist monopolies develop to share the world among themselves; and (5) capitalistic powers divide the world territorially.

The English writer John Hobson theorized that surplus capital stems from oligopolistically organized industries' producing goods in the midst of mass underconsumption caused by insufficient aggregate demand to absorb the output.[45] More recently, Baran and Sweezy have focused on oligopolies' problems of rising surplus capital and declining profit opportunities in mature economies, such as the United States.[46] Among non-ideologically oriented writers, Brooke and Remmers, in their management guide, *The Strategy of Multinational Enterprise,* quote an English journalist: " 'If you could be a fly on the board-room ceiling, I think you might be surprised at the number of times a surplus of funds and managerial talent was a major factor in setting a company off on the diversification trail.' "[47]

Putting aside the argument that stagnant industrialized economies motivate foreign direct investment, let us examine other aspects of the surplus funds theory. A careful analysis of theories emphasizing the surplus funds emanating from domestic operations and the limited uses of such funds in domestic activities fails to square with empirical evidence relating to the source of funds for foreign corporate expansion. Funds for foreign direct investment may come from three sources: (1) exclusively from the parent corporation or from capital markets in the home country; (2) exclusively from the capital and/or money markets in the host country (local banks, branches or subsidiaries of American banks, Eurobond and Eurocapital markets, public financing agencies); or (3) a mix of parent funds (especially in the form of loans) together with local (host) sources and/or retained earnings of a foreign subsidiary or earnings from licensing operations. In point of fact, only a relatively small portion has come from direct transfers from the United States.

A 1969 United States Department of Commerce study of 313 large American firms indicated that between 1966 and 1969 60% of the total required funds was obtained within the enterprise. More significantly, funds provided by the parent American corporation comprised only 13%

of the total. Capital generated internally by foreign subsidiaries, in the form of depreciation and retained earnings, totaled an aggregate of 46%. Funds from outside a multinational enterprise, including foreign loans and equity investments, comprised, respectively, 39% and 2% of the total.[48]

Another analysis of the source of funds to finance American direct foreign investments indicated that between 1957 and 1965 only 15% came from the United States, and of the remainder 20% came from non-American (local) sources and 65% from the reinvestment of funds generated by foreign subsidiaries. From 1957 to 1965, funds provided by American sources comprised the following percentages of the total sources of capital: 15.7% in Canada, 20.2% in Europe, and 11.4% in Latin America. For all areas, from 1957 to 1965, funds from the United States amounted to 15.3% ($12.8 billion); from foreign sources, 20.1% ($16.8 billion); and from the operations of foreign enterprises—from net income 40.1% ($33.6 billion) and from depreciation and depletion 24.5% ($20.5 billion).[49]

Thus, the overabundance of capital allegedly generated in the past by American corporations has not found an outlet abroad. American companies have made substantial investments in developed nations, which also, presumably, face a capital surplus.[50] Most American companies have generated funds from a mix of sources, with retention of earnings and depreciation deductions by subsidiaries playing a paramount role. The mode of ownership of a foreign operation and the level of technology have also affected corporate financing. Parent corporations have generally made funds available more readily to wholly owned subsidiaries than to joint ventures. High-technology firms, based on the extent of research and development expenditures as a percentage of sales, are more likely to borrow locally and use nonbank finance sources than are low-technology firms of the same size.[51]

Firms have borrowed locally to gain four advantages: (1) automatic protection against devaluation of a local currency; (2) lowered costs; (3) avoidance of local restrictions on funds a parent could bring in; and (4) improved relations with local institutions, especially banks. Although United States–based corporations have employed local debt capital in all regions, the existence of more sophisticated capital markets in Western Europe has led subsidiaries in that region to tap local debt capital to a greater extent than affiliates, for instance, in Latin America. With the imposition by the United States of a voluntary foreign direct investment program in 1965 and the mandatory sanctions in 1968, which were withdrawn in 1974, the activity of American corporations in the Eurobond market mounted rapidly, as corporations sought to meet their capital needs yet stay within governmental requirements.

American corporations have also sought local equity investments while retaining control over foreign subsidiaries. The amount of local investment has depended on the availability of funds in the host country, local attitudes toward foreign investment, and government regulations and other pressures. Companies have desired local financing, especially in politically or economically unstable countries. If funds are raised in a host nation, multinational corporations have reasoned, citizens of that country are more likely to protect the affiliate. Better community and labor relations could be generated and conflicts with host governments minimized.[52]

The next part of this book analyzes the economic and political problems for developed nations raised by the growing interpenetration of global firms. On the economic front the new challenges include: (1) the possible obsolescence of significant portions of traditional economic theories of the competitive market and Keynesian fiscal and monetary stabilizers; (2) the possibility that foreign direct investment by multinational firms has adversely affected the balance of payments positions and created currency instability for developed countries; and (3) the rapid rise of transnational commercial banking and the unregulated Eurodollar market. Problems regarding industrial concentration and the specter of technological dependency will also be considered, as well as labor's contention that United States–based global firms have reduced the number of domestic jobs and redistributed income in the United States. The involvement of multinational firms in the political process of both home and host countries will be scrutinized. Finally, policies suitable for implementation by developed countries will be recommended.

PART TWO

THE IMPACT OF MNCs ON DEVELOPED COUNTRIES

4

ANALYSIS OF THE ECONOMIC
CONSEQUENCES OF MNCs

The intertwining of the economies of the United States, Western Europe and Japan (stemming in large measure from a panoply of activities of multinational corporations and banks), the tapping by global enterprises of capital and technology in various countries, and the resulting transnational flow of information and ideas have diminished the regulatory capacity of individual nation-states on both the macro-economic and micro-economic levels. National economic units have become subordinated to a world economic system based on transnational entities. This chapter considers the challenges raised by multinational enterprises in the following areas of economic policy: national economic planning and controls; multinational banking and the Eurodollar market; and industrial concentration and technological dependency. Chapter five considers the impact on jobs and income distribution. The actual and possible responses by industrialized nations to the growth of multinational corporations and banks are also considered. Alternatives discussed include national devices and the creation of transnational institutions to deal with these problems. The possibility of a speedy implementation of schemes for the transnational regulation of international banking and the Eurodollar market seems remote.

NATIONAL ECONOMIC PLANNING AND CONTROLS

The challenge to national economic sovereignty stemming from the new global business activities has upset nationally oriented monetary and fiscal stabilization policies and long-term economic and developmental planning, which view policy formulation and planning as taking place in isolated nation-states. The effectiveness of policy wanes in the tableau of the world economic system.[1]

For example, a nation may impose credit restraint policies on business with the hope of dampening inflation. Although a gap may exist between the opportunities for flexibile responses by multinational enterprises and the actual exploitation of such opportunities by global firms, multinational corporations reduce the effectiveness of national economic policies because of their ability to draw on different resources. A multinational firm may borrow outside a nation imposing restrictive credit policies or obtain financing through the retained earnings of subsidiaries in other countries. Multinational banks, as analyzed further in this chapter, have utilized the Eurodollar market to circumvent national credit restraints. Thus, a restrictive national monetary policy falls most heavily on domestically oriented corporations and banks, particularly small firms that are not adroit at avoiding monetary tightness. Conversely, if a nation pursues an easy money policy, the resulting availability of credit may be tapped by multinational firms.

The international flow of funds may also cause a certain loss of national autonomy. National money and capital markets, and particularly their interest rates, may be intertwined, thereby rendering more difficult the efforts of any one nation to stabilize its domestic economic activity. The integration of money and capital markets through the Eurodollar market has facilitated an international equalization of interest rates. Central bank officials in any country experience increasing difficulty in moving counter to the direction of international money and capital markets.[2]

Global corporate and banking operations may also disturb national economic plans for social welfare and economic stability by reducing a government's ability to predict the reaction of the private sector to governmental plans and proposals. Multinational corporations may outflank the government in order to avoid the impact of new or existing policies. Global firms may also render more difficult the construction of a viable balance among government, the private business sector and organized labor. The validity of countervailing concepts may be upset, and policies based on labor, industrial and governmental cooperation may be negated. In short, a world economic system has evolved beyond present national regulatory mechanisms.

Two specific problems, namely, the impact of multinational corporations on currency instability and spiraling balance of payment deficits, must be considered in detail. Allegations abound that capital movements by multinational corporations, stemming from the speed with which such firms can act, their ability to coordinate financial management, and their expertise and knowledge, precipitated currency crises in the late 1960s and early 1970s, particularly the two devaluations of the American dollar. Professor Joseph Nye contends, "The ability of a few score corporate treasurers, thinking globally and acting nationally, to transfer vast sums with extraordinary rapidity was one of the factors that contributed to the inability of countries to maintain an international monetary system based on fixed exchange rates."[3] Two other academic observers concluded, "That these largely American multinational corporations precipitated the devaluation of the American dollar in the monetary crisis of March 1973 as speculators unloaded dollars and purchased German marks and Japanese yen is beyond doubt."[4] Observing the magnitude of currency movements into the Federal Republic of Germany and Japan and out of the United States in anticipation of exchange rate realignments which appeared to involve financial institutions, nonfinancial institutions and multinational corporations, a study by the United Nations Department of Economic and Social Affairs noted:

It is possible that in the long run the natural tendency of the multinational corporations to concentrate their vast funds in hard currencies, coupled with their enormous ability to shift these funds internationally even in the presence of strict capital controls, will tend to increase the frequency of parity changes or amplify exchange rate fluctuations.[5]

A monetary crisis beyond the control of any national government might be triggered by global firms' short-term movements of their allegedly enormous sums of liquid assets. Estimates place the liquid assets held by United States multinational corporations at over $268 billion at the end of 1971, or approximately twice the total of all international reserves held by all central banks and international monetary institutions in the world at that time.[6] The magnitude of these assets led the United States Tariff Commission to conclude that movement of a small percentage of such assets could be "quite sufficient to produce a first-class international financial crisis."[7]

The possible drastic impact of collective and individual financial decisions by multinational corporations on national and international currency reserve positions is tempered, however, by a further analysis of the amount of liquid assets owned by American multinational corporations. Careful recalculations, which excluded inventories and receivables not immediately convertible into cash and the assets of American and foreign banks and their branches, placed short-term cash and near-cash assets of United States–based multinational corporations at the end of 1971 at approximately $14 billion.[8]

The juggling of assets other than cash or current assets in an attempt to shift the risk of exchange fluctuations might also trigger a monetary crisis. An example would be the so-called leads and lags technique. Leads and lags involves timing the settlement of intracorporate dealings. Payment of obligations to an entity in a nation whose weak currency is expected to be devalued is delayed; at the same time, payments are hastened to a subsidiary in a nation with a strong currency that is expected to be revalued upward. The potential for disruption is considerable if multinational enterprises take what has become relatively routine action, that is, delaying or speeding up payment on intracompany accounts. A report by the United Nations Department of Economic and Social Affairs noted that intrafirm loans to subsidiaries of American firms rose from $1.4 billion in the first three quarters of 1970 to $2.7 billion during the same period in 1971, apparently in anticipation of a devaluation of the United States dollar.[9] Thus, corporations and banks, even in the absence of a predatory motive, might frustrate a country's monetary policy.

Although it is difficult to establish the responsibility for capital flights, because of the unavailability of data regarding liquid short-term capital transactions and because of the anonymity of international finance transactions, currency instability in the late 1960s and early 1970s probably resulted more from underlying economic factors, the overvaluation of the dollar, and the failure of nation-states to recognize the need for exchange rate changes than from the speculative or hedging transactions by multinational corporations that lacked a large pool of liquid nonworking capital.

The alleged ability of global firms to disrupt currency markets is mitigated by three factors: (1) a sensitivity to the charge that their currency transfers are a major cause of exchange crises, (2) a desire to balance assets and liabilities in different currencies so as to minimize the risk of loss, and (3) a preference for denominating assets and liabilities in home currencies because financial statements are reported in home currencies. United States firms and their affiliates participate in currency movements mainly for protective business purposes. Corporate executives do not view international exchange rate uncertainties as a significant profit opportunity. Corporate currency managers try to avoid losses in foreign exchange dealings.

Edward M. Bernstein, president of EMB (Ltd.) Research Economists, in his testimony before the United Nations Group of Eminent Persons investigating the impact of multinational firms, attributed only a very small part of the total outflow of funds from the United States in 1971 and in the first quarter of 1973 before the devaluations of the dollar to American global enterprises. In 1971 between $1 billion and $1.25 billion of extra funds were channeled by American multinationals into foreign subsidiaries. In the first quarter of 1973, investment by United States multinational corporations in their subsidiaries increased by $1 billion more than might have been expected, but this represented only one-tenth of the deficit in the balance of payments during this period. Another expert estimated that the maximum contribution of American multinational firms to the increase in the balance of payments deficit from 1971 to the first quarter of 1972 was 11%.[10]

Edward M. Bernstein also assessed the flow of funds by American banks. United States banks transferred $5 billion to their branches in 1971 in repayment of Eurodollars borrowed in 1969. Repayments to foreign branches of American banks in the first quarter of 1973 may have been related, Bernstein concluded, to their anticipation of exchange rate movements. Although transfers of funds reported by American banks constituted an important part of fund outflow during the 1971 and 1973 dollar crises, such transfers were undertaken on the initiative of bank customers (including of course, a parent entity or the subsidiaries of multinational corporations), not on the initiative of banks themselves.[11] Thus, "transactions originated by foreign [non-US] holders or borrowers of dollars may well have played a substantial and perhaps even a predominant role" in bringing pressure on the dollar.[12]

The present international system of managed floating exchange rates, which allows, for example, the dollar's value to shift against other foreign currencies, substantially reduces the possibility of multinational enterprises' engaging in currency transactions in the hope of anticipating future governmental action that might stem from accumulated pressure on an under- or overvalued currency. The floating exchange rate system, in which members of the International Monetary Fund allow their currencies to move up or down with market forces, is, however, subject to the possibility of central bank intervention to counter disorderly market conditions or erratic fluctuations in exchange rates.[13] Floating exchange rates probably will diminish the "speculative" movement of corporate funds into currencies perceived as strong and out of currencies deemed weak. The presence of nervous currency traders and the existence of fluctuating foreign exchange markets has, however, increased the volatility of currencies and raised the cost of hedging transactions, thereby hampering world trade.[14]

One further item under the topic of multinational enterprises and national currency systems must be assessed. Under the present monetary arrangement, multinational firms may negate the benefits expected by a country that has devalued its currency in order to stem a rising tide of imports. Global enterprises in their intrafirm dealings may decline to raise the price of goods exported by foreign subsidiaries to the parent corporation (or corporate subsidiary) in such a nation. Thus, establishing currency policies, national policy planners, specifically central banks, must not only develop information systems as good as those possessed by multinational corporations and banks; they must also take into account the intrafirm pricing transactions of multinational corporations.

The mounting balance of payments deficits sustained by the United States in the early 1970s, which were reversed in 1975 only to fall back into the red in 1976 because of American dependence on imported oil, stemmed in part from the Vietnam War, which fueled domestic inflation. Rising prices weakened the competitive position of American-made goods in the world market. As American manufacturers experienced greater difficulty in exporting, the national surplus of goods exported over products imported was wiped out. The Vietnam War also added to overseas military expenditures. Critics of foreign direct investment charge that the overseas activities by American corporations drained capital from the United States, displaced America's exports to countries receiving such investments and also to third nations, and increased foreign productivity and competitive efficiency, thereby contributing to the deterioration of the American trade position.[15]

A number of problems exist with this analysis of the negative role of multinational firms. First, it is impossible to determine definitely what would have happened if corporations had not made foreign direct investments. Would the United States firms have continued to export to foreign nations, or would these markets have been preempted? Stated differently, did the goods produced by foreign subsidiaries displace American exports to third countries as well as to host nations? It is difficult, in other words, to establish conclusively whether foreign investments were export-destroying or export-creating. It is also impossible to determine precisely whether foreign direct investment by American firms displaced domestic investment by such corporations or took place in addition to domestic investments.[16] Additionally, as discussed in chapter three, American multinational corporations have generated a substantial portion of their capital requirements for the creation and expansion of foreign subsidiaries from overseas sources, thereby weakening the capital drain argument.

Studies have nearly unanimously concluded that foreign direct investment has had, on the aggregate, a positive net long-term impact on the American balance of payments. The United States Tariff Commission noted that, in 1970, for instance, almost the entire American merchandise trade surplus resulted from parent firms' trading with their foreign subsidiaries.[17]

Factors contributing to the trade surplus center on the exporting proclivities of American multinational firms and the substantial royalties nd fees that accrue from the transfer of American technology to foreign ubsidiaries and other firms. The export pull of foreign subsidiary opera- ions necessitates the shipment of parts and components for further proc- ssing and replacement equipment. Subsidiaries are more effective sales ntities than nonaffiliated distributors because of their interest in promot- ng sales of the products of their parent corporation. Subsidiaries are also ble to fill out product lines, and their presence in other countries may timulate interest in US–made goods produced by the parent entity.[18] In ddition to receipts from subsidiaries for royalties and license fees and for management and other services, American firms may also obtain valuable echnology by acquiring foreign entities and from foreign affiliates.[19]

Finally, foreign direct investment by American corporations apparently as not adversely affected, over the long term, the balance of payments ositions of various developed host countries.[20] Importation by a foreign ubsidiary of capital equipment may negatively affect a nation's trade bal- nce, but over the long run the impact of foreign subsidiaries on a host ountry's balance of trade depends on a variety of factors, including the egree of integration of the subsidiary into a global enterprise, the size of he market in both the host and home nations, the type of operation and he ability of a subsidiary to export to Third World nations, particularly ormer colonies. A degree of caution is therefore, in order. As Professor ack Behrman has stated, "It is impossible to determine precisely what mpact direct investment has on the trade balance of the host country, hough the direction of the change is generally favorable in the advanced ountries."[21]

MULTINATIONAL BANKING AND THE EURODOLLAR MARKET

The growth of multinational banking and the rise of an unregulated urodollar market pose problems for the world economic system and ational economic controls. Banks engage in worldwide operations resently beyond the control of respective national central banks. Central ank regulators lack the information to monitor and the tools to regulate he foreign branches and subsidiaries of commercial banks heavily depend- nt on overseas activities. Parent banking institutions may also lack the bility to effectively scrutinize overseas operations. As one astute London- ased Morgan Guaranty bank official related, "New York knows what I'm oing . . . because I send them the figures—a week or so late, much too late or them to do anything about it."[22]

The international financial debacle in 1974 forced national authorities o explore the possibilities for rudimentary controls over transnational banking operations, including surveillance of the foreign activities of commercial banks. In the United States the Federal Reserve System and the Comptroller of the Currency engage in such surveillance of the foreign activities of commercial banks. But the scope of the surveillance remains unclear, as does the implementation of additional reporting by, and an examination of, American banks operating abroad. In addition to improving the information process, other tasks confronting regulatory bodies include delineating the range of permissible activities by United States banks in foreign countries, fixing the adequacy of the capital of American banks in consideration of their foreign activities, and establishing capital reserves for American banks in light of the risks of international banking. The impact of international banking on domestic monetary policies must be considered, as well as who will serve as lender of last resort.

The scope of operations of American banks, especially Edge Act subsidiaries, remains a difficult regulatory problem for United States authorities. Specifically, should the government establish a list of activities (positive or negative) or continue the existing ad hoc, case-by-case approach? The question of capital adequacy for banks with significant foreign operations presents a thorny question that turns on the risks attached to bank activities, the sufficiency of risk-reducing arrangements, and the ability of a parent to insulate itself from the liabilities incurred abroad. Any type of effective control rests, of course, on timely access to information regarding international operations. Better information systems will aid regulatory authorities in analyzing the condition of a bank and the impact of banks, individually and collectively, on the economies of separate countries and on the worldwide economic system.[23]

The regulatory responsibility for international consortium banks, which may be jointly owned by commercial banks in the United States, Japan and Western Europe, remains undetermined. Doubts as to the viability of consortium operations have been eased by the respective parent banks' giving so-called "comfort letters," which, although carefully hedged, pledge a pro rata backing of the consortium. Some national central banks, such as the Bank of England, have also secured commitments from the parent banks involved in a consortium for support beyond their original capital commitments.[24]

It is easy to delineate alternate means for national authorities to exert greater control over the foreign activities of parent banks under their respective jurisdictions. However, the placement of such impediments on multinational activities by any one nation would probably induce bankers to charge that that country was unfairly placing banks under its jurisdiction at a competitive disadvantage. In addition to these restraints on national controls, barring an international financial crisis, there is no impetus for transnational regulation of multinational banking. Governments are reluctant to surrender their national sovereignty.

National authorities probably face an even greater challenge than multinational banking—the unregulated Eurodollar market.[25] The Eurodollar market, which contains a money pool in excess of $200 billion, constitutes a new form of international currency and the largest money market in the world. A Eurodollar consists of an American dollar on deposit in a bank outside the United States or such a deposit created by complicated bookkeeping entries. The Eurodollar market (in reality, the broader Eurocurrency market, composed of bank deposits in foreign currencies other than the dollar) serves the needs of at least three different groups: national governments wishing to hold dollars outside the United States, beyond the reach of American regulatory authorities; corporate executives seeking an international currency; and commercial banks desiring to make loans without the reserve restrictions imposed by central banks.

The development of the Eurodollar market stemmed from the existence of higher interest rates in Europe than prevailed in the United States, the removal of foreign exchange controls by Western European nations in the late 1950s, and confidence in the currency used—the American dollar. Other reasons for growth of the Eurodollar market include the United States' enactment (since rescinded) of an interest equalization tax in 1963, which blocked access by foreigners to the American capital market, and efforts by the United States to control the amount of money American firms could take out of the United States to invest in foreign subsidiaries. Another factor was American banks' desire to avoid Federal Reserve Board restrictions imposed on interest rate ceilings on domestic bank deposits.[26]

As an offshoot of the Eurodollar market, a Eurobond market developed. The increased demands by multinational corporations for capital stimulated the growth in the volume of funds channeled into the longer term Eurobond market, which corporations and countries tapped by floating debt issues.[27] The Eurobond market, regulated by the rules of the Association of International Bond Dealers, consists of issues underwritten by international syndicates and sold to purchasers able to pay in funds not subject to exchange controls. The creditors receive the payment of the interest and principal on the obligations without any national withholding tax deductions.

The Eurobond market arose when the United States introduced in 1963 an interest equalization tax that made it difficult for Europeans to raise money in the United States. When the United States government restricted the outward transfer of capital, American corporations also tapped the Eurobond market to meet overseas capital needs and to secure funds more cheaply and on better terms than in the United States. Continued imposition by the United States government of a 30% withholding tax on the interest paid to foreign investors has kept foreign borrowers out of the American capital markets and permitted the Eurobond market to flourish.

Only a preliminary analysis of the impact of Eurodollars on inflation, the balance of payments and monetary policy within individual nations exists. For example, monetary theorists take the position that an increase in Eurodollars raises the world's money supply, thereby contributing to inflationary pressures.[28] A more refined examination reveals the impact of the Eurodollar system on the growth of deposits in the respective national banking systems, especially central bank deposits, creating money in other countries and thereby spreading inflation.[29] With respect to the balance of payments problem, a leading observer of the Eurodollar market has concluded that until 1969 the Eurodollar system had a slightly positive net impact on the United States balance of payments, but by the end of 1973 the Eurodollar market had exerted a slightly negative net impact, with a particularly deleterious influence in 1970 and 1971.[30]

Regarding domestic monetary policy, Andrew Brimmer, a former governor of the Federal Reserve System, asserts that tight credit, which restricts the amount of funds American commercial banks have available for loans, may be circumvented by bank borrowings in the Eurodollar market. Brimmer maintains that during the second half of 1968 and the first half of 1969, multinational banks were less affected by domestic credit policies and were able to postpone cutbacks to business borrowers.[31] In contrast to the position that the Eurodollar market reduced the effectiveness of the monetary policies of individual nations, another expert has concluded that bank Eurodollar borrowings did not actually increase the volume of reserves available to the banking system, but that multinational banks adjusted more successfully to tight money conditions. Thus the existence of the Eurodollar market may have had only a slight impact on the overall efficiency of American monetary policy but may have aggravated the capital flows from the United States during speculations against the dollar.[32]

In the midst of this contradictory and often confusing analysis what stands out boldly is that, with few exceptions, the pool of Eurodollars, as one observer put it, is "sloshing around the world money systems"[33] in a high-speed market free from regulation or a lender of last resort except as a head office may turn to its central bank for help. Three possible dangers inherent in this situation must be examined: (1) massive withdrawal of bank deposits, (2) widespread defaults and rescheduling of Eurodollar indebtedness by developing nations, and (3) threat to a bank's liquidity stemming from a collapse of the inter-bank Eurodollar borrowing system.

Eurodollar depositors include American banks, their branches and subsidiaries, corporations with spare funds, central banks having large accumulated dollar reserves, and foreigners, most recently Middle Eastern nations. The magnitude of deposits by oil-rich nations and the possibility of a sudden withdrawal of such funds arguably raise two problems: (1) the liquidity and capital structure of banks may be in doubt; and (2) the Eurodollar system may be vulnerable to political pressures by nation states.[34] However, the present level of Middle Eastern deposits, which do not exceed 5% at various leading American banks, lessens the potential adverse consequences of a politically inspired deposit withdrawal.

Eurodollar borrowers include banks, their branches and subsidiaries, corporations, central banks and government agencies. Particular attention has focused on developing nations who borrowed in the Eurodollar market after 1973 to finance balance of payments deficits stemming in part from mounting oil and food bills and to engage in vast construction projects. The magnitude of Eurodollar borrowings by the governments of developing nations, which reached $50 billion by the end of 1975 (with about one-half from private lenders[35]) out of a total external debt of $123 billion, and the relation of debt servicing to the export earnings of the respective borrowers, raise the risk of defaults and reschedulings, the exposure of the private financial system, and possible catastrophic repercussions. Some observers fear that a debt crisis in one country would lead to further difficulties and a breakdown of the world monetary system.[36] However, even a massive rescheduling of the indebtedness of developing nations probably would not bring on a worldwide depression. Central banks could respond by increasing the reserves of private banks, and government guarantees, such as provided by the United States Export-Import Bank on loans by American banks, and the ability of the International Monetary Fund to extend new credits to developing countries lessen the risk. Furthermore, the exposure of banks to the risk of default and rescheduling is limited, as these loans constitute a small and seemingly manageable portion of the portfolios of American banks.

A flourishing inter-bank Eurodollar market has developed, enabling one bank to borrow from other banks. Through the inter-bank system a branch of an international bank may tap funds that may in turn be recycled to other branches or back to the parent institution. The pattern of commercial banks borrowing funds for the Eurodollar market for short time periods and relending to business borrowers for a longer term may be rational from a bank's viewpoint because of two factors—short-term rates are lower than long-term rates, and business borrowers want longer term loans. However, the inter-bank loan pattern creates the possibility of a liquidity crisis in the event a bank cannot repay its short-term borrowings as a result of the default by debtors of the bank or the withdrawal of funds by one or more major depositors. The collapse of a West German financial institution in 1974 led to an unwillingness by members of the New York Clearing House Association to enter payments to correspondent banks until other correspondent banks had entered balancing payments to the Association. During the second half of 1974, the credit-worthiness of participants in the inter-bank market came under scrutiny, leading to the creation of a differential premium structure for various tiers of banks participating in the Eurodollar market. Differential interest rates forced the departure of smaller banks from the Eurodollar market.[37] The possibility, therefore, exists for foreign branch bank failures which may place great stress on the various national commercial banking systems and diminish the capital cushions of banks.

Bank regulatory systems traditionally used reserve requirements to prevent liquidity crises. At present the only reserves in the transnational Eurodollar system are the deposits that foreign branch banks have in their respective home offices. The system depends on the liquidity of the parent banks and whether national central banks would engage in rescue operations of distressed parent banks. Apparently, monetary authorities have agreed to provide funds to any bank under their respective jurisdictions needing funds to cover losses from foreign currency operations. But home office banks, in time of a panic, may, in the absence of further assistance from one or more central banks, be unable to provide sufficient funds to repay short-term borrowings by their foreign branches.

In a world marked by the circulation of vast sums of money without rules and regulations, such as those relating to reserve requirements, for instance, which nation-states have considered prudent for decades, two possible kinds of control exist: national and/or international regulation of multinational and consortium banking and the Eurodollar market. On the national level, central banks in various nations have reassured commercial banks, or at least the foreign branches of banks under their respective supervision, that they will act as lenders of last resort in case of trouble. However, no blanket guarantees have been given. Each rescue operation will be judged individually in terms of the conduct of the bank, particularly its loan operations and other related practices.[38] More formal structures for the involvement of national central banks on a regular basis would constitute a stabilizing influence and would probably prevent the collapse of the Eurodollar market in the event of a default by a limited number of banks or borrowers.

Looking to the future, each central bank might impose reserve requirements on its own banks, limit the ability of the Eurodollar market to add to its domestic money supply, impose charges on foreign deposits to limit the inflow of funds through a Eurodollar conduit, and intervene directly or indirectly in the Eurodollar market. However, the difficulty of achieving harmony in and the coordination of national regulation efforts would probably disrupt such a scheme, and controls imposed by only one or a few countries would probably prove ineffective. A lack of cooperation by other nations, for instance, negated the effort of West Germany to regulate the impact of the Eurodollar market on its domestic monetary policy.[39]

As the international economy cannot be sliced into pieces suitable for national control, regulatory efforts might be focused on the creation of transnational rules and institutions. International harmonization and coordination of monetary, fiscal and economic policies could increase the effectiveness of regulation. As a first step in this direction, monetary authorities of many developed countries have joined together to improve communications and to devise a financial early warning system. Central bank officials from the United States, Japan, West Germany, France, Belgium, the Netherlands, Sweden, Italy and the United Kingdom have begun meeting regularly.[40]

Other possible transnational regulatory techniques include subjecting all banks, such as those operating in the European Common Market, regardless of nationality of the parent bank, to a code of conduct including rules of good behavior. Nations in Western Europe, Japan and North America might establish institutions for collective money management, including the consolidation of monetary systems and reserves and banking machinery, and attempt to harmonize national economic policies.[41] The International Monetary Fund could be transformed into a world central bank with power to impose reserve requirements on the foreign currency holdings of nation-states. The Fund could mandate the turnover of a specified portion of the foreign currency holdings by governments to the IMF in return for access to a new international currency, so-called Special Drawing Rights. To regulate multinational banking, the International Monetary Fund could be authorized to impose interest rate ceilings on inter-bank transactions, thereby hampering the ability of multinational banks to circumvent the monetary policy of various nations. Instead of the problems inherent in formulating and securing the observance of a code of international regulation, such a system would require only an agreement by each country to enforce the interest rate ceiling on inter-bank transactions as set by the IMF.[42]

Whether the international regulation of transnational economic activities, including multinational banks and the Eurodollar market, will succeed remains doubtful. First, nation-states may in the absence of a worldwide crisis cling to the concept of national sovereignty and refuse to surrender national autonomy to an international regulatory body. A divergency of national interests may capsize any transnational regulatory scheme. Secondly, joint regulation by Western European nations and the United States might lead the Eurodollar market, presently centered in London, to financially less sophisticated centers that evidence little interest in subjecting the Eurodollar market to stringent controls. Finally, and perhaps most importantly, despite the difficulties inherent in the Eurodollar (and more generally the Eurocurrency) market, it serves useful purposes for nation-states. Governments, in time of a financial crisis, may tap the market as a source of capital. The market also steers petrodollars accumulated by oil-rich nations into the developed world. It is, therefore, unlikely that nation-states will unduly constrain the Eurodollar market.

INDUSTRIAL CONCENTRATION AND TECHNOLOGICAL DEPENDENCE

On a micro-economic level, multinational enterprises in oligopolistic industries have upset the traditional economic market based on the forces of supply and demand. The economic market is conceptualized as generating price signals that provide information for decisions about resource allocation and income distribution. Both domestic and multinational oligopolistic firms, especially vertically integrated entities, may be able to avoid the market's constraints by cutting output and stabilizing (or increasing) prices in the face of slumping demand. Such firms may also possess the ability to pass on spiraling costs to consumers. Intracompany transactions by a multinational enterprise, involving a global parent and its subsidiaries, may also enable such firms to bypass the market price established for component parts or items. These intrafirm exchanges, known as transfer pricing, replace market transactions and enable multinational corporations to evade many of the constraints on corporate behavior imposed by national regulations.[43] A multinational company can locate profits in a foreign subsidiary with lower tax rates (and, conversely, restrict profits where taxes are higher) in order to reduce the corporation's total tax burden on its worldwide operations; and it can reduce prices on goods sold to a subsidiary, thereby generating capital and permitting the financing of the subsidiary. Intrafirm transactions, particularly by pharmaceutical firms, have come under scrutiny in a number of Western European countries, including the United Kingdom, West Germany and Austria.

Although the generation of profits by the manipulation of prices and other means is not without consequence, multinational firms may present two more significant problems from the standpoint of an industrialized host country. By dominating certain industrial sectors, especially in growing high-technology industries, multinational firms may produce a sense of technological dependency that pervades a society. In a few developed nations subsidiaries of multinational companies represent the dominant percentage of all enterprise, by assets, sales or profits. One such country is Canada, where American companies account for approximately 60% of the total manufacturing output. In addition to a heavy concentration in manufacturing, direct investment by American corporations in Canada dominates the petroleum and natural gas, mining and smelting and financial fields. American-based control is highest in Canadian industries where taste formation and technological and product innovation are crucial. Significant foreign ownership also exists in Australia in the following areas: motor vehicles, telecommunications, pharmaceuticals and toilet products, soap and detergents, and petroleum refining and distributing.[44] Even in Western Europe, where United States manufacturing subsidiaries recorded only about 6% of aggregate manufacturing sales in the 1960s, American firms established preeminence in advanced technological industries, such as computers, and in certain manufacturing sectors, such as ball-bearing, carbon black, petroleum refining, and telecommunications equipment.[45]

The extent of foreign dominance is even more apparent from an analysis of specific industries in different countries. The ball-bearing industry is 100% foreign owned in Italy and 80% in France. The carbon black production is 75% foreign controlled in the United Kingdom and 95% in France. In France in the 1960s, the synthetic rubber and margarine industries were each 90% foreign owned and agricultural equipment was 70% foreign owned; telecommunications equipment, 65%; with 50% of the electric lamp, office equipment, tire and plumbing equipment industries in foreign hands.[46] In developed countries, then, foreign firms evidence a high concentration of direct investment in industries characterized by fast growth, high technology and an orientation toward exports. But what is the consequence of the concentration of foreign direct investment in certain sectors and the foreign dominance of certain industries?

The dominant position of foreign-owned firms in different industries, especially in concentrated industries characterized by product differentiation, may introduce or further patterns of industrial concentration or artificial product differentiation. A worldwide pattern of concentration and product differentiation may be extended into a nation, reducing competition and making more difficult the entry of independent, locally owned firms. In short, foreign direct investment and industrial concentration go together. However, the growth of foreign subsidiary manufacturing corporations in industries already characterized by a high degree of concentration may lead to a lessening of concentration by increasing the number of competitors.[47] One study of industrial patterns in Canada indicates that the prevalence of foreign ownership has not increased. or decreased the degree of competition in terms of industrial concentration and merger activity.[48]

Foreign control of key technologically advanced sectors, such as computers, electronics, and space research, may undermine national scientific and industrial independence. Moreover, nations must face a larger problem, namely, the creation of a so-called branch-plant mentality among the citizens of a developed host country, a mentality characterized by the lack of decision-making power over key issues affecting foreign subsidiaries, which spreads to a more general lack of political, social and cultural independence. Multinational corporations may make decisions affecting the entire economy of host countries. As decision making on many issues shifts outside a host country, remote corporate control may fail to grasp national problems. Decisions may be made without considering local consequences. An environment may be created that permanently dampens local entrepreneurial effort. The capacity of a host country in managerial, technical and financial aspects of business may be stunted. The educational system and the media may train citizens of a host country for lives as consumers and workers in an American-style society. In addition to spawning a cultural colony, economic dependency may adversely affect a nation's capacity for making independent political decisions as the country becomes locked into various relationships with another nation.[49]

A particular danger feared by host nations is the possibility of becoming technologically dependent on the advances of a parent corporation for growth and product development.[50] Technology transfers may be withheld by a parent corporation on orders from its home government. Lacking national sources of technological advancement, the argument runs, the host nation's economic development may be hindered and its political influence reduced. A nation may be frozen into production and education patterns determined elsewhere.

To meet the fear of technological subservience in the late 1960s nations in Western Europe channeled public funds into certain industries to subsidize domestic research and development and to encourage or compel nationalization or acquire majority ownership positions. Governments also sought to promote national and transnational mergers.[5] National efforts to rationalize and strengthen the position of domestic firms lessened competition.

Governments also pressured foreign corporations to establish local research and development facilities to alter the pattern of corporations concentrating the bulk of their research and development activities in central research headquarters located in the home country or in a very few developed nations.[52] The centralization of research has stemmed from several factors, including a desire to cut the required capital investment and a belief that a large research and development organization working on many projects generates feelings of success, while the decentralization of research and development may pose the problem of where to allow innovation if a foreign research and development facility produces a successful result. Even if a multinational firm does establish a research unit in a developed country, no assurance exists that such a facility will pursue independent research efforts in the local interest. Indeed, a corporation may deliberately funnel more research funds to a foreign subsidiary because of lower costs. Moreover, research and development undertaken by foreign subsidiaries may reduce the supply of scientific and engineering talent available to local firms, thereby stifling the growth of domestically oriented research.

The fear of technological dependency among most developed nations in Western Europe has abated as a result of several factors: the efforts of Western European nations to strengthen local firms and increase research and development activities by domestic and multinational enterprises; a decline in the technological preeminence of American industry in many fields; and the cross-penetration of European firms into the United States. This fear still lingers, however, in Canada and in France. Moreover, although there is little evidence to indicate that foreign firms have engaged in widespread plant closings in Western Europe, isolated cases have had a marked impact on particular firms, industries, or regions, and actual or threatened closings arouse strong fears.[53]

5

THE CHALLENGE OF MNCs TO LABOR AND TO THE CONCEPT OF DECENTRALIZED PARTICIPATORY WORK STRUCTURES

Beyond the effect of multinational enterprises on the micro- and macro-economic sectors, global firms, labor unions allege, have a more personal and deleterious impact on workers. Labor claims that US–based multinational firms have reduced the total number of jobs in the United States and shifted the domestic distribution of income to capital factors and away from the labor sector. The validity of such claims is weakened somewhat by a careful analysis of the assumptions on which the various studies are based and by the disaggregation of the figures. Yet, the foreign expansion of multinational corporations has definitely produced a shift of jobs in the United States among industries and among particular job skills, and national policy planners must devise means to creatively utilize the talents of individual workers displaced by structural employment shifts brought about by the operations of global firms. An additional problem is the fact that multinational firms also perpetuate, on a global basis, the hierarchical division between management and workers, rendering attempts to devise participatory organizational structures difficult, not impossible.

IMPACT ON JOBS AND INCOME DISTRIBUTION

Organized labor unions in the United States, specifically the AFL-CIO have vociferously charged that American multinational corporations accounted for a significant share of the jobs lost in the United States the late 1960s and early 1970s, with a resulting harmful impact on many individuals and communities. Labor spokesmen have estimated that the

American economy lost 500,000 job opportunities between 1966 and 1969, while the new job possibilities lost grew more than a million between 1966 and 1972.[1] Employment plummeted in the domestic manufacture of radios and televisions and in the electronic components and accessories industries.[2] An academic study corroborates the aggregate job loss possibility figures and points to a net loss in 1970, for instance, of 160,000 jobs in the United States attributable to overseas investment by American multinational manufacturing firms, especially in the machinery, electrical equipment and chemical industries.[3]

Unions developed the aggregate job loss possibility figures by comparing the number of jobs required to produce the equivalent value of imports competitive with domestic products in given years, less the number of job opportunities attributable to the higher United States merchandise exports. In short, foreign investment is linked to the growth of imports, and a causal relationship is posited with domestic employment. It is difficult to quantify competitive imports, which vary from industry to industry and are dependent on seasonal and cyclical factors. Linking foreign subsidiaries of American multinational corporations with the growth of imports into the United States is also speculative. Furthermore, different factors govern foreign direct investment and domestic employment, with the latter more influenced by the general state of the domestic economy, the phase of the business cycle, aggregate demand, and domestic monetary, fiscal and and tax policies.[4] Structural shifts in the location of operations by certain industries and firms, however, cannot be ignored.

Labor starts from the premise that United States–based multinational enterprises reduce domestic jobs by producing in foreign nations goods that otherwise would have been manufactured in the United States and exported abroad and by using the plants of foreign subsidiaries as bases for the exportation of goods to the United States and to other markets. The shift of production to so-called export platforms in low-wage countries, which goods, it is assumed, could have been produced by American workers, has been of particular concern. The net result of these developments, so the argument runs, is the displacement of American workers and a shifting of the economic base of the United States to a service economy. The impact of multinational enterprises in changing employment patterns exposes organized labor's vulnerability in times of high unemployment and underemployment and highlights organized labor's weakness outside the manufacturing sector. In addition, the ability or the threat of multinational corporations to shift production, temporarily or permanently, from one country to another, the use of different plants in different countries to produce the same item, and the fina cial ability of global firms to withstand a strike raise additional challenge for nationally based labor unions and for the regulatory power of individual nation-states. To a certain extent organized labor may overestimate the flexibility of multinational firms. A corporation desiring to shift production faces a number of costs under local laws, such as severance pay requirements, and transfers of operations may not be possible on short notice as plants may not be conveniently relocated and existing units may lack sufficient excess capacity. Union leaders are also disturbed by the lack of sufficient information to engage in collective bargaining with multinational corporations and by corporate decision making in central headquarters beyond the reach of a local union. Labor faces the additional challenge that the threat of a plant closing in a given country may also cause a union in that nation to moderate its demands.

Underlying labor's job loss argument is the assumption that a high proportion of the production generated by foreign direct investment could be retained in the United States, specifically that foreign markets could continue to be served by the exportation of goods from the United States. Foreign investment, it is postulated, adds to (or replaces) local investment in a host country, thereby reducing investment in the United States. Workers could be employed indefinitely domestically, the argument goes, if only capital remained at home; employment in the United States also declines because subsidiaries export back to the United States goods that would otherwise have been produced domestically.

Other analysts, proceeding from different assumptions, maintain that foreign investment by American firms has preserved and generated domestic jobs. A study by the United States Department of Commerce concluded, "A reasonable interpretation of available evidence leads to the conclusion that U.S. foreign direct investment is not contrary to the interests of U.S. workers but may, in fact, be a positive factor in stimulating U.S. employment and economic activity."[5] One commentator has stated that under almost any assumption gross dislocation by US-based global corporations is quite small compared with the annual growth of the US labor force. Industries with high foreign direct investment exhibit faster than average domestic growth and rarely displace absolute numbers of workers.[6]

Estimates place the number of jobs created in the United States, directly or indirectly, by foreign direct investment in the late 1960s at 590,000, including 220,000 direct production jobs, 250,000 white collar jobs in home offices, 100,000 openings in supporting services, and 20,000 jobs in transportation and warehousing.[7] A number of studies indicate that domestic employment by United States-based multinational firms grew nearly three times as fast as total manufacturing employment.[8] One expert, however, estimates that the net overall impact of American global firms on domestic jobs is probably negative if more than 12.5% of the foreign production of new subsidiaries displaces U.S. exports.[9] Nonetheless, eliminating the automobile industry figures, the correlation between foreign direct investment and domestic market penetration by imports from foreign subsidiaries of American corporations remains insignificant.[10]

Although it is difficult to assess the impact of foreign direct investment on employment in the United States (because of the problem of isolating the impact of all multinational corporations, the variety of industries, individual firm trends, labor practices and conditions of work, and ultimately the multitude of causal relationships between jobs and foreign investment) cyclical and other factors may outweigh the impact of foreign direct investment. Observers stressing the positive contribution of multinational corporations to employment trends in the United States move from the premise that firms go abroad to combat a potential erosion of corporate competitive positions in foreign markets. They assume that American exports lacked competitiveness and maintain that foreign competition would have overwhelmed American exports. The choice was: Go overseas, or face a substantial decline in total sales and profits. Domestic investment, for most firms, simply was not a real alternative to investing abroad. Failure to engage in foreign direct investment, it is argued, would have resulted in a loss of jobs in the domestic manufacturing sector. These analysts also contend that the flow of imports into the United States in such categories as textiles, shoes, steel and automobiles emanates from foreign-owned firms, not American global giants.[11] Turning to the positive impact, defenders of United States multinational corporations also maintain that foreign direct investment created jobs in various ways: by stimulating domestic production of capital goods to be used in new overseas plants and components to be processed and assembled overseas; by using a foreign subsidiary as a vehicle to open export markets for other products of the parent corporation; and by providing increased opportunities for white-collar workers and scientific and technical personnel, who furnish engineering and research and development services.

The fallacy with the conclusions reached by both defenders and opponents of multinational corporations lies in their failure to disaggregate the figures. The effect of foreign direct investment on domestic employment varies among industries. How many jobs were created or displaced in each category, by job classification, by skill level and by geographical area? Studies also fail to assess alternate use of corporate funds (such as the payment of dividends, investment in the production of other goods or utilization of other domestic outlets) and whether an individual, if not employed by a given firm, would continue to remain unemployed. A pioneering study indicates that foreign production by global companies caused a shift of demand to "higher" level labor skills (i.e., more "professional" and away from blue-collar positions in industries facing competitive imports and export industries that have lost their competitive advantage.[12] But the questions of how many jobs could have been created if American plants had not gone abroad, and whether American-based production could have remained competitive in export markets (and for how long) or whether sales in overseas and domestic markets would have been lost to foreign competition remain difficult to analyze. Particularly hard to analyze is the question of whether United States firms require foreign subsidiaries to compete effectively under all conditions or just in certain circumstances.

The increase in foreign direct investment in the United States may create new jobs if new technologies, industrial techniques or product ideas follow the inflow of capital. If, as seems likely, the minor technological improvements accompanying foreign capital may produce only a limited long-run contribution to expanding the American job base, the borrowing and utilization of American technology and industrial ideas by non-US global corporations may diminish the number of job opportunities for US workers in export-oriented industries.[13]

Thus far, shifts in the numbers of workers and sectors of gainful employment have been analyzed. Foreign production may, even in the absence of a diminution of jobs, redistribute national income away from labor, particularly among the lower levels of blue-collar workers. Estimates of the reduction in the absolute level of labor income in the United States below what might have occurred if American corporations had invested funds only domestically run to over $6 billion a year.[14] In addition to shifting income, foreign direct investment decreases the capital stock with which Americans work, thereby reducing the productivity of labor and real wages.[15] Foreign direct investment thus reduces the rate of growth of labor income and the share of labor in national income.

The alleged adverse impact of global firms on the distribution of income in the United States rests on three points. The first point is that foreign direct investment acts as a substitute for domestic investment. This premise is questionable because of the means by which American corporations finance overseas operations. Capital from the United States does not constitute the sole or even the most significant means of financing foreign direct investment. A more reasonable premise might be that corporations deploy funds to finance both foreign and domestic activities. If, however, foreign investment supplements domestic investment, the growth rate of labor's income would not be reduced; but labor's share of national income, both foreign and domestic, would still fall in the face of in increased growth rate for the income of capital. The second point is that corporations could readily find outlets for funds in the mature American economy, for example, by fulfilling unmet social needs in areas of health and mass transit. However, even if net returns from foreign operations (after payment of foreign taxes) are less than domestic returns before the payment of taxes,[16] the strategy of investing abroad at a lower rate of return may be sensible if a corporation thereby maintains a continued higher profit rate at home. Placing additional funds in domestic operations may only lower a firm's overall rate of return. Expansion of corporate activities abroad may fulfill an enterprise's need for growth apart from the profit consequences. The third point is that all income derived from foreign operations goes to the capital sector of the American economy.[17] To the contrary, it appears more likely that foreign investment creates (or at least preserves) a certain number of jobs, albeit in different work categories, so that some of the gains generated by foreign operations flow to workers, although not necessarily to the same individuals whose jobs were displaced.

In response to the alleged adverse impact of foreign direct investment on American jobs and the revenue loss for the federal government, estimated to exceed $4 billion per year,[18] Senator Vance Hartke (D–Indiana) and Representative James Burke (D–Massachusetts) introduced the Foreign Trade and Investment Bill of 1973, embodying tax changes and controls over the outflow of capital and the imports of goods.[19] The bill sought major shifts in the United States' taxation of the foreign operations of American corporations. Under the proposal, foreign taxes paid would be deductible from corporate taxes instead of, as now, entitling the subsidiaries of American corporations to domestic tax credits. Opponents of the present credit approach argue that the national return to the United States on corporate foreign investments should be the return net of foreign taxes, while return on domestic investment should be the return before American taxes, as foreign taxes paid on foreign profits are lost to the United States government. The credit approach equalizes gross returns at home and abroad, which may not be desirable from the viewpoint of the United States. Giving only a deduction would put the foreign investment decision to more demanding test, as the rate of return net of foreign taxes would be required to equal gross returns on investments in the United States.

The tax deduction approach, however, would place United States firms at a decisive disadvantage. American multinational corporations presently face foreign tax rates as high as the rates imposed by the United States government. If American firms received only a deduction for foreign taxes paid, then subsidiary operations abroad might not remain competitive with corporations headquartered in other nations because of the increased tax burden imposed on the foreign subsidiaries.

The Burke-Hartke bill also proposed termination of the present deferral system, which permits the reporting of income generated by foreign subsidiaries of American corporations to be deferred until the repatriation of income in the form of dividends from foreign entities. Since a significant portion of the net earnings of foreign subsidiaries are reinvested, the deferral actually constitutes an exemption from taxation. The deferral thus promotes the growth of American enterprises outside the United States through the reinvestment of foreign profits to expand overseas operations.

Elimination of the tax deferral, however, might force corporations to pay a tax on earnings retained abroad from domestic funds, thereby reducing the capital available for the expansion of plant and equipment in the United States. Although, in theory, the interposition of a foreign-based entity instead of a domestic corporation does not constitute such a fundamental change as to justify a difference in tax treatment, a foreign subsidiary cannot always control the timing of dividend payments. The requirements of host nations, the imposition of capital controls, and the rights or wishes of other shareholders restrict the freedom of foreign affiliates. The forced repatriation of funds might conflict with a policy of a host nation or create ill will in the eyes of a foreign country, especially if the subsidiary is not wholly owned.

The proposals to change the present system of taxing the foreign activities of American multinationals rest on the premise that the United States tax system constitutes a prime motivation for foreign direct investment by American firms. As discussed in chapter three, this premise is flawed. Unilateral action by the United States forcing American global firms to eliminate or cut back overseas operation would permit Western European and Japanese firms to fill the void, with little assurance of a long-run positive impact on the number of domestic jobs or the expansion of investment at home.[20]

If further research establishes that foreign direct investment imposes too great a cost on American labor and domestic economic development, then the tax deferral provisions should be revamped. Possible modifications include phasing out the deferral over a specified time period or subjecting a portion of the earnings of foreign subsidiaries, perhaps in certain industries, to United States taxation, whether or not such earnings are repatriated. In any event, the credit should continue for foreign taxes paid on the earnings of overseas subsidiaries.

In the long run, consideration should be given to the need for corporate expansion abroad and the multitude of domestic and foreign ramifications from global corporate activities. If such an overall reappraisal produces evidence that the present method of taxing the foreign subsidiaries of American corporations creates too great a tax advantage for foreign direct investment, then it may be deemed desirable to remove such tax incentives, provided that some transitional cushion is offered for corporations. However, the idea of a dramatic restructuring of the tax system calls forth a grim prospect: To suddenly deprive American corporations of their foreign earnings probably would produce a devastating impact on the United States economy. One survey of 45 global firms indicated that 60% of these firms anticipated catastrophic or permanent damage from a total pullout of all their foreign operations.[21] The impact on corporate global activities emanating from a change in the United States tax system remains, of course, unclear; but once the adverse consequences of tax changes were established, the federal government could undertake efforts to direct corporate resources and establish priorities through national economic planning tools. Such a system might spur corporations to take advantage of domestic business opportunities in fields outside those in which they presently operate, particularly fields that would fulfill unmet domestic social needs.

The Burke-Hartke proposal, around which critics of the domestic impact of United States–based multinationals rallied, also would have empowered the president of the United States to regulate or prohibit any person within the jurisdiction of the United States from engaging in the direct or indirect transfer of capital out of the United States when such a transfer would result in a net decrease of employment in the United States. The bill also mandated the imposition of quotas on imports.

The United States probably would receive little cooperation from other nations in enforcing a program to control the international flow of capital and technology. The imposition of import quotas, in particular, would invite retaliation by foreign countries.

In retrospect the Burke-Hartke proposal constituted a bludgeon rather than a surgical instrument to meet the domestic problems posed by the overseas activities of American global firms. The foreign activities of United States multinational firms have produced structural changes in domestic production and employment. Rather than wedding American corporations to existing fields or keeping the American labor force tied to particular jobs on the production line, the nation's economic system should be flexible and allow the country to concentrate its resources in high growth areas. But a shift in the composition and number of jobs causes suffering on the part of the affected workers and their families. These structural transformations, therefore, raise the question of whether a corporation or its labor force should bear the cost of shifting production abroad, particularly to low-wage countries.

It is recommended that the United States government lessen the impact on displaced workers and their families through a variety of programs, including compensatory programs, public works projects and the licensing of new foreign endeavors. Compensatory programs for displaced workers and their families could take the form of guaranteed income payments for a specified period of time, retraining for jobs in high technology or service industries, and payment of relocation expenses. Precedent exists for such proposals. When Congress created a public corporation, Amtrak, to consolidate American railroad passenger service, the legislation provided protection for dislocated workers with the following assurances: (1) a worker who was laid off or downgraded as a result of the creation of Amtrak would receive his full wages and fringe benefits applicable to his old job, plus any subsequent increases in wage rates or improvements in fringe benefits for a period of time equal to his previous railroad employment, up to a maximum of six years; (2) a worker transferred to a railroad job at another location would receive full reimbursement for all family moving expenses; (3) a worker could choose to receive funds for retraining and a lump sum severance pay instead of income maintenance benefits. The Trade Act of 1974 made workers eligible for trade-adjustment assistance when increased imports contributed importantly to the absolute decline in sales and production and the total or partial layoff of a significant number of workers.[22] Despite the complex procedures requisite to the receipt of benefits and the surrounding bureaucratic maze, a number of workers, particularly in the automotive and clothing fields, have received trade-related jobless aid.

Compensation proposals must deal with a number of technical problems. Consideration must be given to the time limitation on benefits, protection of social security and unemployment compensation rights, provision for family health benefits and loss of seniority, and provision must be made for older workers who may not be able to find suitable jobs. The fact that a corporation may cause the dislocation of not only its own workers but also employees in other firms and industries renders more complex the compensation question.

Federal public works projects may also be required, as well as federal control over the location policies of corporations. Public works projects could be funded by general tax revenues or by the imposition of a special tax on corporations that displace workers by moving production facilities abroad. If the latter route were selected, this additional levy might not only lessen the attractiveness of a foreign plant but also reduce the competitive position of a product in both world and American markets.

The federal government might also require a license before any United States corporation could undertake foreign direct investment, including the reinvestment of profits in foreign subsidiaries. A license applicant would be required to show that the proposed investment would serve United States interests and be free from harmful political consequences. The license requirement might also be tied to a corporate guarantee of full compensation for the loss of wages, fringe benefits and seniority rights sustained by any United States worker or, in a more limited form, by any employee of a corporation adversely affected by such foreign activities, because of either imports or the loss of export sales.[23]

IMPACT OF WORKER PARTICIPATION IN CORPORATE MANAGEMENT

A most profound human crisis involves a two-fold inquiry: Why should people perform meaningless work in inhumane organizations? and Why should workers take orders from leaders they do not choose? Through meaningful work, individuals may realize their potential. In an attempt to give more widespread access to corporate decision making, a number of Western European nations, led by West Germany, have undertaken steps to restructure corporate decision making by mandating worker participation on the management level. Worker representatives are given a specified number of seats on the board of directors of a corporation or on a new supervisory board constituting part of a new, two-tier management structure. More extensive efforts at worker self-management, which may be harbingers of the future, have attempted to revamp authoritarian organizational hierarchies and seek to involve employees in decision making throughout the enterprise. But the multinational structure casts doubt on the possibility of meaningful participation by workers.

The term "multinational corporation" suggests an enterprise with international ownership and management. In reality ownership and management usually rest in the hands of the nationals of the respective home countries. The shareholders of multinational corporations are overwhelmingly nationals of the country of incorporation, with perhaps 2–3% of the outstanding shares held by foreigners.[24] Two notable exceptions to the pattern of ownership and control in one nation are Royal Dutch Shell and Unilever; British and Dutch interests jointly share the ownership and control of these two corporations.

Internationalization of the share ownership of a parent corporation probably would be a waste of time and effort. Proposals to create worldwide ownership of parent's stock are impractical for the following reasons: ownership and management of an entity would be separate; a subsidiary would remain tied to a worldwide system; and foreign shareholders might not continue to hold shares. Unless a requirement were imposed that shares distributed to foreigners be kept in a particular nation, such shares might come to rest in the hands of nationals of the home country. In any event, managers would probably disregard the foreign shareholders.

Few corporations have achieved international integration of management, that is, the assignment of executive responsibility without regard to nationality. Nationals of a home country predominate as officers and directors of a parent corporation. A survey of the 150 largest (in terms of sales) United States manufacturing corporations indicated that non–US nationals composed 20% of the total employment of such firms, but only 1.6% of top management entered the United States as foreigners after age 25 (or remained outside the United States). Foreign nationals filled less than 1% of the senior headquarters positions.[25] Another study notes that only three (Shell, Nestlé and Exxon) of the twenty-five largest American and twenty-five largest West European firms have more than three nationalities represented on the corporate board of directors and top management. Foreigners comprised .9% of members of the board and the management of American corporations and 2.9% of such positions in European corporations.[26]

Although placing increasing numbers of nationals from a host country in important managerial positions in foreign subsidiaries,[27] corporations have found it exceedingly difficult to move foreign nationals into corporate-headquarters positions. Observers of multinational firms indicate that with few exceptions, including some American banks, Alcan, and Nestlé, rarely are younger, abler individuals from subsidiaries in developing countries assigned for three-to-five year periods to managerial and professional posts in a developed country.[28] Generally the rise of foreign nationals in a corporate hierarchy stops at intermediate coordinating centers on a continent-wide level. One of the key problems is the centralization of decision making, which leaves personnel in subsidiaries ill prepared to make the jump to corporate headquarters. Cost incentives exist for American corporations to recruit United States citizens for top executive positions. Moreover, foreign nationals manifest a reluctance to live in a headquarters country as a result of language barriers and a lack of social confidence.

In the future, more foreign nationals may cross the threshold to executive positions at corporate headquarters. A recent assessment of the management of global firms concluded that the almost imperceptible progress toward internationalization of top executives has occurred only in corporations with 75 to 100 years of international experience and has been brought about by horizontal mergers, the worldwide diffusion of skills in various industries, the need for higher level jobs for foreigners who would otherwise leave and by political pressures.[29] As firms think in terms of a global perspective, perhaps currently best exemplified by IBM among American corporations, enterprises will require more managers who can analyze the foreign environments in which enterprises presently or may in the future operate. These globally oriented corporations may seek the best people, regardless of nationality, to solve problems and formulate strategy.[30] The advancement of foreigners to corporate headquarters may, however, render firms vulnerable to charges of contributing to a "brain drain."

In light of the worldwide corporate hierarchy coordinating the planning, production, marketing and finance operations of multinational firms and the difficulties inherent in internationalizing the management of global giants, doubt exists as to the possibility of creating and implementing a viable structure for worker participation within a global business organization. Even if the managers were willing to share some of their power, the logistics of a multicontinent system of meaningful worker involvement in corporate management and the development of the information systems requisite to meaningful participation boggle the imagination.

Participation in global organizations may prove impossible. The technical specialization inherent in complex organizations may make an oligarchy inevitable. Workers may lack sufficient information, and the systems of representation may prove inadequate. Discontinuities of communication and interaction compound the problem.

The growth of multinational corporations creates the haunting vision of a hierarchical ordering not only of a firm but also of economic activity on a global scale. The vision of centralized decision making in certain key developed countries, with the remainder of the earth confined to lower levels of activity and income, has spurred increasing resentment on the part of those at the low end of the present system.

Surmounting the obstacles may require an examination of the impact of multinational firms on participatory concepts. Such an analysis may lead to a development of smaller, decentralized communities and corporate entities. These more humane units would meet human needs in a variety of ways. Smaller economic units would enable workers, the non-experts, to be more informed and to assume responsibility for the social consequences of an enterprise by participating in a wide range of managerial decisions.[31]

6

THE IMPACT OF MNCs ON THE POLITICAL PROCESS OF DEVELOPED NATIONS

The impact of multinational corporations on political process in home and host countries remains a controversial topic. In the making of post–World War II American foreign policy, corporations played a key role in setting the dominant ideology and supplying top policy makers. With the change in relative power position of the United States in the 1970s, the role of corporations in foreign policy evolved. Business interests may not be as readily translated into foreign policy decisions. Home and host nations may use international firms as tools of influence for governmental policies. Revelation of questionable payments abroad by American multinational corporations has focused renewed attention on the impact of global firms on the political decision-making process.

After the war, American business executives sought corporate growth and expansion domestically and abroad. At home, business needed a national government that would provide subsidies to business (with the costs borne by the American taxpayers) and spur the consumption of goods and services, thereby promoting prosperity and maintaining the basis of a private enterprise economy, while at the same time lessening pressing social and economic problems. Business desired the federal government to promote an "open door" for American economic penetration abroad as part of a national system to protect and facilitate the interests of business. The world had to be made safe for the continued presence and the expansion of business. Corporate executives sought a foreign policy based on an expansionist ideology, stability for private firms, preservation of the existing distribution of world economic wealth, status and power, perpetuation of spheres for trade and investment, and an uninterrupted flow of cheap raw materials from developing nations.[1]

The American business community is, of course, not homogeneous. Larger firms with plants abroad are generally more interested in the protection of foreign direct investment, while smaller enterprises engaged in international trading operations desire the government's promotion of exports. But almost unanimously, business executives would agree on the need for government promotion of various types of foreign corporate expansion.

To meet the overseas needs of corporations in the post–World War II era, business executives created an ideology that provided a framework for American political action in the international arena and shaped the formation, dissemination and enforcement of foreign policy attitudes and assumptions. In addition to setting the general consensus out of which national security and foreign policy were established, the interchange of personnel between government and business marked the symbiosis between corporations and the American corporate state.

Individuals holding many of the key foreign policy and national security posts were drawn from the business community, including attorneys serving the needs of corporate clients. These individuals shaped the policymaking institutions and developed the criteria by which their successors and the rapidly growing bureaucracy made decisions. Business-oriented individuals sponsored policy-planning and consensus-developing organizations, such as the Council on Foreign Relations, which serve as a transmission belt for corporate influence. These organizations perform a number of functions, including creating and spreading an expansionist ideology, acting as moderators of the conflicts within top business groups, and providing a training ground for individuals who will eventually assume appointed governmental posts.[2] In commenting on the importance of a policy-planning network G. William Domhoff concluded:

First, it provides evidence that businessmen, bankers, and lawyers concern themselves with more than their specific business interests. Second, it shows that leaders from various sectors of the economy do get together to discuss the problems of the system as a whole. Third, it suggests that members of the power elite who are appointed to government are equipped with a general issue-orientation gained from power-elite organizations that are explicitly policy oriented. Fourth, it reveals that the upper-middle class experts thought by some to be our real rulers are in fact busily dispensing their advice to those who hire them.[3]

Beyond inferring power from the disproportionate number of business-oriented people in high position, how can we ascertain that businessmen actually wield power in government? When the United States held unquestioned sway as the world's most powerful nation, the federal government, in the area of foreign policy, generally served the interests of business: "The foreign policy decision-makers' view of American society and America's role in the world is derived from the same social and intellectual sources as that of the businessman."[4] The continued expansion of and security for the overseas operations of multinational corporations necessitated a counter-revolutionary foreign policy. The United States provided economic and military assistance, beginning with the Marshall Plan, to further the expansionist desires of American corporations, in addition to humanitarian and national security motivations. The Central Intelligence Agency intervened in Iran in 1953 and Guatemala in 1954 to remove governments considered an actual threat to business interests.[5]

The interpretation of American foreign policy formulation as a reflex of business interests becomes less viable, however, when American military intervention in Vietnam, Laos and Cambodia is assessed. The Vietnam agony probably did not arise as foreign-policy makers' response to corporate interests with a stake in foreign markets and investments. These interventions may better be viewed in terms of the ideology of militant anticommunism and the domino theory, as protection against insurgent revolutionary organizations in other countries that threaten the desired pattern of stability and the confidence of foreign elites in the ability of the United States to secure their privileged position. When business executives perceived that the costs of intervention in Vietnam exceeded the alleged benefits of safeguarding American supremacy and the "private enterprise" system, they broke with government policy and advocated a deescalation of the war.[6]

The failure of America's attempt to intervene in Vietnam and the decline of the United States' hegemony have brought about a more complex business-government relationship. The government continues to promote the interests of American business abroad but increasingly will not apply overt sanctions against an offending country. For instance, the United States has generally pursued a low profile in Latin American by not taking an aggressive posture on behalf of the subsidiaries of American firms facing nationalization.[7] A major exception was the covert effort by the Nixon administration to wage economic warfare against Chile, particularly the closing of access to loan funds; collaboration among officials from government and the private sector hastened the overthrow of former President Salvador Allende. Corporations such as Gulf Oil in Angola came to realize that their economic power was perhaps greater than the military might or political clout of the United States government.

The trend toward a separation of government and business interests in the foreign policy arena is best exemplified in the Middle East.[8] Despite strenuous corporate efforts, American policy makers have heeded interests other than those of American corporations. On the other hand, during the 1973 oil embargo, United States oil companies curtailed shipments of petroleum to the United States armed forces, confirming fears that the companies feel little direct allegiance to the United States.

Corporations have not controlled government policies in a number of areas. The United States government has used multinational corporations, particularly their information-gathering capacity, to pursue its own political, economic or military objectives. Taxes from the operations of global firms finance America's political and military positions.[9] To further containment policies, the United States has pursued restrictive trade policies. Prior to the detente between the United States and the People's Republic of China, the American government restricted trade by domestic corporations and their foreign subsidiaries with the People's Republic. Against the wishes of multinational firms, the United States government has pressed for extraterritorial application of laws, particularly in the anti-trust field, often in contravention of the laws and policies of host nations.

Multinational firms have had an impact not only on the political process of a home country but also on host nations in both the developing and developed world.[10] American corporations have engaged in a wide spectrum of activities to insure the success of their foreign endeavors. One prevalent activity has been the payment of money to persons or officials who are in a position to further the interests of the corporation. This practice has included direct payments to foreign consultants and agents, campaign contributions to political parties and bribery of government officials. Corporations have channeled millions of dollars through these payments, which often extend over a period of years. Legal and illegal corporate political contributions in host countries comprise a sizable portion of the overseas payments. These political payments are often justified on the grounds that they are essential to protect democracy (an argument particularly recurrent with regard to payments in Italy) or to continue doing business in the respective host nations.

A large portion of overseas corporate payments goes to "consultants" and foreign agents in the form of commissions and fees. The role of these consultants and sales agents, who are often former high-ranking American and foreign military officials, is controversial. Despite the apparently legitimate services performed by some consultants in providing technical, legal, financial and marketing advice in a manner similar to consultants in the United States, consultants may serve as conduits to transmit bribes to influential officials in foreign governments.

Corporations have also expended funds abroad in efforts to overthrow or "destabilize" host governments. The desire to gain relief from unfavorable policies of a government in power or the desire to prevent the election of officials who might jeopardize company interests has led firms to undertake such a course of conduct. The most infamous example of this conduct is the activities of the International Telephone and Telegraph Company in Chile in 1970.[11]

These activities, which comprise an integral part of the strategy of global corporations, cast doubt on the ability of host governments to withstand pressure from multinational firms. The political process in nations may constitute a shadow game, with the real power held by global enterprises. In short, multinational corporations may curtail or destroy the sovereignty of nation-states. Disclosure of the pattern of corporate payments abroad and acceptance of funds by high-ranking governmental officials in Western Europe and Japan may lead to political instability in such nations and damage governmental relations with nations friendly to the United States. National and transnational efforts at regulating the conduct of multinational firms and national and regional steps taken by Third World nations to lessen the power of global firms will be examined in Part III.

PART THREE

THE IMPACT OF M N Cs ON
DEVELOPING COUNTRIES

7

M N Cs, THE THIRD WORLD AND DEPENDENCY

Developing countries perceive multinational corporations and the worldwide capitalistic system as perpetuating the dependency of the Third World on industrialized nations, even with the passing of formal colonial relationships after World War II. By securing effective economic, political and cultural dominance for certain countries, notably the United States, over the remainder of the world, multinational corporations have redistributed wealth, in the view of Third World nations, from the under-developed periphery to the centers of industrial power and decision making.[1] One example of the outward sanction effect is Chile, which traditionally has relied on the exportation of a single raw material. (Copper comprises approximately 80% of Chile's exports.) Foreign firms penetrated and dominated Chile's economy and repatriated profits out of Chile. From 1945 to the early 1970s, American firms remitted $7.2 billion from Chile while providing only $1 billion in capital.[2]

Critics of multinational enterprise, using the dependency analysis, warn that participation in the world capitalist system of trade, investment and organization of production creates an international polarization between the sophisticated industrialized countries in the center of the system and the developing nations at the periphery of the system. The needs of industries in the center set the order of priorities. Income, status, power and consumption patterns radiate from the multinational corporations headquartered in world cities located in the center of the capitalist system. Centralized corporate hierarchies in a few global cities make strategic decisions, provide a framework for the control of giant firms, determine global business strategy, innovate a never-ending flow of new products, and radiate information, thereby confining the remainder of the world to lower levels of activity, both within and outside the sphere of business.

Dependency theorists divide the world outside the capitalist center into two levels—an intermediate stage and the periphery. One step below the corporation headquarters in world cities are the plants located in the lesser cities, at the periphery of the center or at the core of the periphery, which manage the day-to-day activities of the firm. These lesser cities adjust to the commands emanating from the upper echelons and engage in, coordinate and supervise the production and distribution of goods. Finally, at the periphery, nations produce raw materials needed by the center and carry out certain phases of industrial production under foreign control.

The global plans and the expansionist needs of multinational firms, according to the dependency theory, shaped the growth and development of the world capitalist system. Multinational firms, with their integrated vertical hierarchical structure, control their far-flung operations based on a global strategy originating outside of and without regard to the interest of Third World host nations. Foreign subsidiaries of global giants conduct truncated operations—not a full line of functions—in developing nations.

Under the theory of dependency, the growth of the developing nation occurs as a reflex of the expansionistic drives of multinational firms and the economic systems of the dominant countries. The level of business concentration changes along three lines as the world divides between the center and the periphery: by trading partner, by commodity and by type of activity. The center has many trading partners, whereas a country in the periphery generally establishes trade relationships with only one or two nations. The center produces and trades in a diversified range of products, while the periphery concentrates on a few primary exports to pay for its imports. Capital-intensive, high-skill activities with significant spin-off effects in other areas characterize the center; the periphery, on the other hand, concentrates on labor-intensive, low-skill activities with a limited spin-off thrust.

Economic exploitation results from the incorporation of Third World nations into the world capitalistic system, which in turn produces, according to dependency theorists, underdevelopment, slow economic growth and technological backwardness. The center controls the economic potentials of the periphery. The center's power grows through technological progress. The periphery is relegated to the function of a raw material supplier. The integration of developing countries into the world capitalistic system, therefore, defines and delimits the alternatives available for Third World nations.[3]

This chapter explores the concept of dependency by analyzing the economic, cultural and political impacts of global firms on developing nations. In many instances, multinational corporations have adversely affected the economic, social and political systems of the Third World

ECONOMIC FACTORS

Economic problems constitute the mainstay of the dependency theory. It is alleged that developing countries face declining terms of trade and are plundered by firms engaged in the extraction of raw materials. As part of their manufacturing operations, multinational corporations use transfer pricing techniques and restrictive business practices and support technologies and social structures inimical to well-rounded development. Reliance on foreign technology yields technological dependency and places local firms in an unfair competitive position. Acquisition of local firms by global enterprises lays the basis for foreign control over a nation's industrial base. Multinational corporations also gain control over the fragile financial and capital markets in Third World nations. The activity of multinational corporations in the raw material and manufacturing fields generates "excess" profits, which global firms repatriate to their home countries, adversely affecting a host nation's balance of payments. The outflow of national wealth weakens a country's capacity to develop its local capital markets and its capacity to create an independent technological base. The growth of indigenous firms is stunted.

RAW MATERIALS, TERMS OF TRADE AND RESENTMENT

The intertwining of the Third World's raw material resources with the world capitalist system has led Third World nations to experience declining terms of trade and to direct resentment against multinational firms and industrialized nations. Analyzing the long-run downward trend in the terms of trade between the manufactured products exported from Great Britain to Latin America and the primary products imported into Great Britain from Latin America since the late nineteenth century, Raúl Prebisch viewed the benefits from technological change and increased productivity as spreading to the center of the world system.[4] Although Prebisch's historical work is subject to criticism on a number of grounds, including the composition of the commodity terms of trade index used and the fact that the decline in the prices the British paid for primary products from 1876 to 1905 stemmed from a substantial drop in freight rates,[5] Prebisch sparked an increased awareness of and interest in terms of trade analysis. The declining terms of trade concept underpins the argument that the world capitalist economy automatically and inexorably works against Third World countries.

Developing countries repeatedly allege that their respective raw material and commodity exports, even apart from the ownership of such materials and commodities by global firms, face declining terms of trade. Terms of trade deteriorate when the prices of imported goods in Third World nations rise faster than the prices enjoyed by the exports from such coun tries. A widely held belief exists that the prices of Third World raw mate rial and commodity exports have failed to keep pace with the upwar spiral in the price of manufactured goods imported from industrialize nations. In support of the theory of declining terms of trade, a study b the Secretariat of the United Nations Conference on Trade and Develop ment (UNCTAD) indicates that between 1953 and 1972 the terms of trad of the commodities covered, which included about two-thirds of th total value of commodity exports excluding petroleum, declined c the average about 2.2% annually.[6] The report concluded: "The analys presented in . . . this note would appear to establish fairly conclusive that the net barter terms of trade of a large number of primary commod ties, accounting for the bulk of the commodity exports (excluding petr leum) of developing countries, have deteriorated substantially over th last 25 years."[7]

However, another study for the secretary-general of UNCTAD foun that for a broad range of commodities, again excluding petroleum, th prices of raw material exports during a twenty-five year period in th post-World War II era rose about as much as prices of imported manu factured goods. Although the terms of trade were subject to substanti short-term fluctuations, this group of experts found no clear evidence of long-term deterioration in the terms of trade of developing countries

Nonetheless, it appears likely that prices of raw material and commodi exports from developing countries, in relation to manufactured import have declined since the 1950s. As a *New York Times* reporter conclude "In the 1950s prices fell, although from a high and untypical peak. In th 1960s, using the old techniques of measuring, terms of trade fluctuate around a fairly flat mean. And now in the 1970s, after a short boom, the are moving downward again. And once the double factorial method refined we may well get confirmation that a much grimmer situation h prevailed."[9]

Further studies, however, must be undertaken regarding terms of trad analysis. Past and future studies must be approached critically because the problems inherent in constructing terms of trade indexes. Difficulti include comparing the value of import packages that shift compositic because of technological change, the appearance of new materials, suc as synthetics, and the growing emphasis on recycling. The rising servi sector in the economies of the developed countries may also adverse affect the demand for primary commodity products. In addition, a shi has occurred in the pattern of the quality and quantity of traded good Productivity changes must also be taken into account. The use of inde numbers involves such questions as the weighting system, a suitable ba period, the selection of countries for inclusion in the index and whether the index is based on actual price quotations or unit values derived from trade statistics.[10]

In addition to the likelihood that raw material and commodity exports from developing countries encountered declining terms of trade subsequent to 1950, the ownership and exploitation of agricultural land and natural resources by global firms enraged Third World nations. Multinational corporations engaged in the extraction of raw materials were viewed as drawing nonrenewable resources too rapidly from the soil, seeking only high profits and lacking any interest in balanced local development.[11] Considerable skepticism pervaded Third World nations regarding the value returned to such countries by direct foreign investment in mineral extraction. The mere existence of raw material–producing foreign-owned enclaves, but in particular their isolation and self-sufficiency, also constituted a source of resentment.

Defenders of global firms emphasized, however, the contribution of foreign capital to local development through the generation of foreign exchange and tax revenues.[12] Stressing the benefits of multinational firms, these observers pointed to the inadequacies of Third World nations in a number of areas, especially capital, know-how and international sales network, as barriers to local development of raw material wealth.[13]

Increasingly, Third World countries have rejected this line of reasoning. Governments seized from global firms ownership and control of the extraction and, where possible, of the processing of raw materials.[14] The costs of foreign operations were perceived to exceed the benefits.

THE MANUFACTURING OPERATIONS OF MULTINATIONAL ENTERPRISES

In the 1950s Third World countries turned to a new development strategy, namely, the encouragement of foreign direct investment in manufacturing industries in an effort to reduce their dependency on the importation of manufactured goods. But, together with the relentless quest by multinational corporations for expansion, the trend toward establishing foreign manufacturing subsidiaries exacerbated the economic plight faced by the developing world. Foreign-owned manufacturing subsidiaries posed a number of problems for developing nations, including the use of transfer pricing, various restrictive business practices, the transfer of inappropriate technology, lack of local research and development, and an adverse impact on a nation's industrial organization, its capital markets and its balance of payments position.

Transfer Pricing. Intrafirm transactions between a parent and its subsidiaries enable a multinational corporation to maximize its global profits.

These intrafirm exchanges replace market transactions and enable multinational firms to evade many of the checks on corporate behavior provided by national laws. Intrafirm transactions may take a number of forms, including: (1) locating profits in a subsidiary in a country with lower tax rates (conversely restricting profits where taxes are higher), thereby reducing a corporation's total tax burden on its worldwide operations; (2) withdrawing funds from a given subsidiary (for example, in the face of limits on the repatriation of profits or the expectation of foreign exchange losses if a country devalues its currency) by increasing prices on the goods sold to that subsidiary by other subsidiaries or by the parent entity in a multinational corporate network; (3) financing a subsidiary by reducing prices on goods sold to it by other subsidiaries or the parent in a multinational enterprise. Other transfer pricing techniques include juggling the allocation of overhead and joint costs (such as exploration, research and development and advertising) and overpricing the plant and equipment used to set up or expand a foreign facility.[15]

From the viewpoint of a developing country, transfer pricing means that a subsidiary located in such a nation must pay higher prices for imports, especially for so-called intermediate goods, than prevail in the so-called free market. These intrafirm transactional techniques, particularly the reduction of prices of exported items, may produce a loss of taxes and foreign exchange earnings for a developing country. Low reported profit levels may also deter local competition and perpetuate dependence.

From the vantage point of a multinational corporation, a number of factors, some of them external, are involved in a firm's decision of whether or not to engage in transfer pricing. These factors include tariff barriers in effect in an importing country, the absolute and relative difference in tax rates among various nation-states, and a host government's policies regarding the remittance of profits. Additionally, a parent entity may drain profits from a subsidiary facing difficult labor negotiations. Or, assessing actual and expected exchange rate differentials, a global firm may attempt to evade currency devaluation. Internal reasons motivating the use of transfer pricing include the following: varying degrees of ownership of subsidiaries, with a natural desire to place profits where a firm enjoys the largest ownership position, and using pricing techniques to allocate markets among subsidiaries.

A number of studies indicate that multinational corporations generally engage in transfer pricing in developing countries. Global firms usually overprice the goods imported by developing countries and underprice the export items produced by such nations. One leading study, undertaken by the Colombian government, indicated an overpricing of a wide range of pharmaceutical imports by global firms, 155% above world market prices in 1968 and 87% in 1967–1970, as compared with a 19% overpricing on the products imported by locally owned firms. Selected rubber imports were overpriced by 44%, in comparison with zero overpricing by local firms. Some chemical imports by subsidiaries of global firms were overpriced by 25%, and electrical components by 54%. For eleven of the fourteen foreign firms surveyed in Colombia in 1966 and 1967, the profits accruing from overpricing exceeded declared profits. The Colombian pharmaceutical industry in 1968 reported that profits comprised 3.4% of the effective return, royalties 14% and overpricing 82.6%.[16] A similar pattern of overpricing imported items pervaded the foreign subsidiaries of the drug companies in other Latin American countries. In the Chilean pharmaceutical industry, imports by foreign subsidiaries were overpriced by a range of 30–500%; in Peru, by a factor of 20–300%.[17] Transfer pricing helps explain why a number of foreign subsidiaries may show "losses" each year, yet mysteriously continue in business.

Conversely, foreign subsidiaries of multinational corporations in Colombia underpriced a number of export products, including timber, processed fish and precious metals.[18] Another study of Latin American exporters of manufactured goods in ten Latin American countries during the 1966–1969 period suggests that multinational enterprises underpriced exports from their affiliates by an average of 40%.[19]

The extent to which multinational firms have used intrafirm transactional techniques in the past and may continue to do so in the future is unclear. Methodological infirmities exist in past studies of transfer pricing.[20] One critical problem involves establishing independent world market prices as a basis of comparison. Facile statements abound by multinational enterprises that they price goods according to a uniform standard involving the cost of production of an item plus a fixed markup, which may evidence "minor" fluctuations because of volume.[21] Empirical studies also dispute the pervasive existence of transfer pricing. One survey of 130 United States firms indicated that many of these corporations treated foreign subsidiaries as "unrelated" parties and charged competitive prices.[22] Another analysis, of eight American firms with overseas interests, revealed that only two regularly used transfer prices to maximize worldwide after-tax profits. Among the remaining six, arm's-length pricing was used to avoid conflicts as to which subsidiary showed the highest profit and to project a good-citizen image with host countries.[23]

Despite this evidence, one expert noted: "It is practically beyond question that multinational companies manipulate internal price relations so as to locate their profits either in the country of the mother company or in countries where taxes are lowest."[24] A few anonymous multinational corporations even admit juggling prices. According to the *Wall Street Journal*:

An executive of one big international oil company says prices between subsidiaries are controlled by the company's headquarters, which "tilts" the prices one way or another, depending on the situation. . . .

The treasurer of another company says he sometimes resorts to manipulation, especially when a foreign government blocks a subsidiary's profit remittances to the parent.[25]

In the future, several internal structural factors may lessen the scope of transfer pricing techniques utilized by global enterprises. The latitude available to firms depends on what percentage of a subsidiary's total output is represented by its local expenses. A report by the United Nations Group of Eminent Persons studying the impact of multinational corporations estimated that more than one-quarter of the value of all international trade is in goods of an intragroup character.[26] Additional intracorporate transactions occur in services, research and development and administrative functions. The Group of Eminent Persons concluded, "The scope for price manipulation is therefore quite extensive."[27] Other experts place the value of American exports that bypass the market as high as 50% or as low as 10%,[28] with a relatively higher percentage of goods involved in such transactions going to developing, as opposed to industrialized, nations. But if, as current trends indicate, an overwhelming percentage of the value of manufactured goods in the future will be produced in developing nations, then less room exists for a multinational firm to enjoy the benefits accrued from overpricing imported goods or component parts.

The size and complexity of organizations force managers to dull their pencils somewhat and rely on rules of thumb, not the most sophisticated tools.[29] Studies shown that medium-sized firms, but not large corporations, tend to favor more flexible pricing procedures that take into account varying circumstances and relationships between a parent and its foreign subsidiaries.[30] Corporations that spend greater than average amounts on research and development seem to be more reluctant than other firms to utilize financial techniques that might upset local authorities.[31] Thus, the presence of larger, more technologically oriented firms may limit the use of intrafirm transactions. The use of transfer pricing may also pose intrafirm morale problems and conflicts among executives in a parent entity and the subsidiary corporations.

Finally, governments of industrialized and Third World countries are attempting to constrain the use of transfer pricing and to force the attainment of arm's-length intracorporate pricing standards. Corporate officials point out that in most cases transfer pricing poses no problem because transactions are under the scrutiny of many authorities who would react to evidence of a zigzag policy. Business-oriented academic experts conclud that organizational impediments, together with governmental requirements, have rendered the use of transfer pricing substantially below its indicated potential.

However, certainly in the past global enterprises have possessed, and probably in the future they will possess, the balance of advantage regarding transfer pricing. Governments face a number of difficulties in controlling intrafirm transactions. Doubts exist as to the ability of a nation to gain sufficient knowledge and to administer the laws and regulations controlling transfer pricing in a noncorrupt manner. The small number of expert nation-state personnel further contribute to the power of multinational firms. As George Ball recently stated, "Though the host government can insist on seeing the books of the local subsidiary, it cannot examine the books of the parent, and even if it could, it would not have the highly trained manpower to make informed reallocations of earnings and costs."[32] It also is difficult to establish an arm's-length price for goods, especially in oligopolistic markets, for complex products. In a world pervaded by currency fluctuations and language barriers, the ingenuity of firms is boundless. Sophisticated intrafirm transactional techniques, such as the ability to juggle royalty and management fees and other overhead costs, may become more prevalent.

Restrictive Business Practices. The dispersal of manufacturing activities in Third World countries encouraged multinational firms to impose restrictive business practices on their foreign subsidiaries. During the post-World War II era, developing countries encouraged foreign direct investment in manufacturing plants that would produce import substitute items. These industries required, however, additional imports in the form of capital goods, plant and equipment, and raw materials. Lack of a sufficient home market impeded profitability. Developing countries then sought to penetrate markets in other countries by exporting items to earn vitally needed foreign exchange and to absorb excess plant capacity.[33]

The export restrictions imposed by the headquarters of multinational corporations over foreign subsidiaries tended to thwart the export-oriented strategy of Third World nations. The existence of export restrictions contributed to a relatively poor export performance by the foreign subsidiaries of United States corporations in Latin America. Manufacturing affiliates in Latin America exported less than 10% of their total sales; while in Europe, American subsidiaries averaged 25% of their total sales.[34]

The imposition of restrictive business practices, including export constraints, by multinational corporations on their foreign subsidiaries appears pervasive. A study by the Andean Common Market of over 400 transfer-of-technology contracts revealed that approximately 81% of such contracts prohibited the use of the transferred technology for producing exports. An analysis of 451 contracts by country showed the following prohibitions on exports: Bolivia, 77% of the contracts; Colombia, 77%; Chile, 73%; Ecuador, 75%; and Peru, 89%. Overall, by different industries, the figures were as follows: textiles, 88% of the contracts; pharmaceuticals, 89%; chemicals, 78%; and food and beverage, 73%. The contracts surveyed also contained a high percentage of export restrictions, for example, to certain countries or areas. Two-thirds of the technology contracts in Bolivia, Colombia, Ecuador and Peru, which the Andean Group analyzed, also had tie-in clauses requiring the purchase of intermediate and capital goods from the same source as the know-how.[35]

Other studies, by the United Nations Conference on Trade and Development, have indicated the extent of restrictive practices. For instance, one study indicated that 40% of the technical collaboration agreements between foreign corporations and public and private firms in India contained export restrictions.[36] Sixty-five percent of the contracts analyzed in a Philippines study embodied provisions restricting exports.[37]

The restrictive business practices, particularly the territorial arrangements accompanying the licensing of patents and know-how, are customary and, from the standpoint of a multinational enterprise, probably rational. The parent entity desires to control the knowledge it disseminates and the management of its affiliates. The global headquarters uses export market allocation to preserve its distribution channels and network. Firms producing highly specialized industrial products cannot completely avoid export restrictions, and the economic conditions in various nations may require such measures. Defenders of multinational corporations point out that export restrictions may stem from cost-raising import substitution policies and maintenance of an overvalued currency by Third World nations.[38] The existence and pervasiveness of the restrictive practices, however, perpetuate the dependent position of developing nations.

With respect to the export provisions, spokesmen for multinational corporations rely on a comparative advantage argument as theoretically countering the extent of export restrictive practices.[39] The economic interest arguments runs as follows: It is unlikely that firms would restrict exports from subsidiaries that possess the capacity to produce and market their products competitively in terms of price and quality, provided a continuation of the supply of and an expansion of the volume of exports can reasonably be assured. This line of reasoning fails to meet the aspirations of a developing country that desires to secure manufacturing plants and to increase the exportation of its industrial porducts but lacks a significant price or quality advantage. As the Italian firm Olivetti noted:

Local governments' expectation of establishing an uncontrolled export policy and practice has been resisted with a certain success. A global export system has been adopted with due regard however to the aspirations of individual countries in this respect. It is not practical nor possible to meet these aspirations in full and indiscriminately, and therefore there may remain objections and criticisms by individual governments in this connection.[40]

Restrictive provisions, particularly those governing exports, may become less important and pervasive given a continuation of the trend toward the global sourcing of components by complex multinational corporations. But the global firm, not the developing country, still decides on the location of a plant and the quantity of production. In view of the ability of multinational corporations to shift production facilities and to use production sites in developing nations for export purposes, a firm's policy with respect to export restrictions and the prices of items exported from Third World nations will remain of paramount importance.

Technology Quandaries. Whether a developing country seeks manufacturing plants for import and export purposes, reliance on the foreign subsidiaries of multinational corporations creates a number of problems, including the appropriateness of the technology transferred (whether in the form of managerial skills, know-how or production techniques), local employment possibilities, types of products produced, the lack of local research and development, and a variety of impediments imposed by the existing patent system.

In assessing the employment picture, the Department of Economic and Social Affairs of the United Nations stated, "On the whole, the net employment impact on the host countries is positive since extreme cases of destruction of local industries and wholesale displacement of labour are rare."[41] But opponents of multinational corporations perceive that global enterprises transfer sophisticated technology that is irrelevant to the needs of developing countries, thereby further stunting a nation's capacity for self-sustaining growth. The technology employed in manufacturing facilities of subsidiaries may also reduce job opportunities in economies characterized by unemployment rates in excess of 30%. Underemployment is also extensive. Migrants from the countryside to the cities swell an already redundant urban labor force.[42] An assessment of 257 manufacturing firms in Latin America indicated that subsidiaries of multinational corporations used almost one-half the number of employees per $10,000 of sales as do local firms.[43] Simply put, not enough jobs are being created for rapidly growing labor forces. But the global employment impact of multinational enterprises must be viewed with an awareness that sub-sidiaries of global firms provide fewer than 15 million jobs in the Third World.

Although multinational corporations give both general training to familiarize new workers with industrial production and specific job-oriented training and also attempt to improve the general educational qualifications of their employees so as to meet future training require-ments, problems exist with the types of jobs global firms provide. The manufacturing subsidiaries utilizing capital-intensive techniques often create unskilled jobs with minimal training opportunities, relatively low remuneration and limited spin-off benefits for the remainder of the economy. Some trained managers have moved from these subsidiaries into local firms or government service, but employees generally acquire managerial and accounting skills more suited to the operations of a foreign affiliate. Managers may lack skills readily transferable to a local enter-prise.[44] A concern also exists regarding the creation of a labor "elite" and an accentuation of the wage discrepancies between different skill groups and also those between an urban wage-earning minority and a rural majority, which characterize many developing nations.[45]

Linkages between affiliates of global entities and the remainder of an economy are especially important in determining whether local entre-preneurs will flourish as distribution channels and in other service capaci-ties and whether the industrial sector will be segregated from a nation's economy. Although some firms, such as Sears, have involved significant numbers of local suppliers, evidence exists that multinational firms may resist the subcontracting of parts and components to local manufacturers because of alleged difficulties regarding quality control, organization and cost competitiveness.[46] In some cases multinational subsidiaries have caused the replacement of artisan workers by mass production industries.

Multinational corporations, moreover, because of their self-interest and in view of the small size of the markets in most developing countries, have manifested a reluctance to modify or adapt existing policies, prac-tices, products or social problem-solving technology capable of pro-ducing cheap, basic goods. For example, American firms were reluctant to concentrate on small, efficient cars (or mass transit vehicles) to meet the transportation requirements of developing countries. Even after the introduction of subcompact cars in Latin America, parent corporations required their subsidiaries to concentrate the bulk of their advertising on larger, more profitable vehicles. General Motors and Ford delayed in ad-dressing themselves to the problem of designing a vehicle for low-income consumer needs and smaller scale production requirements. General Motors finally began assembling a low-cost basic transportation vehicle in

Ecuador, the Philippines and Malaysia; GM's Vauxhall plant in the United Kingdom supplied the required engines, transmissions, suspension, rear axle and steering systems for this vehicle. Ford assembles in the Philippines for sale in the Asia-Pacific region, a multipurpose vehicle with its power train supplied by high-volume Ford plants. Apparently, auto manufacturers have given little thought to the production of mass transit vehicles for Third World nations.[47]

In the interest of economic efficiency, multinational firms wish to introduce standardized products and to construct and operate capital-intensive plants using Western technology. A firm's experience generally militates in favor of capital-intensive technology. Lower capital costs, including the sunk costs involving the knowledge of capital-intensive technologies, prevail if a firm utilizes existing capital-intensive technology. A subsidiary wishing to compete in the world market probably requires sophisticated technology. Stated differently, goods produced by means of labor-intensive technology may not be competitive for export purposes.[48] A capital-intensive plant in a vertically integrated multinational enterprise may more easily respond to unexpected fluctuations in demand and/or production. Although limits exist on the effectiveness of capital-intensive plants in Third World countries, including the small size of local markets and the difficulty of maintaining sophisticated equipment, a capital-intensive plant better protects a manager from a variety of risk and uncertainty factors.

The importance of engineers and executives with an engineering background in the selection of technology cannot be minimized.[49] Engineers generally prefer sophisticated equipment, with machine or automatic controls, to a reliance on people as determiners of quality, which is implicit in more labor-intensive techniques. Sophisticated, capital-intensive equipment also permits an engineer to function at a level for which he was trained and at which he has been functioning in a more "advanced" economy.

Managers wish to avoid the problems associated with supervision of a large work force in developing countries, particularly the difficulties involved in dismissing workers because of slack demand or because of individuals' low level of productivity. All of these reasons may be rational from the viewpoint of a multinational enterprise, but the resultant corporate strategy has failed to meet the social needs of developing countries, particularly with respect to the creation of new jobs.

Further empirical research must be undertaken comparing the type of technology, whether capital- or labor-intensive, used by subsidiaries with that used by local firms that manufacture for import-substitution or for export. One study, undertaken for the United Nations Department of

Social and Economic Affairs, concluded that except for the influence of scale and the ability to avoid price competition the techniques and behavior patterns of multinational subsidiaries and local firms are similar. Multinational corporations are more likely than a domestic firm, however, the use labor-intensive second-hand equipment because of the ability of global firms to locate and evaluate the effectiveness of such equipment.[50]

Other pioneering studies have revealed that national and foreign firms may not behave differently with respect to the type of technology used. A comparison of pairs of matched foreign and local firms in the Philippines and in Mexico indicates that the American subsidiaries used more capital per worker, which is more heavily invested in buildings, but do not use significantly more equipment per factory worker than their local counterparts.[51] The subsidiaries of American corporations surveyed, therefore, did not use more capital-intensive methods than did local producers.

Although firms generally transfer advanced technology to their manufacturing subsidiaries in developing countries, the particular industry and the type of product affects the choice of technology and may limit a firm's flexibility to select labor-intensive techniques. One report concluded that many multinational corporations, as a result of carefully checking the possibilities for modifying technology, made a limited number of adaptations in their materials, handling, construction and repetitive operations. These modifications occurred most notably in the fields of food processing and pharmaceutical packaging.[52]

Competitive pressures may lead a corporation to use more labor and less capital per unit of output. On the other hand, a study of the technologies used in different plants, local and foreign, in the same developing country concluded that the firms competing primarily on the basis of brand-name identification rather than prices, were more likely to employ capital-intensive technology. Holding the basis of competition constant, no significant difference was found to exist between the behavior of a domestic firm and that of a foreign-owned factory with respect to the type of technology used.[53]

The technology question involves other problems, including the lack of local research and development and impediments posed by the patent system. Developing countries rely on multinational corporations to gain access to new research and products. Cognizant that in the modern world the control of a society may rest largely on technology, Third World countries decry the centralization of research and development in industrialized nations and the accompanying "inadequate" levels of local research and development. Factors favoring the centralization of research and development include cost considerations, the need for a large market and the need for contacts among personnel in laboratories, corporate headquarters and universities. In addition to these general arguments, spokesmen for multinational corporations assert that a lack of technical experts and support services in most Third World nations and the inadequacy of local educational facilities and governmental subsidies perpetuate the reliance on foreign technology. Corporate executives view research and development as a function for a parent entity. According to the Exxon Corporation, "The overall level of R & D in developing countries is low and it is true that MNCs conduct only limited amounts of research in developing countries. It is unlikely that MNCs will sponsor significantly higher levels in the near future."[54]

This attitude on the part of global firms has not lessened the developing countries' fears of technological dependence. Few multinational firms, if any, have evidenced an interest in building up the educational and technical skills of nations in the periphery.

Even if a nation does mandate increased levels of local research and development, subsidiaries of multinational firms may absorb scarce scientific talent, making it more difficult for local firms to compete. Similarly, it is charged that multinational enterprises contribute to a brain drain, an omnipresent problem in developing nations, by causing the migration of scientists, professionals and businessmen to advanced countries in search of better-paying jobs and an environment thought, at least by Western standards, to be more stimulating and desirable.

The existing patent system may present a fundamental barrier to the technological independence of Third World countries. A concentration of patent holders exists in developing nations. For example, in Colombia, in the pharmaceutical, synthetic fiber and chemical industries, 10% of all patent holders, all of whom are multinational corporations, own 60% of the patents.[55] Studies also indicate that the overwhelming percentage, on the order of 90 to 95%, of the patents granted to foreigners by various Latin American countries are never utilized or exploited.[56]

The current patent system and the high percentage of unused patents enables multinational firms to preserve markets for overpriced imported components or final products. Lacking access to the technology monopolized by multinational firms through the patent system and the know-how and human technical skills that global firms have accumulated, local firms fall behind in the competitive race. To the extent that a subsidiary of a multinational corporation does in fact work a patent, depending on the value of the output generated and the ability to export the product, the payments made by affiliates for the technology, the patents and the accompanying know-how may adversely affect a developing nation's balance of payments position.

Impact on Industrial Organization Patterns. The presence of multinational corporations in Third World nations may increase economic concentration and produce a loss of local entrepreneurial opportunities. The fears manifested by developing nations regarding foreign industrial dominance and control of key industries have been realized. Recent statistics from several countries indicate the extent of foreign industrial dominance. Among the 500 largest manufacturing firms in Brazil, foreign subsidiaries controlled 37% of the total output; multinational enterprises owned 100% of that nation's auto and tire production, 67% of the machinery output and 68% of the electrical appliance machinery output; multinational corporations controlled 59 out of the 100 largest manufacturing concerns. In Mexico, 100% of the output in rubber product transportation materials was foreign controlled, with 75% of the industrial chemical and tobacco industries under foreign control. In pre–Allende Chile, in each of seven key industries from one to three foreign firms controlled at least 51% of production.[57] As one expert concluded, "The world level of concentration is much higher than it would be if foreign investment and domestic mergers were restricted."[58] Following in the path of foreign industrial dominance, American-style oligopolistically organized industries, resting on brand names and consumer preferences, have come to pervade many developing nations.

Foreign subsidiaries thwart local competition in a variety of ways. Affiliates of multinational firms have grown by acquiring firms in the main sectors of a country's private economy.[59] For example, more than one-third of the direct private investment by American firms in Peru and Colombia during the period from 1958 to 1967 involved the acquisition of local firms.[60] The absorption of local entrepreneurs retards self-sustained national development. By producing machine-made products that destroy native handicrafts, global corporations have a negative effect on a local economy. Global firms may, however, create opportunities for suppliers of component parts, for retailers and repair shops and provide training for employees, some of whom may take their skills into other lines of endeavor.

Impact on the Balance of Payments and Capital Markets. Multinational enterprises also place a drain on a nation's balance of payments and on local capital markets. Part of this difficulty emanates from the profit rates generated by foreign affiliates. The rates of return enjoyed by successful subsidiaries in extractive industries have often been exorbitant. A study of an American mining firm in Peru estimated that from 1953 to 1966 the company's annual profits on its capital invested in Peru ranged from 29.7% to 132.6%, depending on the accounting method used.[61] Subsidiaries in extractive industries are usually much more profitable than those in manufacturing operations, but manufacturing returns generally are understated because of the exclusion of fees and royalties and the use of transfer pricing. Leading the profit parade for manufacturing firms, fifteen multinational drug subsidiaries in Colombia showed rates of return on their respective investments in excess of 136% in one year (1968).[62] Barnet and Müller estimate that the minimum rate of return on investment for manufacturing subsidiaries of United States–headquartered firms in Latin America during the 1960s was at least 40% per year.[63] Multinational firms assert, of course, that in view of the risks undertaken and the considerable instability of developing countries, such profits are not excessive.

Passing the question of establishing a "fair" rate of return for operations in Third World nations, the repatriation of profits generated by foreign subsidiaries and charges for patents, trademarks, licenses, know-how, management and service fees adversely affect a nation's balance of payments. Between 1960 and 1968, American multinational firms repatriated 79% of their net profits from Latin America operations, while from 1965 to 1968, 52% of profits generated by the manufacturing subsidiaries of United States firms operating in Latin America were repatriated to the parent corporations.[64] A one-sided flow of payments for technology and know-how exists in favor of the Western countries. A study of 13 developing countries that represent 65% of the population and 56% of the total gross national product of all Third World nations showed the total cost, in the late 1960s, for patents, licenses, trademarks, know-how, management and service fees, to be in excess of $1.5 billion per year, or more than half the amount of direct private investment in these developing countries. The costs for these items grew at the rate of 20% per year, thereby absorbing an ever-increasing share of export earnings.[65]

The net result is an outflow of funds from Third World nations. According to one estimate, between 1946 and 1967, for each dollar entering Latin America approximately $2.70 left.[66] Between 1965 and 1970, the net investment inflow to 43 developing countries was 30% of the outflow.[67] The interminable nature of the remittances and the lack of guarantees of new capital inflow exacerbate the suction effect of foreign direct investment in developing countries.

A word of caution is in order. The comparison of outflow and inflow of capital created by multinational firms may be misleading. Despite the existence of restrictive business practices (i.e., a limitation on exports and the requirement of tie-in purchases) and transfer pricing policies employed by global firms, defenders of multinational enterprises argue that foreign investment in new productive facilities, as opposed to the takeover of existing firms, enables a developing nation to reduce its imports and increase its exports. The positive impact of foreign direct investments on exports and imports is illustrated by the fact that in 1966 United States subsidiaries in Latin America exported $4.5 billion worth of goods and imported only $1.3 billion in materials and supplies.[68] Foreign subsidiaries may also stimulate the establishment of complementary domestic industries.[69] However, the generation of income by foreign subsidiaries probably raises consumption levels, thereby reducing the supply of goods available for export. Furthermore, foreign-owned import substitute industries may import capital goods and machinery, causing a negative impact on a country's balance of payments.

Royalty figures may also be deceptive, especially those paid from wholly owned subsidiaries to a parent corporation. Royalty and other forms of payment for technology and knowledge represent one way of taking money out of a subsidiary in response to corporate strategy or governmental policy.

A number of critical questions must be asked in order to determine the impact of foreign investment on balance of payment figures: (1) Could local investors possibly replace foreign direct investment? i.e., does the foreign subsidiary's output truly supplement or only substitute for what otherwise would have been produced? (2) What is the impact of foreign direct investment on import substitution by a developing country (this may be further divided into impact of new subsidiaries as opposed to older affiliates)? (3) Were the earnings of the foreign subsidiary reinvested in the nation or remitted to the parent corporations? More generally, how would local resources have been directed in absence of foreign direct investment?

Global enterprises tap local capital markets, especially for short-term working capital, drying up domestic firms' sources of financing. Also, subsidiaries of multinational banks may control increasing amounts of scarce savings in a host country. The propensity of American multinational banks to lend to foreign subsidiaries of United States corporations, stemming from the long-range global interests of the banks, denies local enterprises a possible source of funds.[70] Meanwhile, debt repayments by Third World nations to private sector banks and public sector organizations (both bilateral organizations, such as the United States Agency for International Development, and multilateral agencies, such as the World Bank) contribute to the capital drain from developing countries.

CULTURAL AND SOCIAL FACTORS

The economic penetration by multinational corporations shapes and distorts cultural patterns in developing countries. The Westernization, particularly the Americanization, of culture presents a formidable threat to the cultural integrity of the non-Western world. Multinational firms transmit the values and life styles of global capitalism. The elite in developing countries follow consumption patterns of advanced countries. By imitating Western consumption patterns, the elite create a pattern that others attempt to replicate. Local employees of a foreign subsidiary adopt a life style modeled on the image established by the parent corporation and its executives and employees. The ethic of consumption soon pervades the other sectors of society.[71]

Multinational firms reproduce the products and ideas originated in developed countries. But the taste and consumption patterns that follow the use of these products, which local industry must emulate to remain competitive, may fail to meet the needs of the mass of citizens in developing countries. Two examples illustrate the dichotomy between social needs and the requirements of profit-oriented production. First, the manufacture and sale of automobiles in a developing country absorbs resources that might better be utilized for mass transportation, creates environmental problems and requires the importation of petroleum, unless available and refined locally, thereby increasing a nation's balance of payments difficulties. Second, firms have successfully promoted, through advertising campaigns, food products, such as soft drinks, that provide little if any nutritional value and drain the disposable income of individuals who can ill afford to waste money. Food and beverages developed for richer, consumer-oriented societies may displace more nutritious, traditional foods, especially among lower-income consumers. The over-zealous promotion of infant formulas in developing countries may divert a significant portion of a family's income and create severe health hazards among the poor.[72] The probability of an over-dilution of the formula to stretch utilization produces an inadequacy of nutrients, which contributes to malnutrition, illness and higher infant mortality rates. The serving of contaminated formula in bacteria-laden bottles led one organization to identify infant milk formula as a "baby killer" in developing nations.[73]

With foreign direct investment comes a surfeit of products and a reliance by global enterprises on sophisticated marketing techniques to create and mold consumer wants and needs in order to sell their goods and services. A loss of national control over communications media may result from the domination of consumption patterns by multinational corporations. Television and radio carry messages designed to stimulate consumption. Motion pictures and televison create the images of Western society and its values—the thrill of violence and consumption.[74] Global advertising firms, particularly American advertising agencies, account for an increasingly larger proportion of advertising in developing nations.[75]

The harmful impact of marketing and sales techniques, which observers have deemed inappropriate, may be seen in a shift from local beverages (or local soft drinks) to international brand-name soft drinks; likewise, the spread of 400 Kentucky Fried Chicken outlets (a division of the American firm Heublein, Inc.) to 30 countries and the international activity of McDonald's and Burger King (Pillsbury Co.) evidences the worldwide proliferation of American "culture."[76]

The cornucopia of efficiency and advertising affect the values of Third World citizens. Instead of meeting the basic food, health and housing needs, the consumption pattern fostered by foreign direct investment stimulates wrong appetites, misallocates resources and contributes to a worldwide homogenization of life styles and values.

POLITICAL FACTORS

In addition to an enfeebled economic system—characterized by an outward flow of capital and a lack of or lessening of competition from local businesses—weak political structures, including antiquated governmental and legal systems and the absence of competent, independent and knowledgeable administrative experts, have pervaded Third World nations. These institutional structures and the rise of a Western-oriented consumer society, critics of global firms allege, co-opt the elite of developing countries, who become closely tied to multinational corporations and the international capitalist system. According to this line of reasoning, global giants create client groups whose interests, privileges and status derive from their ties to foreign firms. These client groups have a vested interest in perpetuating the preeminent position of multinational corporations in a local economy. A symbiosis is posited to exist between foreign investors and the members of local oligarchies that form the backbone of reactionary political parties. In a political process characterized by a lack of widespread participation, the ability of multinational firms to detach a national elite from the masses enables these entities to undermine national political autonomy and to diminish national identification.[77]

Other observers reject this pessimistic view of the co-optation of local groups and the submergence of the national political process. A study of foreign copper companies and their alleged conservative retinue in Chile from 1955 to 1970 indicates that leaders of the traditional upper classes in Chile did not oppose, and in some instances led, the movement to restrict the activities of foreign copper producers. The nationalistic urges of local conservative groups may, therefore, preclude a symbiosis with foreign investors.[78] Local businessmen competing with foreign subsidiaries have perceived their own independent economic interests and generally sought to limit the activities of multinational corporations. Nationalistic bureaucrats have tended to make increasing demands on foreign interests to garner additional governmental revenues and perpetuate their claim to power.[79] These bits of evidence support the view that foreign interests in developing countries, especially in the natural resource field, have few permanent domestic allies.

Facing unpredictable and often inhospitable environments and desiring to perpetuate conditions favorable to foreign direct investment, some global firms have attempted to subvert a nation's political process by more direct means than the promotion of a consumer society. Multinational corporations have actively intervened in the domestic affairs of host developing countries. Internal cleavages, which make the politics of developing countries penetrable and fragile, facilitated these efforts. In some instances, for example in Chile prior to and under the regime of President Salvador Allende, multinational firms sought to subvert (or, that wonderful euphemism, "destabilize") the local political process by supporting and collaborating with forces hostile to a legitimately constituted political authority. On other occasions, global enterprises sought to utilize their broad financial power to develop close (and, it was hoped, favorable) relationships with government officials through a variety of means including bribery. Corporate funds have also been used, whether legally or illegally under the laws of a host nation, to support particular political parties. Global firms have pressured, with diminishing success, their home countries to intervene in the domestic affairs of a host nation. The most conspicuous example of this pattern of behavior was the economic strangulation of Allende's regime by the United States government, which resulted, in part, from the urgings of American business interests. The United States government also blocked credits to Peru after that nation expropriated an Exxon subsidiary in 1968.[80]

Beyond the predatory practices characterized by blatant corporate self-interest, the presence of multinational enterprises in developing nations engenders the fear of a loss of national sovereignty and identity on the part of nation-states and reduces the policy choices available for a host country. Removed from the rarified atmosphere of the world cities and centralized corporate headquarters, a nation may develop a branch-plant outlook, which affects its spirit of independence and its ability to engage in independent decision making on a broad range of economic, political and social issues. A suspicion exists that the leaders of periphery nations may be unable or unwilling to assert the position of their respective countries and satisfactorily resolve the conflicts existing between the economic goals of a corporation and the broader social policies of a nation-state.

Critics of multinational corporations present the economic, cultural and political strands of dependency as a continuing situation. They contend that a world capitalistic system, which necessarily involves continued corporate expansion and exploitation of the Third World, predetermines and limits the possibilities for socially constructive growth and development. But despite the power of multinational corporations, developing countries have sought to break free from the grasp of global firms and to limit or end their economic, cultural and political dependency. The efforts of developing nations to extricate themselves from the so-called iron law of dependency have included national devices, organization of regional groups and ultimately the formation of cartels of raw material producers. These steps mark one of the decisive turning points for world development in the twentieth century.

8

THIRD WORLD EFFORTS TO BREAK FREE
FROM THE GRASP OF DEPENDENCY

Seeking a greater utilization of a nation's potential and a degree of self-determination with respect to national economic and political policy making and socioeconomic development, including participation in the management of subsidiaries of foreign business enterprises, Third World countries have gradually abandoned their previously passive role. Venezuela's President Carlos Andres Perez aptly expressed the view of many Third World leaders in declaring, "Today, industrialized nations must share decision-making with us. We believe in interdependence, but interdependence among equals rather than an interdependence in which there are subordinates."[1]

The winds of nationalism and a greater awareness of the costs and benefits of multinational enterprises have spurred a more activist position. Changes occurring in the composition of local ruling groups and in the value structures of such groups have resulted in elites, in many countries, that act less and less as the pliable allies of global firms. Control over vital raw materials has shifted the balance of economic power to nations controlling those natural resources. Third World countries have become aware of the opportunities for bargaining and for entering into coalitions.

This chapter examines the steps taken by Third World governments to alter arrangements involving the manufacturing operations of foreign subsidiaries. Pursuit of national economic and political objectives evolved through three phases: bargaining to renegotiate the benefits enjoyed by foreign subsidiaries; strengthening national legislation; and, finally, creating regional programs. These strategies generally pursued the same objectives vis-à-vis manufacturing firms, namely, dissassembling the package—the organization, management, technology and access to markets—

possessed by global firms and capturing excess oligopoly profits. Nations hoped that increased local ownership would promote development by encouraging entrepreneurship and changing the selection of products, the technologies to be used, and marketing methods. The next chapter analyzes the response of multinational firms to developing nations' efforts to restructure the operations of foreign manufacturing subsidiaries; the following chapter examines the techniques used by the Third World to seize control over and deploy their most powerful lever in the global arena—raw materials.

STRENGTHENING A NATION'S BARGAINING POSITION

During most of the post-World War II era, developing countries bargaining with multinational firms operated from a position of weakness. A lack of knowledge regarding the impact of global firms on a nation's economic, cultural and political situation and a lack of the requisite technical and administrative skills thwarted national efforts to assess the impact of and regulate global giants.

Increased knowledge regarding the operations and the impact of multinational corporations led nations to reassess their bargaining position vis-à-vis global enterprises. Governments of developing countries acquired the expertise to oversee the activities of foreign subsidiaries by training nationals in negotiation, taxation, accounting, and production; by hiring top rank international lawyers, accountants and economists and other academicians; and by employing both foreign and local industrialists, as well as personnel from state corporations and advisors from international institutions.[2]

Moving from a more enlightened position and a growing supply of or access to trained personnel, countries commenced rudimentary assessments of the costs and benefits of multinational firms.[3] Third World nations became aware of the excessive costs of the package traditionally provided by manufacturing subsidiaries of multinational corporations. They observed that firms transferred inappropriate modes of technology and adversely affected economic and cultural patterns by minimizing employment possibilities, discouraging local entrepreneurs and stimulating consumption.

A number of other factors improved the nation's bargaining position. Competition by labor-intensive industries for new sources of cheap labor benefited developing countries. The growing markets in developing countries also worked to make these areas more attractive to global enterprises.

And once a multinational firm located a plant in an underdeveloped country, that operation became a hostage that the local government could squeeze.

In more intensive bargaining with foreign firms, Third World nations pursued two informal paths. First, these host governments imposed and collected higher taxes and other fees and restricted the financial and operating policies of existing foreign manufacturing units. But the increased complexity of industrial processes and products—the supposed genie of progress—lent an esoteric character to the manufacturing activities. The regenerative nature of manufacturing operations, as opposed to the extractive activities in the raw material sector, rendered the former less vulnerable to governmental renegotiating pressures.[4] Faced with these difficulties regarding the regulation of established manufacturing operations, Third World governments turned to controlling the entry of new foreign firms into domestic markets as their primary regulatory strategy.

The second path in negotiations with foreign firms involved the realization by governmental leaders that any of a number of firms could supply the required types of technologies. The ability to negotiate with multinational firms from different nations strengthened a developing nation's bargaining advantage. Techniques used by Third World governments included competitive bidding, encouraging new foreign competitors to challenge established manufacturing operations, and providing local firms with capital and other forms of assistance to prevent key industries from falling under foreign domination. In addition to diversifying the sources of technology and foreign investment, Third World nations sought new trading partners and markets. They also took advantage of the economic and technical assistance provided by centrally planned economies.

However, several factors impeded the development of new bargaining strategies. As multinational corporations from the United States, Western Europe and Japan became aware of the bargaining process used by a nation, these firms formed new oligopolies to prevent that nation from playing off firms from different countries. Additionally, multinational firms headquartered in different nations could conspire to upset the strategy of competitive bidding. More significantly, limitations on governmental expertise, the pervasiveness of corruption, the limited size of a market in most Third World countries and the amount and profitability of existing foreign direct investment restricted the ability of developing nations to break their dependence on foreign manufacturing subsidiaries and traditional sources of technological knowledge. The ability of global firms to introduce new goods and manufacture more complex products enabled them to retain their bargaining leverage.

FORMALIZING A BARGAINING POSITION
THROUGH NATIONAL LEGISLATION

Cognizant of their increasing bargaining power, developing countries turned to legislation to extract a larger share of the profits, jobs, markets, technology and managerial skills created or controlled by global firms. This legislation pursued three basic strategies: (1) limiting the entry of foreign firms by preserving certain areas for local firms and by nationalizing key sectors of the economy; (2) requiring local participation in the ownership, management or control of existing and/or new foreign subsidiaries; and (3) controlling the transfer of technology through the registration of technology contracts and/or governmental evaluation and approval of such contracts.

The major efforts to control global firms centered on screening foreign direct investment and only permitting entry on stringent conditions agreed to at the outset. Countries modeled their requirements on the Japanese foreign investment laws. To achieve self-sufficiency and sound economic development, Japan, commencing in 1950, screened foreign direct investment and permitted only those investments that could make a positive contribution to the Japanese economy. The existence of a large market with sufficient internal demand and the presence of a large, innovative industrial sector enabled Japan to implement restrictive policies. The government encouraged the licensing of technology to protect domestic industry. The criteria used for screening investment projects were generally vague, giving government officials added latitude.[5]

With the dramatic resurgence of the Japanese economy over the past quarter century, Japan gradually relaxed its foreign investment restrictions. By the early 1960s, Japan was allowing the entry of foreign investment that would not unduly oppress small domestic firms, seriously disturb the industrial order or impede the local development of industrial techniques. Liberalization took the form of permitting joint ventures equally owned by Japanese and foreign interests in an expanding line of product groups. Only recently has Japan permitted wholly owned foreign subsidiaries, and then only in product areas where local firms assert nearly undisputed competitive superiority.

The Japanese example inspired nationally oriented leaders in developing countries to delineate, by legislation, general guidelines, subject in each case to an assessment by an administrative agency, covering the activities of multinational corporations in a number of areas, including which industries would be open for foreign investment, ownership patterns in foreign subsidiaries, and restrictions on the remittance of profits, on transfer pricing and other business practices regarded as harmful. A general pattern has evolved in developing nations. Certain economic activities, such as transportation, communications, banking and insurance, are reserved solely for domestic, either public or private, enterprises. In other areas of economic activity, these nations welcome new foreign investment but mandate local participation, by the public or private sector, or a specified percentage of the ownership of a foreign subsidiary. Legislation usually covers both new foreign investments and takeovers of existing local firms.[6]

Mexican legislation exemplifies the trend to delimit the industries in which foreigners can invest and to regulate the ownership position of multinational corporations in their affiliates. The 1973 law to promote Mexican investment and regulate foreign investment reserves certain activities for the state or local private firms and limits future foreign investment to a maximum of 49% participation in all areas not covered by previous legislation and decrees. An administrative body, the National Foreign Investment Commission, may increase or decrease the maximum percentage of foreign ownership in certain geographical areas or economic activities. The 1973 law also requires prior approval by the National Foreign Investment Commission before foreign investors can acquire more than 25% of a local company's capital or more than 49% of its fixed assets. Rather than imposing rigid rules, Mexico encourages bargaining between the government and multinational corporations.[7]

The Mexican statute follows the nonretroactive pattern of legislation to control foreign investment. The Mexican government recommends but does not require that existing foriegn subsidiaries make available a portion, preferably a majority, of their shares for purchase by the Mexican public.[8]

A few nations have mandated foreign divestment, either complete or partial, in certain activities. For example, Jamaica required that its nationals obtain 51% ownership of certain foreign-controlled commercial banks within a specified time period.

Several variants of foreign investment legislation exist. At one extreme, India favors technical collaboration agreements with foreign corporations but without any foreign ownership, or with a minority ownership position. By administrative action, the Indian government has permitted foreign majority ownership in fields where India has made little industrial progress, where the cost of imported equipment remains high, or where export possibilities stand to reduce the strain on the country's foreign exchange resources. For example, when IBM set up a subsidiary in India, the company insisted on and obtained a 100% ownership position because of the complex nature of the industry and the export guarantees given by the corporation.[9]

Canada has established an elaborate system of administrative regulation.

Under the Canadian Foreign Investment Review Act of 1973, as amended, the Canadian government screens the proposed takeovers of domestic firms by foreign corporations and foreign direct investment in new lines of business in Canada, including expansion by foreign companies already operating in Canada. The criterion is the extent to which the proposed takeover or investment will generate significant benefits for Canada. As part of the administrative process, the screening agency in the Canadian Ministry of Industry, Trade and Commerce also attempts to bargain with foreign firms to improve the benefits for Canada resulting from a new investment. In addition, a government-organized Canadian Development Corporation has promoted new Canadian-controlled corporations by pooling management skills and capital, thereby providing a local alternative to operations by foreign subsidiaries. The Canadian Development Corporation has also provided funds to secure greater national participation in the ownership and control of foreign corporations engaged in Canadian industry.[10]

The transfer of technology and intrafirm pricing have come under increasing scrutiny and regulation by developing nations. Governments have sought more information about the different components of the technology package multinational corporations provide. From their studies, developing nations have concluded that the global firms levy what are regarded as "exorbitant" charges for the technology transferred to their controlled subsidiaries or to local firms. Beyond an assessment of the cost benefit ratios of foreign technology transfers, countries have realized that the failure to control technology may doom nation-states to a low-status role in the present world system. Increased knowledge and a better perception of the technology transfer problem have led to national legislation.

The 1972 Mexican Law on the Transfer of Technology and the Use and Exploitation of Patents and Trademarks illustrates a national effort to regulate the purchase of technology by means of disclosure, registration, evaluation, negotiation and control so as to prevent excessive royalties and eliminate contractual clauses that might impede local development. Under the Mexican statute, contracts and documents pertaining to the transfer of technology must be registered with a government records office. Agreements that, among other items, impose excessive royalties, restrict the export of goods or services by the local technology user, limit the licensee's management powers, or prohibit the use of complementary techniques, are not eligible for registry and, therefore, have no legal effect. Unlike the Mexican foreign investment law, the technology statute is retroactive. Companies have been forced to rewrite contracts and present them to an administrative commission, which has reduced royalty levels from an annual range of from 5 to 15% of a licensee's annual sales to under 3%.

Licenses in excess of the 3% figure have been approved, however, for products with high research and development costs.[11]

Mexico has also moved to eliminate patents in certain areas, including pharmaceuticals, chemicals, agriculture, nuclear energy and pollution. Nonrenewable investor's certificates, which permit companies with new products to collect royalties but not to control licensing, have replaced patents. The duration of new patents, in fields where they are still allowed, has been reduced.

Governments have also moved into the thorny area of controlling transfer pricing. Difficulties to be surmounted in this area include checking intrafirm prices and then comparing them with market prices. Establishment of an arms-length standard may be impossible if the items are not freely traded in a market. Nevertheless, host nations have spot-checked areas most vulnerable to manipulation and have used current infractions as grounds for reopening back tax returns. By enlarging the share of local equity held in a foreign subsidiary, it is hoped that nationals, with the requisite business abilities and the time, will monitor intrafirm pricing arrangements.

Developing nations have also imposed other restrictions on multinational corporations, including requirements that nationals comprise a specified percentage of a subsidiary's personnel, its management team and its board of directors. Limits have been imposed on profit repatriation and local borrowing by foreign affiliates of global giants.[12]

However, there are significant impediments to unilateral efforts to regulate the manufacturing operations of multinational corporations. Cost factors, including the acquisition of information, administrative staff requirements and the training of personnel, may place the effective implementation of these programs beyond the reach of many developing countries. A national effort to control multinational corporations requires periodic appraisal procedures and a centralized agency to review the activities of those firms and develop regulatory criteria. The potential for political corruption based on the continuance of personal ties between global firms and a local elite still exists. Moreover, nations fear that regulation will mean the loss of existing and future foreign investments as firms turn to less restrictive locations. As a major result of these regulatory dilemmas, nation-states have formed regional economic alliances to promote their interests.

REGIONAL EFFORTS TO REGULATE THE ACTIVITIES OF M N Cs

Although impediments to regional cooperation abound, including differences in background, resource and administrative ability, regional groupings strengthen the bargaining positions of developing countries and support the development of techniques suitable for dealing with the problems posed by global enterprises. A regional bloc can impose rules and extract concessions that few nation-states could obtain alone. Regional arrangements also rule out competition among participating nations which would weaken the bloc's position in bargaining with global firms. A potential attraction of regional blocs to foreign investors is access to a regional free trade zone, an inducement that might encourage foreign investors to operate under the region's regulations.[13]

A leading example of regional cooperation is Decision 24 of the Commission of the Cartagena Agreement, promulgated in the early 1970s by the Andean Common Market, composed of Bolivia, Chile, Colombia, Ecuador, Peru, and more recently, Venezuela. Decision 24 has spun an intricate web covering present and future foreign direct investments and the transfer of technology, including trademarks, patents, licensing agreements and royalties. The divestiture sections of Decision 24 constitute an innovative approach, short of nationalization, to the problem of foreign control and dependency. To be eligible for the trade concessions offered by the members of the Andean Common Market, every existing foreign controlled affiliate from outside the region, must sell a majority of its equity shares to local investors within a specified time period, from fifteen to twenty years; and new investors from outside the region must also asume minority ownership positions. Foreign firms that fail to comply with the divestiture provisions will, of course, be placed at a disadvantage in trading activities within the Andean group in comparison with local entities and firms meeting the local ownership standards. Several sectors including banking, mass media and domestic transportation, are closed to future foreign investment. Current foreign investors in such sectors are given a specified time period in which to divest themselves of at least a majority of their ownership to Andean nationals.

The Andean group regulates technology transfer and the remittance of profits. Royalties for technology are limited in the hope of encouraging price reductions and preventing foreign firms from using royalties to extract excess profits. Restrictive business practices, including tie-in provisions and exports restrictions, are prohibited.

The Andean Pact also provides for the creation of state-owned regional multinational enterprises. These entities may be the first in a series of regional enterprises in developing countries that will ultimately invest in and conduct activities in other nations outside their region.[14]

Despite the efforts of regional blocs to increase nationals' ownership in existing and future foreign subsidiaries and to control the payments for the transfer of technology and the remittance of profits, nation-states implementation of regional policy goals may vary according to national assessments of the costs and benefits of multinational firms. Also, competition by some members of a bloc for foreign direct investments may produce inducements and other national legislative programs not in accord with the regional scheme. Even if a bloc surmounted the variety of national perspectives, administrative staffs would be handicapped by inadequacies.[15]

AN ASSESSMENT OF INFORMAL AND FORMAL REGULATORY PROGRAMS

In seeking to reduce dependency and capture excess profits, developing countries must carefully analyze the costs and benefits entailed in regulating the entry and activities of manufacturing operations of multinational corporations and breaking up the package provided by such entities. This requires accurate information. Nations will apply different cost-benefit ratios depending on the economic sector under examination and the total situation of the country.

Countries wishing to tap the skills and resources offered by global firms must establish a minimum level of return that will attract corporations. Efforts to dissemble the package provided by multinational corporations and to separately price and obtain skills and technology raise two significant questions: What will be the impact of excluding foreign capital and technology? and, In the absence of, or drastic limitation upon, foreign direct investment, how will a nation generate sufficient capital for its development projects?

A program to exclude private foreign investment rests on the assumptions that (1) eliminating the economic drain caused by multinational corporations will create a new wellspring of local capital, and (2) through national economic planning, a government can rationally allocate capital to certain sectors, particularly labor-intensive industries, thereby meeting pressing social needs.

Few studies exist as to the impact of a withdrawal of foreign capital from a nation. It has been estimated that if no foreign capital of any sort were present in Canada (assuming a continuation of the existing production processes, the existing capital-to-labor ratio applied to government and business, and a maintenance of current Canadian official overseas loans and holdings of foreign exchange assets), the Canadian gross domestic product would decline by over 16% and gross national income would be reduced by 2.9%.[16] Nations contemplating the elimination of foreign investment must be willing to accept similar consequences.

In the absence of private foreign direct investment, a government apart from local capital sources, could pursue several strategies to raise necessary capital. A nation could float debt issues on the Eurodollar or other capital markets. Credits could be sought from international financial institutions. Reliance could be placed on centrally planned economies to provide capital. Transnational public sector financing organizations, under Third World control and funded by oil rich nations, may be developed in the future.

Despite potentially adverse consequences, a nation may conclude that the nationalization of foreign holdings and a program of economic isolation, at least from Western nations, offers the best hope for achieving desired social goals. In pursuing this goal, nations may be handicapped by a lack of trained local manpower. Also, foreign participation may be needed to maintain distribution channels and marketing outlets. Without a clear vision of how to proceed in the absence of expansive developmental and infrastructure programs, a program of autarky may prove difficult. But it is not impossible.

9

THE RESPONSE OF M N Cs TO THIRD WORLD REGULATORY EFFORTS

As developing nations, either unilaterally or through regional programs, have sought to obtain technology, management and other benefits from global firms and to achieve a larger share of the ownership in foreign subsidiaries, multinational firms have responded with a variety of new business arrangements, including joint ventures, management contracts and licensing agreements. The emphasis placed by developing countries on the ownership of multinational firms may obscure the sophisticated efforts of such enterprises to perpetuate their control over foreign manufacturing ventures.

JOINT VENTURES

A joint venture involves a partnership composed of public sector agencies, a host government or local private interests in a developing country on the one hand and a global firm on the other. A multinational corporation may contribute to the joint venture through equity or debt funds, patents, trademarks or essential operational factors such as a plant and equipment. A nation may limit the amount of capital a multinational enterprise can place in the joint venture. In some instances, global firms may enter into contractual joint ventures in which they make no capital investment. The joint venture structure enables a global corporation to share in profits and participate in policy making, planning and management functions.[1]

Third World nations favor joint venture arrangements. The hope exists that such a business structure will facilitate the more rapid transmission of managerial know-how and appropriate forms of technology and will prevent a variety of abuses, including excessive industrial concentration and improper political influence. The opening of an equity ownership position for local interests may, it is believed, promote more meaningful participation in and control over a business.

Developing nations have sought to emulate the joint ventures Eastern European nations entered into with Western firms. Yugoslavia took the lead in amending its foreign investment law in 1967 to permit joint ventures. Western interests could receive equity positions in such joint ventures and own fixed assets in Yugoslavia, but a management committee composed of Yugoslav and foreign representatives had to make, by consensus, all important management decisions. In the early 1970s Hungary and Rumania authorized joint ventures. Western equity participation is limited to 49% ownership in Hungarian and Rumanian joint ventures; while in Yugoslavia, in certain cases, a foreign partner's equity share may exceed 50%. Hungary and Rumania have restricted joint venture arrangements to certain sectors of their economies and do not permit Western partners to control fundamental management decisions.[2]

Global firms have resisted joint venture arrangements in developing nations, especially those entailing a minority ownership position. Multinational enterprises seek both majority ownership and voting control because of a parent corporation's desire to coordinate and integrate the worldwide production and marketing operations of a far-flung network of subsidiaries. Businessmen are wary of having a governmental or public agency partner assume a majority ownership position and make decisions that are not based on profit-oriented criteria.[3]

More sophisticated businessmen, however, see the need to enter into joint venture arrangements in order to neutralize the local political and other interest groups, including elites, bureaucrats and businessmen. Moreover, tapping local capital is seen as reducing the risk of foreign operations. Also, local businessmen may provide valuable information regarding local markets and products, and they constitute a source of knowledge regarding governmental policies and the activities of labor unions.

Against these advantages accruing from a joint venture must be placed several disadvantages. First is the fact that the local partners share in the profits previously enjoyed solely by the multinational corporation. Second, local equity may be in scarce supply. Third, the new local shareholders who possess a different time frame and often desire a quicker dividend pay out than old shareholders, pose new problems for the multinational enterprise; they may challenge existing cost allocations between operations and the control over reinvestment or pay out of joint venture profits

The top-heavy debt structure of a joint venture may also be vulnerable to start-up and other short-term losses.

If the government of a developing country mandates that foreign investors may establish only minority ownership and voting positions in a joint venture, a multinational corporation may compensate by entering into special arrangements with local majority partners or attempt to control the enterprise through a variety of techniques, including technology and management contracts. In industries in which technical change is critical, control may be exerted through a technology contract delineating the flow of technology from the parent firm to the joint venture. The technology contract may also provide that a multinational firm will supply key supervisory personnel with the requisite know-how to utilize the technology or that any such personnel hired locally will be satisfactory to the foreign investor.[4] Two knowledgeable observers have concluded: "Nevertheless, although a number of foreign investors likewise feel that voting and technical control should always be linked, a majority of them consider their technical superiority an adequate means of exercising a lasting *de facto* control over the foreign joint ventures where they are in a minority position."[5] A global enterprise may also wield control through a management contract that provides for the placement of key management personnel from the parent corporations in operating posts.

If local majority shareholders lack a common purpose, have no interest in exercising control, or are on friendly terms with foreign interests, this will also facilitate the control aspirations of multinational corporations. A small local elite may repeatedly participate in a number of joint ventures in a nation because of the difficulty, if not impossibility, of broadening the base of private local investor involvement. The elite group may be unresponsive to national priorities or governmental objectives, thus providing ineffectual representation of national interests. The dispersal of a majority local ownership position among a number of shareholders may create a passive, nonunified group, enabling a minority foreign interest to perpetuate its control position.[6]

Beyond the problem of actual control, joint venture arrangements may fail to cure other problems inherent in the manufacturing activities of multinational corporations. One study concluded that a joint venture may not, in the long run, produce any greater contribution to a nation's economic and social development than would a wholly owned foreign subsidiary.[7] Joint ventures may pay more for technical and managerial services in the form of royalties and other fees than do wholly owned subsidiaries. A majority-owned subsidiary will generally receive greater access to the global distribution channels of its parent corporations than a joint venture. Also, a multinational firm may attempt to exercise more control over the export decisions and distribution patterns of minority-owned joint ventures in order to protect and enhance its global marketing strategy. Use of know-how and trade names may be restricted by contract to certain geographical areas.

It is true that joint ventures generally pay lower prices than do wholly owned foreign subsidiaries for intermediate goods purchased from multinational firms. However, higher charges for know-how, trade names, management and technical services and other overhead expenses may counterbalance the gain achieved by diminished transfer pricing.

Joint ventures place a double burden on a local capital market by using the financial resources of local partners as well as tapping local credit sources, thereby reducing the amount of capital available for other businesses. The impact of using local debt and equity capital sources to finance a joint venture depends on an assessment of how a nation's private and/or public sector would otherwise deploy such funds.

In an attempt to extricate a nation from the yoke of dependency, a developing country may mandate joint venture arrangements and pay an economic price, at least in the short-run. To reduce the drawbacks of joint ventures, Third World countries have turned to a careful scrutiny and appraisal of the control techniques used by foreign interests, even those occupying minority positions. Several corporations may be invited to serve as the foreign partners for a venture. The bargaining positions of developing countries in the regulation of joint ventures depends, in the final analysis, on several factors, including the type of technology required, the size of the local market and the number of multinational firms possessing the requisite technological, managerial or marketing skills.[8] If a nation wishes to enjoy the benefits offered by multinational corporations but avoid the encroachment of Western ideas and values, the establishment of industrial enclaves in which joint ventures will conduct their operations may become necessary.

OTHER ARRANGEMENTS EXCLUDING FOREIGN DIRECT INVESTMENT

A country wishing to avoid foreign equity or debt investment may gain technological and managerial know-how by requiring multinational corporations to license their technology or enter into management and marketing contracts.[9] The experience of Eastern European nations provides a useful guide for developing countries. Major contractual techniques used by Eastern European countries to achieve an inflow of intangible managerial, administrative and technical skills include technology licenses, turnkey contracts, production arrangements and management contracts. The licensing of technology, know-how and other forms of knowledge involves the payment to Western firms, in cash or with deliveries of products in kind, of fixed or variable fees (the latter linked to performance of the venture) over a limited time period. Contractual arrangements may be subject to renegotiation at specified intervals. Turnkey concepts include having a Western firm provide the design and technology for a new plant and furnish the more sophisticated equipment, while the Eastern European government or agency assumes responsibility for constructing the plant and supplies less sophisticated technology. Or, foreign interests may be brought in to supervise the building of a plant that a government will operate upon its completion. In one notable example of the turnkey technique, the Soviet Union engaged Fiat to build an automobile factory. Under a production arrangement, a Western corporation supplies the necessary production technology and/or part of the product line, while the Eastern partner furnishes part of the production line and perhaps some of the technology. The final product, under a production contract, may be jointly marketed or marketed by each partner in its own national market or in a regional trading area. A management or marketing contract may also be employed in East-West business dealings. Under such an agreement a foreign corporation receives a fixed payment for future services that it will render over a specified time period, with possible provisions for incentives to spur successful performance.[10]

Unless a Third World government permits a foreign corporation to remain in or enter a market by transferring skills, not capital, the attitude of multinational corporations to contractual arrangements varies depending on a number of factors. If a nation's market is too small to warrant an investment, or if a firm lacks sufficient capital, then contractual techniques will be favored. Many corporations, however, desire to invest in their foreign ventures. Firms possessing a technological lead or those having incurred substantial research and development expenditures generally evidence a lack of interest in contractual arrangements. Such firms strive to maintain control over their technological and experiential inputs and do not wish to impart valuable know-how as part of a contractual deal. Although these firms probably would achieve sufficient protection through a contract, they manifest a desire to supply an entire package, including capital, to a venture. Other multinational companies avoid contractual arrangements out of a desire to control prices and market allocations and to prevent any threat to established market and distribution positions.

A developing country that forces multinational corporations to untie the package and, by contract, transfer technology, know-how, management and marketing, but not capital, faces at least three dangers. First, a certain percentage of firms will not enter into such arrangements. For example, IBM desires wholly owned foreign subsidiaries so as not to dilute corporate decisions regarding prices, profit remittances and the firm's international allocation of resources. Because of IBM's technological superiority, nations accede to the firm's position. Depending on their clout, some firms may successfully renegotiate a government's terms of entry.

Secondly, some corporations will enter only into contracts containing formal or informal restrictions that, in fact, increase the cost of the intangibles provided. The restrictions may permit a global firm, even in the absence of any capital investment, to control a foreign venture and utilize an operation as part of its worldwide system. A perpetuation of dominance occurs because the knowledge and expertise possessed by multinational firms generates the need for undeveloped nations to continually tap their skills. The location of expertise and the decision-making capacity in the corporate headquarters may frustrate the monitoring ability of a local venture on a developing nation.[11]

Thirdly, if a contractual set-up will generate a return deemed inadequate, a firm may transfer less sophisticated technology or skills. Each contractual supplier may also raise the price of the ingredients it furnishes, realizing that the prospective return from a venture depends on the use of other factors not under its control.

To counteract the attempts by multinational firms to control ventures utilizing contractual arrangements, governments have turned to outside expert advice and trained nationals to monitor operations and manage businesses. Prime responsibility must, of course, be placed on effective surveillance by local employees, officers and members of boards of directors. Lack of sufficient numbers of capable local personnel and a continued need to import knowledge and technology perpetuate the dependency syndrome. But governments are aware of the variety of restrictive and harmful business practices and have, at least, made a start to curb these abuses.

DIVESTMENT

To tap the financial resources, technology and the intangible expertise, including skills in management and marketing, offered by multinational corporations, developing nations, unilaterally or on a regional basis, may increasingly utilize a fade-out divestment scheme for future ventures involving global entities, and perhaps for existing foreign subsidiaries.[12] Divestment contemplates the conversion, within a specified time period, of existing or prospective wholly owned foreign subsidiaries into joint ventures in which local interests participate as equity owners or into totally domestically owned businesses. The stake owned by foreign investors, including a profit interest and the ownership of intangible and tangible assets, would be sold or given to local investors in the private or public sector. Divestment turns on obtaining the maximum advantage from a multinational corporation during the limited time period a global entity has made or will make its key contribution to a developing nation. Each nation must, therefore, assess the time period after which the benefits provided by foreign firms generally, by foreign enterprises in a particular field or by a specific foreign subsidiary have diminished or will diminish, so that a foreign-owned company may revert, in whole or in part, to local ownership.

In addition to fixing the interval before divestment becomes effective, a divestment scheme faces other problems from the standpoint of both multinational corporations and developing nations. Business executives generally view fade-out arrangements with considerable skepticism.[13] A fear exists regarding an increase in control and regulation by the public sector and the fear of nationalization without adequate, timely compensation. Firms that tightly integrate their subsidiaries into a worldwide production and marketing network may find divestment unattractive. One study revealed that 70% of the American companies surveyed might be candidates for fade-out arrangements in Latin America, depending on the actual terms and conditions, specifically whether foreign firms could avoid divestment for a sufficiently long period to obtain a return deemed adequate and after divestment retain a minority interest.[14] Depending on how executives assess the viability and profitability of foreign operations, corporations may reappraise mandatory divestment arrangements.

From the vantage point of a Third World country, mandatory divestments raise significant problems. Global firms may fail to provide, on a continuing basis, the latest technology or the best management. The inability of a corporation to perpetually tie the activities of a subsidiary to its worldwide production and marketing network may impede foreign investment and also lessen the desirability, from the viewpoint of local interests, of operating a business after divestment. Faced with a limited time frame in which to generate profits, global enterprises may seek "excessive" profits and repatriate earnings quickly, placing additional pressures on a host country's balance of payments. If a divestment arrangement includes compensation for foreign investors, raising capital locally or borrowing funds may prove a difficulty, whether undertaken by the nation's public or pirvate sector. A government considering this arrangement must decide whether capital should be allocated to replace existing or future foreign investments rather than to meet social needs or finance new domestically owned enterprises. Local partners may be relegated to secondary roles, in such activities as sales, publicity or labor relations, if foreign firms, owning a minority interest after divestment, continue to control such key activities as operations, financing and marketing.[15] The apparent slowness with which the members of the Andean Common Market have pursued the divestment concept attests to the difficulties in implementing such a scheme, particularly in assessing and projecting the price to be paid and determining the point in time when the benefits provided by a foreign affiliate will be outweighed by the costs. The need to acquire new technology and tap the access to foreign markets, along with the positive benefits provided by multinational corporations, probably will discourage nations or regional blocs from embarking on a far-reaching divestment approach.

10

THE RAW MATERIALS LEVER

To redress the abuses of dependency, particularly declining terms of trade, many Third World nations have used the bargaining position of their prime economic resource—raw materials needed by industrialized nations. Governmental techniques have included the establishment of control over a nation's land, its minerals and agricultural produce. Nations have also formed producers' cartels, most notably the Organization of Petroleum Exporting Countries (OPEC). The success enjoyed by OPEC has sent tremors throughout the Western world. OPEC has strengthened the bargaining position of the Third World regarding raw materials assiduously sought by industrialized nations, giving rise to Third World demands for a new international economic order.

With the growing awareness of developing countries regarding the value of and demand for their natural resources and the availability of information regarding the activities of the multinational corporations engaged in raw material extraction, Third World governments have pursued two nationally oriented strategies: obsolescence bargaining and nationalization. Multinational corporations initially have possessed greater bargaining power when they have sought to tap the raw materials located in developing countries. Access to capital, technical skills and the world market enable global firms to attain attractive concession terms. But once a firm has invested capital and made its mineral discoveries, its bargaining power declines.

Nations have come to view the returns generated by multinational corporations as no longer appropriate to the attendant risks. Governmental leaders have perceived an economy heavily reliant on the exportation of one or two raw materials as vulnerable to changes in the prices for such resources. Accompanying the sense of exploitation and dependency has come a resentment at the isolation of foreign enclaves conducting extractive activities.

Before significant steps could be taken to gain a larger share of the profits, nations had to strengthen their bargaining techniques. Local individuals and public or private corporations had to acquire technical skills and marketing knowledge; the ability to generate capital grew. Host nations realized they could hire independent advisors.

Moving from an improved knowledge and bargaining position, governments engaged in obsolescence bargaining and renegotiated existing concession agreements.[1] Demands for contractual revisions came to be viewed as part of the game. Increased bargaining strength also affected new agreements. Companies in extractive industries risked new investments on terms established by host governments that would previously have been regarded as unacceptable.

In addition to obsolescence bargaining, the concept of foreign concessions came under attack. Regimes seeking to demonstrate power over multinational enterprises nationalized foreign concession sites, agricultural landholdings, and mineral and commodity processing facilities. In the mid-1970s, Venezuela nationalized its petroleum industry; bauxite mining and processing came under government control in Jamaica and Guyana; Middle East nations, including Iraq, Kuwait and Saudi Arabia, gained ownership over their oil resources. In seizing the assets of an American iron-ore firm, Peru's minister of mines and energy, Jorge Fernandez Maldonado, charged the corporation with violating its contracts with the Peruvian government, wasting ore lodes, and causing "serious damage to our country by actions typical of the immoral conduct that the great multinational consortiums traditionally exercise."[2]

Rhetorical flourishes aside, multinational firms have posed at least two major challenges for the national aspirations of developing countries, especially as manifested in the expropriation of foreign assets in extractive industries. First, vertically integrated firms control processing facilities, such as expensive aluminum smelters, and marketing networks outside a particular nation. A government might try to mitigate foreign control of these facilities by using its bargaining position to force a firm to engage in more local processing prior to nationalization, by allocating capital for the development of local processing after the nationalization of concession sites, by investing in local industries, such as petrochemical and fertilizer, that consume large quantities of indigenous raw materials, by developing its own marketing network, and by locating new trading partners, including countries with centrally planned economies and maverick Western nations.[3]

Recognizing a continued dependence on global petroleum firms, countries such as Venezuela, even after nationalization, have entered into agreements to obtain the technical and managerial expertise of multinational corporations, as well as access to their marketing networks. The involvement of foreign firms in the exploration for crude oil in Venezuela will continue. Joint venture arrangements may emerge when new exploration must be undertaken to bolster Venezuela's oil production.[4]

A second challenge posed by multinational firms is the development of international alliances. In the copper industry, for example, global firms, realizing the difficulties involved in recapturing oligopoly profits downstream after the nationalization of extractive activities, turned to international alliances to bolster their position and ward off the threat of nationalization, or at least increase the compensation to be paid for expropriated assets. Kennecott pioneered in such strategies by raising funds for new joint venture projects from a consortium composed of the host government, customers in Europe and Asia and international financing institutions, with repayment provided from the output generated by a project. Kennecott hoped to pressure a nationalistic Chilean government not to void Kennecott's management contract for the project or repudiate the governmental guarantee for debt obligations issued by the joint venture. If a subsequent government failed to assume the guarantee obligations, Kennecott reasoned that creditors could threaten legal action against other commercial transactions involving Chile. Thus, even if support by the United States government was not forthcoming in a crisis situation, other interests, namely, customers and financial institutions in different nations, would have a direct stake in making certain the Chilean government did not repudiate its obligations. The second part of Kennecott's plan involved lining up governmental supporters in the United States so that the threat of nationalization would produce a face-to-face confrontation between the United States and Chile. Despite this well-planned protective web, Chile nationalized Kennecott's assets; but the government had to pay more in compensation than if such strategies had not been used.[5]

By the 1970s, the nationalization strategy had become a familiar aspect of international business, but the creation of cartels of raw material producers raised new quandaries for the world. Oil-producing nations formed the Organization of Petroleum Exporting Countries to raise the prices of crude oil and to assist in securing national control over the production of petroleum. The success of OPEC, in increasing petroleum prices and using this tactic as a political weapon, led nations producing other commodities to form cartels, with the aim of using economic power to redistribute the world's wealth, to achieve local control and increase domestic processing, to conserve diminishing resources and to force changes in the foreign policies of consuming countries.

Based on the consumption of a seemingly inexhaustible supply of cheap

Middle East oil—the artery of prosperity—the economies of the United States, Western Europe and Japan had blossomed after World War II. Between 1950 and 1973, United States oil consumption rose from 2.37 to 6.3 billion barrels a year. In Japan, the demand for imported oil rose from 100,000 barrels a day to almost 6 million barrels a day. Western European imports of oil rose to over 15 million barrels a day in 1973, up from 1.5 million barrels a day in 1950.[6]

Supported by the governments of the United States and the United Kingdom, seven multinational oil corporations—Exxon, Mobil, Texaco, Standard Oil of California, Gulf, Shell, and British Petroleum—controlled the production of oil and allocated markets for the sale of petroleum. The cartel activities of the major oil corpoations span much of the twentieth century. The 1928 Achnacarry Agreement enabled major oil firms to achieve a stable economic arrangement, and after World War II, these corporations reestablished their encompassing marketing and pricing agreements. The control of these major firms was gradually eroded in the 1950s however, by independent American and European producers that obtained contracts for Middle East oil. To expand their markets, these independents turned to price cutting and lessened the effectiveness of the international oil corporations.[7]

After the formation of OPEC in 1960, its member nations at first bided their time, because of the abundance of oil and an inability to agree on production controls. OPEC members realized, however, that the economic survival and expansion of industrialized economies rested on a continuing supply of petroleum.

Events turned in OPEC's favor in 1973. An economic upswing was underway in industrial nations generally characterized by weak governments. In addition to a temporary tightness in the world oil supply, geographical concentration and political cohesion worked to the advantage of major petroleum exporting nations. The Shah of Iran and King Faisal of Saudi Arabia agreed to act in concert. King Faisal hoped to exert his influence to free Jerusalem from Israeli control, while the Shah hoped to tap the wealth of his declining oil reserves. The relative abundance of wealth enjoyed by OPEC members, who generally produce oil for export and lack significant internal interests pressuring for petroleum price reductions, extended the cartel's time horizon. In the short run, at least, the lack of alternative sources of supply and the lack of a substitute commodity facilitated the cartel's action. Under these conditions, the cartel of oil producing nations became a political and economic reality.

In the fall of 1973, OPEC unilaterally quadrupled the prices of crude oil exports, posting an additional price increase in 1974 and 1975. The celebrated seven-sister multinational oil corporations were reduced to the status of tax collectors for OPEC revenues. During the winter of 1973-74, Arab members of OPEC embargoed petroleum shipments destined for the United States and the Netherlands and cut back shipments elsewhere, in an attempt to use economic pressures to influence the resolution of the Arab-Israeli conflict.

The oil price increases contributed to a worldwide inflationary spiral, produced a fear of collapse in world financial markets, generated a fear that Arab interests would appropriate massive amounts of Western industrial and real estate properties, and drove oil-importing developing nations to a precarious financial position. Yet, the fears of calamity flowing from OPEC actions must be viewed critically. Recent estimates indicate that OPEC price hikes were responsible for only 20 to 25% of the 1974 rise in the United States' consumer price index. Because of the greater dependence of Japan and Western European countries on imported oil, such nations were harder hit than the United States. The OPEC price spiral caused about one-third to one-half of the inflation in those countries in 1974.[8] Looking to future OPEC price rises, their impact on worldwide inflationary pressures, although considerable, probably will not toll the end for Western economies.

The specter of the worldwide disruption of financial markets and a "large" concentration of funds and resources in the small number of OPEC hands seems, likewise, exaggerated. Although estimates differ, depending on a number of imponderables (including the worldwide demand for petroleum, future economic conditions in the West and the effectiveness of conservation measures), projections indicate that by 1980 surplus revenues enjoyed by OPEC members may turn into annual deficits because of the growing imports by Middle East nations to develop infrastructures, raise living standards and arm themselves. The development plans of populous nations like Iran and Algeria will permit such countries to generate only a small surplus, if any, while cash will probably continue to pile up in Kuwait and Saudi Arabia. Some OPEC members, including Iran, recently turned to foreign loans to finance their development plans.[9]

Estimates place OPEC's wealth by 1980 at 2.4% of the world's capital stock, with a smaller percentage of the world's total financial and real assets.[10] These figures appear manageable. OPEC members, furthermore, probably will not buy out Western firms on a massive scale but, more likely, will use their oil revenues to buy armaments, pursue social development programs and build their industrial capacity, especially in the field of crude oil processing and the production of petrochemicals.

One threat appears valid, namely, the plight faced by Third World nations that import oil. OPEC price hikes have increased the balance of payments deficits incurred by oil-poor developing nations heavily dependent on imported oil as an energy source. The so-called Fourth World experienced an aggregate balance of payments deficit of $35 billion in 1975, a substantial portion of which was attributable to the high cost of oil. Estimates of the trade deficit in 1976 indicate a slight decline to $30–35 billion.[11] Rising prices of agricultural commodities imported to meet food shortages also strained the resources of many Third World nations. The cumulative impact of petroleum and food price hikes led to massive long-term and short-term borrowing by developing nations, estimated at more than $130 billion.

To satisfy the financial and developmental needs of oil-poor developing nations, OPEC members have diverted a portion of their revenues to the Fourth World countries. Arab members of OPEC set up a number of development funds and banks to compensate poorer Arab nations. Venezuela has eased the burden of oil bills by selling oil on the following terms: half in cash and the balance in the form of low-interest long-term loans. Venezuela has also made substantial contributions to the Inter-American Development Bank and the Caribbean Development Bank. OPEC members have channeled funds to international institutions, particularly the Special Oil Facility of the International Monetary Fund, to finance balance of payment deficits incurred by members of the International Monetary Fund.[12]

Despite loans and other forms of financial support made available to Fourth World nations, the prospect of further OPEC price hikes raises increasing doubt as to the financial viability of some developing nations. Continued infusions of funds from OPEC members and international financial organizations will be required to avoid widespread defaults and re-schedulings of loan obligations.

Speculation continues to abound regarding the long-term viability of OPEC and the cartel's ability to significantly increase petroleum prices. Three questions stand out. Will Saudi Arabia continue to limit its oil production? What will be the worldwide demand for petroleum? The continued recovery of Western economies from the depressed conditions of 1974 and 1975 enhances OPEC's prospects. What will be the impact of new oil supplies under the control of industrialized nations, for example, from the North Sea and the North Slope of Alaska? The combinations of these new high-cost sources with the desire to stimulate the development of synthetic fuels and other energy sources may force industrialized nations to seek a stable floor price for petroleum and not drive the price back to pre-1973 levels. Assuming OPEC remains in business, members of OPEC will probably allow multinational oil companies to continue to sell OPEC production in order to prevent under-the-table attempts by member nations to increase sales.

To date, OPEC has not collapsed but has served instead as a model for the formulation of cartels by developing nations exporting other raw materials. A long history lies behind recent efforts to organize raw material cartels. During the 1920s a number of producing firms (or sometimes producing governments) entered into commodity agreements to drive up prices by means of export controls and quotas. Because these firms lacked sufficient market power, the agreements failed to prevent dramatic declines in commodity prices during the Great Depression. The inter-governmental commodity agreements of the 1930s in tin, rubber and wheat aimed to benefit producers through export restrictions and taxes. World War II brought an end to these agreements. The decline in prices after the Korean War produced a series of intergovernmental agreements in wheat, sugar, tin and coffee designed to halt plummeting prices and reduce price instability. These agreements included interests from produc-ing and consuming nations. For example, the 1962 International Coffee Agreement, signed by over 50 consuming and producing countries, estab-lished export quotas. Arrangements governed the world coffee market until 1972, when the economic provisions of the agreement lapsed.[13]

Following OPEC's success, in quick succession nations formed cartels or associations for a variety of raw materials, including bauxite (Inter-national Bauxite Association), tin (International Tin Agreement), coffee (International Coffee Council) and copper (Intergovernmental Council of Copper Exporting Countries).[14] These arrangements strive to achieve a common, and hopefully beneficial, pricing strategy for producing nations and to prevent multinational corporations from playing one country against another.

Although the cartel of bauxite producers probably has the greatest possiblity for success, nonpetroleum raw material groups face a multitude of problems. In recessionary or nongrowth economic periods, cartels generally experience difficulty in raising prices. The financial staying power of many raw material–producing countries differs from, and is inferior to, that of oil-exporting nations. Developing nations must produce, export and sell their raw materials or commodities or face financial ruina-tion, especially in times of mounting oil prices. For commodities requiring more labor-intensive processing operations than petroleum, cutbacks in output spell increased unemployment. Some commodities, bananas, for example, cannot be stored. The inability of a cartel to control a sufficiently large share of world output or reserves, the presence of geographical and political diversities and the absence of shared experiences among pro-ducers create additional impediments. The problem of internal dissension, particularly with respect to the allocation of production quotas, is always present. Fear that price increases will generate a decline in demand or a shift to the consumption of near substitute materials hampers a cartel, as does the possiblity of the development of natural or synthetic substitutes and greater emphasis on the recycling of raw materials. The existence of a cartel may also encourage new producers to enter the field, and it may force importing nations to stockpile raw materials against the time when the cartel may increase its prices. Only in the case of petroleum does the cost of a raw material constitute a large percentage of the selling price of an intermediate or end product.[15] Finally, the efficacy of nonpetroleum cartels may turn on the willingness of OPEC members to provide financial assistance, particularly with respect to the stockpiling or destruction of surplus stock or the enforcement of a limitation on production.

Despite these problems, in addition to petroleum, bauxite appears the raw material most suitable for cartelization. Forty percent of the world's production of bauxite is concentrated in four Caribbean countries—Jamaica, Surinam, Guyana and the Dominican Republic. The four Caribbean nations, together with Australia and the Soviet Union, aggregate over 75% of the world output. Six multinational firms, Alcoa, Kaiser, Reynolds, Alcan, Pechney and Alusuisse, account for over 80% of the smelting capacity in the noncommunist world. As with petroleum, the existence of a few, large vertically integrated firms enhances the operation of a cartel. Market dominance facilitates corporate efforts to pass along added costs, including higher raw material prices, to consumers. Developed nations are heavily dependent on the importation of bauxite. Price hikes seemingly do not produce a decline in demand. Bauxite also lacks a readily available low priced substitute. In addition to fluctuations in the demand for bauxite, the cartel faces one critical problem, namely, difficulty in fixing the price for bauxite because of differences in quality among bauxite deposits and the lack of an accepted benchmark standard. Because of the reliance of some nations, such as Jamaica, on the foreign exchange generated by bauxite exports, the ability of nations to hold off the world market significant amounts of bauxite appear problematical.[16]

The success of OPEC has also had a far-reaching symbolic significance for the Third World nations. OPEC meant that at last some developing nations had broken free from the grasp of dependency. This realization spurred developing nations to propose transnational solutions to challenge the existing world order and the problem of dependency.

11

TRANSNATIONAL APPROACHES AND THE THRUST TOWARD A NEW WORLD ORDER

Riding the wave of OPEC's success, yet cognizant of the long-range ability of developed countries to generate new sources of supply for Third World–controlled raw materials, innovate synthetic substitutes, engage in conservation measures and recycling and build stockpiles, developing nations sought, in the mid-1970s, to develop a new international economic order based on their apparent position of power. From this effort emerged a far-reaching attempt to redistribute income and decision making in the world, to minimize the severe jolts to economies which accompany violent swings in world commodity prices and to achieve wider opportunities for industrialization in developing countries. Using a transnational approach, the Third World moved on two fronts: (1) raising the prices of and controlling the availability of raw materials; and (2) attacking the problems presented by the manufacturing operations of multinational corporations in developing nations.

RAW MATERIALS

After the success of OPEC, the quest for the new international economic order began in 1974 with the adoption by the United Nations General Assembly of the Declaration on the Establishment of a New International Economic Order in May and the Charter of Economic Rights and Duties of States in December. After asserting that each nation-state possesses full and permanent sovereignty, not subject to any form of external coercion, over its natural resources and all economic activities, Third World nations called on "rich" nations to share resources with poor countries and alter a system in which developing countries constitute 70% of the world's population but obtain only 30% of the world's income.[1] One hundred ten nations met in Dakar, Senegal, in February 1975 and reached a consensus on concrete proposals for creating a new international economic order. The Lima Declaration of the Second General Conference of the United Nations Industrial Development Organization, held in March 1975, incorporated many of the Dakar proposals.

As part of the new international economic order, prime attention focused on a multifold program to regulate, through a series of agreements, raw material and commodity markets, including prices and supplies. Devices proposed by the Third World to raise and/or support prices and allocate production among nations included the use of buffer stocks, that is, an agreement by producing and consuming nations to engage in purchases or sales of a commodity, when necessary, to maintain prices within a designated range. Buffer stocks would be accumulated in periods of glut and released in time of shortage, thereby protecting producing nations from wild price gyrations. Instead of separate arrangements for each commodity, the United Nations Conference on Trade and Development advocated an integrated commodities plan based on a central fund to finance international buffer stocks for a number of selected commodities, except food grains.[2] Fixed floor and ceiling prices for commodities, as well as various conpensatory and supplementary financing systems to protect export earnings, were considered. The indexation of commodity prices was also proposed. An indexation program would gear the prices of commodities and raw materials exported by developing nations to the cost of the manufactured goods Third World countries purchase from developed nations.

Faced with the need to structure programs to satisfy the demands of OPEC members and to preserve and bolster Western preeminence in the world capitalist system, the United States government gave up a strategy of confrontation to force down oil prices and sought limited areas of cooperation with developing nations. During 1974 and early 1975, the United States vacillated on how to deal with the Third World, especially OPEC. Some advocated a federal agency to act as the sole purchasing agent for American oil imports; oil purchased under a secret competitive bidding program could then be resold to private firms. Proponents hoped that secret competitive bidding for licenses to import oil into the United States would force members of OPEC to cut prices to obtain a larger share of the American market. Such a program, however, failed to consider the possibility of an OPEC boycott or the submission of similar bids by OPEC members. A federal agency to take over the function of importing oil would also be hampered by problems of capital costs, a lack of experience and the possibility of constituting a larger focus for foreign political pressures.[3] For a time, the United States State Department wanted the United States and the other oil-consuming nations to set a common floor price on oil imports to insure the development of alternate energy sources and full-blown conservation measures, even if OPEC tried to undercut such efforts by slashing oil prices. It was hoped such a plan would serve as an inducement to oil producers to consummate long-term lower-cost arrangements with oil consumers.[4] Considerable attention was also focused on splitting the solidarity of Third World countries by pointing to the adverse impact of spiraling oil prices. Others suggested that industrialized nations build an adequate petroleum stockpile. Two major problems with this proposal were cost and the possibility that other industrialized nations might also commence stockpiling unless the United States made its stockpile available to such countries.

The United States government, in mid-1975, shifted from a hard line confrontation position and manifested an interest in commencing a dialogue with the Third World. A meeting between raw material–consuming nations and raw material producers held in Paris in April 1975 fell apart because the United States wanted to focus only on energy while developing nations wanted to broaden the agenda to include all raw materials and a broad range of development questions. An April 1975 conference witnessed a coalescence of the views of OPEC members and non–oil-developing countries that the agenda should include the protection of the purchasing power of developing countries' export earnings and the indexation of raw material exports.[5] The Third World continued to support OPEC's efforts for at least three reasons: (1) the hope of other nations to be oil exporters; (2) developing nations' desire for assistance and support for their own cartels; (3) and the fact that nearly all developing nations bear the scars of dependency and humiliation. The United States government realized the difficulty in dividing the nation-states of the Third World.

In May 1975, Secretary of State Henry Kissinger evidenced a willingness to broaden the discussion between producing and consuming countries to include all issues of concern to the developing nations and to consider international arrangements for greater price stability of various commodities on a case-by-case basis. This new stance paved the way for the more detailed proposals Kissinger presented to the September 1975 Special Session of the United Nations General Assembly and to the December 1975 Conference on International Economic Cooperation. With reference to commodity trade and production and the stability of the export earnings of developing countries, in September 1975, Secretary of State Kissinger recommended the establishment of a consumer-producer forum for each key commodity to promote the efficiency, growth and stability of the respective markets. He supported a liberalization of the financing of buffer stocks by the International Monetary Fund and the creation within the IMF of a development security facility to stabilize overall export earnings by giving loans to sustain development programs in the face of export fluctuations. Funds available for loans would total up to $2.5 billion per year, with an aggregate maximum of $10 billion. Kissinger also proposed an international system of nationally held grain reserves to meet food shortages and famines. Secretary Kissinger sought to work within the existing institutions of the world capitalist system. He refused to agree to indexation and manifested a desire to avoid international price-support mechanisms for basic commodities.[6]

The Third World responded to these American overtures by indicating a willingness to continue talks with industrialized nations. For example, the resolution adopted at the close of the September 1975 Special Session of the United Nations General Assembly called for a multifaceted program to improve the market structures for the raw materials and commodities exported by developing countries that would include international stockpiling and other arrangements designed to secure stable, remunerative and equitable prices for these raw materials and commodities and the enlarging of existing financial facilities for compensatory financing to minimize export revenue fluctuations. The resolution also called for continued study of commodity indexation schemes by the Secretariat of the United Nations Conference on Trade and Development.[7]

In October 1975, representatives of various developed and developing nations agreed to convene, outside the framework of the United Nations system, the Conference on International Economic Cooperation. The conference's four commissions on energy, raw materials, development and finance, it was contemplated, would propose new economic arrangements reaching beyond issues involving the price and supply of petroleum.[8] The conference would enable the dialogue to continue between the Third World and the industrial nations.

With the heightened prospects for an ongoing dialogue between producing and consuming nations, several problems must be faced regarding stabilizing or increasing the flow of commodities and raw materials. Third World countries seek an end to declining terms of trade and exploitation, which may be defined as forming part of an exchange of goods and services when the goods and services exchanged are quite obviously not of equal value and one party to the exchange uses a substantial degree of coercion.[9] Third World countries, in short, seek at least a "just" price for their commodity and raw material exports. How such prices will be set, for which raw materials and commodities, by what institutions, and whether consumers and producers will participate, remain unresolved. At least four problems exist with nonmarket price and supply arrangements. First, agreements among developing and developed nations, if successful, would provide a floor under world prices, thereby contributing to worldwide inflationary pressures. Indexing, in particular, might freeze prices at arbitrary levels. Moreover, segments of labor and industry within each nation-state capable of achieving parity with rapidly mounting commodity and raw material prices might further exacerbate the inflationary spiral. Secondly, plans to hold up prices in periods of falling demand might reduce the demand for such commodities and raw materials. Higher prices might also spur production of raw materials and commodities in industrialized nations at less than the prevailing prices. Production of synthetic substitutes would also be encouraged. Thirdly, the utilization of a buffer stock mechanism involves difficulties in projecting the future size of a necessary buffer stock in light of long-term supply and demand patterns and the impact of price increases. It also raises the problem of the allocation of quotas, at various production levels, among producing and consuming nations. A decision must also be made on how the burden of contributing to the buffer stocks should be allocated among consuming nations. Finally, a common fund scheme covering many commodities may be unworkable, because such a fund could be manipulated for political ends. Whether a common fund would be less costly than separate funds is also unclear.

Despite these difficulties, stabilization arrangements offer a mutuality of benefits for both producing and consuming nations. Producing nations seek stable (and hopefully increasing) prices to maximize governmental revenues and avoid strains on their ability to plan new investments and to satisfy social demands. Consuming countries want assured access to supplies at somewhat predictable prices that will be consistent with business plans, price levels and sales patterns. Stabilization might minimize cycles of underinvestment and overcapacity as well as inflationary pressures flowing from resource scarcities. Sophisticated corporations in oligopolistic industries, seeking new markets in oil-importing developing nations to absorb their exports of manufactured goods and to extend the reach of the consumer society, and possessing the power to pass on commodity price increases to consumers, may support raw material and commodity agreements. Despite ideologues' arguments to perpetuate the supposed free market, a favorable attitude to some type of arrangement may prevail among business leaders.

The mutuality of benefits flowing from a commodity stabilization system probably will lead to an agreement among nations. Price levels, production quotas and/or buffer stocks arrangements can be arrived at through negotiations, which, of course, will include political and economic factors and considerations of the bargaining power of each side. Such agreements require international arrangements, open to all nations, that will meet, through compromise, the needs of both developing and developed countries and take into account the value of raw materials and commodities to consumer nations and the alternate costs of substitute sources. Consideration may also be given to indexation in order to surmount the problem of declining terms of trade and the impact of inflation exported from industrialized nations.

The most critical question is not which mechanism should supplant the market mechanism, but how to distribute the fruits generated by the efforts of Third World nations to countervail the power of multinational corporations and industrialized countries. The new arrangements may adversely affect nations and other unorganized consumers heavily dependent on the importation of a wide range of raw materials, including agricultural products. Increases in raw material prices will yield benefits for major raw material exporters—the Soviet Union, South Africa, Canada and Australia—which do not fit the stereotype of impoverished developing nations. Future world food shortages may further increase the power of the United States, which already dominates a food producer's oligopoly. In short, commodity and raw material price supports may not facilitate the transfer of income from rich to poor nations.

To meet the redistribution goal, the export earnings of Third World nations could be stabilized (or increased) by means of a transnational arrangement. Such an international program could be modeled after the 1975 Lomé Convention, pursuant to which members of the European Economic Community and certain countries in Africa, the Caribbean and the Pacific agreed to a guarantee program, based on the respective levels of development of the participating Third World countries, for specified nonmineral products. In the event export revenues obtained from specified products sent to the Common Market decline below a certain level, the Common Market will compensate the affected countries for a part of the resulting loss.[10] The experience of the Lomé Convention and the compensatory financing facility of the International Monetary Fund may form the basis for an expanded transnational program to insure export earnings. Export subsidies provided by importing nations may provide the best technique to fulfill a basic need—the quest by developing nations for a measure of stability.

MANUFACTURING OPERATIONS OF MULTINATIONAL FIRMS

The confrontation between consuming and producing countries over the price, supply and availability of raw materials and commodities temporarily obscured the efforts of developing nations to create transnational regulatory mechanisms to control the manufacturing operations of multinational corporations and overcome the specter of dependency. The United Nations system, the focal point for these international efforts, has been active in the following areas: investigation of global enterprises, the creation of new bodies and commissions to engage in research on the impact of multinational corporations, and the consideration and recommendation of a variety of means to regulate global giants. In 1972 the Economic and Social Council of the United Nations requested the Secretary-General of the United Nations to appoint a Group of Eminent Persons to study the role of multinational corporations and their impact on the developmental process and their implications for international relations and to submit recommendations for international action. The Group of Eminent Persons in its report recommended that the Economic and Social Council of the United Nations discuss issues related to multinational corporations at least once a year and that a commission on multinational corporations be created under the auspices of the Economic and Social Council. The Group further advocated the establishment of an information and research center to perform two functions: (1) to make available information to assist developing countries in dealing with global firms, and (2) to provide substantive and administrative services, including the collection, analysis and dissemination of information, for the proposed commission on multinational corporations.[11]

In August 1974, the United Nations set up an Information and Research Center to obtain needed information and analyze and disseminate such information to nation-states. This was followed by the establishment of a permanent United Nations Commission on Transnational Corporations in December 1974. The commission was created to act as a forum within the United Nations for a comprehensive consideration of multinational enterprises, including furthering an exchange of views, conducting inquiries, making studies, preparing reports and assisting the Economic and Social Council in developing a set of recommendations that might form the basis of a code of conduct regulating the activities of global firms and preparing proposals relating to the regulation and supervision of multinational corporations.[12]

Implicit in such steps are a variety of policy alternatives and various mechanisms for implementing the regulation of multinational entities. At least three possible routes could have been chosen: disclosure, international incorporation, or transnational standards for corporations, home countries and/or host nations. The United Nations has chosen to pursue the first and third paths, namely, gathering information and formulating a code of conduct for multinational enterprises.

The foundation of a transnational policy for the regulation of multi-

national firms rests on the disclosure of information by multination
firms and the governments of home and host nations, and on the colle
tion, assessment and dissemination of such data. Information could b
gathered, analyzed and disseminated in a variety of areas, including: inte
affiliate flows of goods and services and their pricing; the internation
distribution of specific activities, including technology and other corpora
skills and equity ownership and control; the origin and nature of inte
national direct investment apart from capitalized know-how and tl
transfer of secondhand equipment; the impact of foreign subsidiaries o
governmental policies, such as tariff, restrictive business practices, cred
availability and the access to alternative sources for the supply of goo
and services.[13] Attention might also be focused on multinational corpora
ownership of land, mineral and other resources in each country; paymen
global firms received for royalties, patents, licenses and management co
tracts from foreign subsidiaries; private sector interlocks with government
together with credit and debt relationship; and the taxes paid by mul
national corporations in each country.

With the present rudimentary knowledge regarding the economi
political and social impact of global firms, particularly in view of the l
disclosure requirements imposed by nations other than the United State
information gathering is a laudable first step. Two caveats must be note
First, although a need for more information exists, corporations ma
have valid reasons for preserving the confidentiality of information.
line must, therefore, be drawn that will respect legitimate corporate nee
but not allow firms to hide behind a screen of business secrecy. Secondl
in gathering the data, certain preliminary judgments must be made to pi
point the most critical information, including implicitly the development
paths of nation-states, the costs and benefits of multinational firms, tl
allocation of such costs and benefits, and the objectives of and the mea
for implementing transnational regulation. A promiscuous gathering
data probably would be self-defeating. But greater disclosure and gatheri
of information, for example, on restrictive business practices and inte
affiliate transactions, form a first step in a pattern of international contr
and indirectly provide a means of substantive regulation.

Beyond disclosure, multinational corporations could formally b
internationalized. Instead of national incorporation and regulation, a
international corporate law could be developed providing for internation
incorporation of certain global firms. A proposal by George Ball envisag
the establishment of an international corporate law administered by
supranational body, composed of representatives from signatory nation
which would exercise supervisory authority over the internationally cha
tered corporations.[14] The share ownership, board membership and to

management of such corporations would also be internationalized. With ownership dispersed, a parent corporation might no longer be regarded as the sole instrumentality of a particular nation.

Proposed restrictions on internationally incorporated enterprises are of particular concern. A firm chartered under the proposed international companies law would agree to be bound by its provisions. Each signatory state would agree neither to impose additional restrictions on the chartered corporations nor to expropriate the subsidiaries of such corporations without prompt payment of adequate compensation. In short, by placing the entire scope of corporate activities under international surveillance and regulation, the proposed law would protect a firm from further interference by host nations.

Another variant envisages the registration with the United Nations of multinational enterprises satisfying certain criteria. Such registered firms would agree to meet certain requirements. In the event a dispute arose between a host country and registered multinational firms, a United Nations body would, after conducting an independent study, produce a report.

The suggestions for global chartering suffer from several impediments. Although the proposed rules would contain restrictions on corporate activities, as would a code of conduct, developing countries would not support lax, imprecise standards and inadequate enforcement machinery. The inability of nation-states to impose additional restrictions on global firms constitutes an impediment, as do the lack of precision in the process of selecting representatives to the supranational body and uncertainties regarding the supranational body's sanctioning powers.[15] In short, global chartering proposals tilt too much in favor of protecting the existing position of multinational corporations.

In addition to disclosure, the heart of the United Nations' efforts center on drafting a code of conduct for transnational enterprises. A code of conduct envisages the establishment and acceptance of basic principles that would serve as guidelines for the activities of multinational corporations.

A proposed General Agreement on Multinational Corporations forms a starting point for the consideration of a code of conduct. Modeled after the General Agreement on Tariffs and Trade, the proposed agreement would lay down a limited set of principles to be administered by an international agency possessing the power to investigate questions submitted by corporations or nation-states and make non-binding recommendations that would, hopefully, be accepted by the affected parties on a voluntary basis. Signatory states and perhaps multinational corporations could consult and bargain regarding policy departures from the agreement and also discuss problems and procedures to facilitate the settlement of disputes. From a few generally accepted principles, it is contemplated, an international treaty of substantial coverage would emerge. The precedents developed by the agency could also form a basis on which to build a supranational system.[16]

One proposal, a General Agreement on Capital and Technology Transfer, encompassed among other items the following specific basic principles: (1) the political neutrality of foreign-owned firms in a host country; failure to maintain such neutrality would void parent government risk guarantees; a firm would be able to influence politics in a host country only by public statements; covert activity of a political nature would constitute a per se violation; (2) adherence by multinational firms to all local laws; (3) recognition by host governments of foreign ownership of tangible assets and the intangible rights of management control for 20 years, unless a shorter time period was agreed to; an investor-contractor would have to adhere to entry conditions unless adherence was made impossible by a host government or a change in circumstances beyond the control of the foreign investor; (4) full acceptance of tax incentives and holidays introduced by other member governments to aid foreign business interests; (5) taxation of earnings by the home government at capital gains rates or not more than 50%, whichever is less; (6) referral of disputes regarding interpretation of rules to an international forum created under the convention.[17]

The existence of a code, and then a treaty, would eliminate the slow, costly procedure of case-by-case bargaining between a nation-state or a regional bloc of countries and a multinational corporation.[18] Multinational firms would, furthermore, know what was expected of them, at least on the issues comprising the code. Signatory nation-states would be legally committed to arrangements covering foreign direct investment, unaffected by pressures from special local interests or the temptation to rely on discriminatory or retroactive, ad hoc measures in regulating global corporations.

Agreement on a basic set of principles remains difficult because of the lack of common interests between developed and developing countries and because of their differing perceptions of the economic, political and social impacts of multinational enterprises. The first meeting of the United Nations Commission on Transnational Corporations in March 1975 produced a split between developed and developing countries on the scope and content of a code of conduct and on whether such a code would apply to host governments as well as to private and/or public enterprises engaged in foreign direct investments.[19] Third World representatives favor a code of conduct that would not impair the sovereignty of host governments. Industrialized nations and executives from multinational firms seek

estrictions on the activities of host nations and a code of good corporate
behavior formulated in general terms. For example, Sir Val Duncan,
chairman and chief executive officer of the United Kingdom-based Rio
Tinto Zinc Corporation, outlined a code of good corporate citizenship
with the following features: a progressive degree of local autonomy in
decision-making, subject to very minimum coordination at the center;
employment of as high a proportion of the nationals of any host country
as possible, including senior management; having the nationals of a host
country serve as a majority of the board of directors of each overseas
corporation; sensitivity to reasonable aspirations of a host nation; and
permitting the population of a host country to participate in major enterprises of that country, after major risk stages have been surmounted.[20]

In view of the support of multinational corporations for a code of conduct establishing general guidelines, industrialized countries and Third
World nations probably can agree on a code covering a narrow range of
issues.[21] Four likely areas of agreement are: (1) barring activities by global
firms that adversely affect competition, such as the takeover of or the
merger with an existing local firm; (2) requiring an end to discrimination
in employment based on sex, age, religion, race or ethnic origin; (3) requiring that qualified local personnel be employed or be trained for
employment; and (4) imposing an obligation on multinational enterprises
to obey local laws and refrain from intervening, directly or indirectly, in
the domestic affairs, particularly the political process, of a host nation.
However, Third World nations may be reluctant to bar corporate bribery
of government officials, directly or indirectly, through the use of agents.
Local laws and customs may not prohibit either bribery or corporate
political contributions.

Beyond this limited range of items, agreement on a code of conduct
may be more difficult because of either the technical questions involved
or differing viewpoints on allocating the costs and benefits of multinational firms. Three areas of disagreement stand out: transfer pricing,
technology, and taxation. Other difficult areas include ownership and
fade-out divestment policies, procedures and methods for nationalization,
the amount and the timing of the payment of compensation, and environmental questions including an assessment of costs and allocation of such
costs.

A statement in a code declaring that multinational corporations shall
not engage in transfer pricing establishes little. Even after more data is
gathered on the extent and effects of transfer pricing, standards and regulations covering a wide range of situations in different industries must be
established. Guidelines of universal applicability appear nearly impossible
to draft. The multitude of means for transferring income must be

considered. A "just" price for tens of thousands of terms cannot be fou
An arm's-length standard of pricing is not helpful in instances of pri
set by a few firms. Determination of the costs, particularly the allocat
of research, administrative and overhead expenses, is difficult. Agreem
on the allocation of a stream of revenue among nations may also pr
difficult. Facing this magnitude of imponderables, the transfer pricing p
visions of a code of conduct may relegate implementation and enforcem
to national or regional bodies with an international agency merely coll
ing, analyzing and distributing data on transfer pricing.[22]

Technology questions present further difficulties. The Secretariat
the United Nations Conference on Trade and Development has formula
a code of conduct for the transfer of technology that includes unbundl
the transfer so that technology may be purchased apart from the t
package of capital, management and expertise; reasonable prices for
technology transferred; time limits on licensing agreements; eliminatio
a variety of restrictive practices associated with the transfer of technolo
including export controls; prohibitions on the acquisition of compet
technologies, and tied-purchases; strengthening of national technolog
capability.[23]

Agreement probably could be secured on the prohibition of cert
restrictive business practices by multinational firms in connection with
licensing of technology. Developed countries, however, representing
interests of global firms, may seek to distinguish price-fixing techniq
from restrictive business practices involving the allocation of expo
Businesses may regard pricing decisions as too sensitive a matter to be
cluded in a code. Industrialized nations may also resist subjecting exist
technology contracts to current and future periodic reviews and the
position of a limitation on the royalties or fees in contracts tr
ferring technology. Multinational corporations stress the need for t
firms to receive what they consider adequate remuneration as a prerequi
to transferring technology; otherwise, global giants threaten to withd
from transferring technology. A requirement that a parent corporat
deploy technologies and production processes capable of most efficie
employing local factors of production would also encounter the opposit
of global firms. Competition from other multinational firms and a vari
of alternative sources may constitute a more effective way to force for
investors to experiment with more suitable technologies. Finally, in v
of regional and national efforts in broad areas of technology problems,
value of a code may be doubtful.

Revision of the patent system by means of a code of conduct rem
controversial and the final result uncertain. A code proposed by
representatives of the so-called group of 77 calls for the abolition

patents.[24] Other Third World spokesmen have advocated the creation of an international patent bank to which public institutions would donate patents. The bank would license patents, without royalties or fees, to developing countries. But developed nations and multinational corporations will probably remain adamant in support of the patent system. They argue that the patent, as a monopoly, forms an incentive for innovation.

As access to the most modern forms of technology probably does not meet the development needs of many Third World countries, revisions of the patent system may fade into the background. The ability to tap more appropriate forms of technology, particularly labor-intensive technology and unpatented know-how, may be much more vital for developing countries. If high technology is deemed critical, nations or regional groupings should consider national or regional legislation containing greater discrimination in the granting of patents, particularly with regard to the standard of usefulness. Such legislation should mandate compulsory patent licensing in case of nonutilization by foreign firms.[25]

Although taxation has traditionally fallen within the orbit of national concern, an international agreement might provide for a universal tax on the global profits of a multinational corporation, with the tax liability assessed by each jurisdiction in which a firm operates in proportion to the profit of the entire enterprise, irrespective of where the profit nominally appears.[26] Such a tax system would remove the incentive to engage in transfer pricing and other manipulations of income. A global tax system would also generate capital for Third World countries.

At least three obstacles exist to an international tax system. First, such a scheme would impede national sovereignty. Second, a formula would have to be devised basing taxation on sales, profits, assets, or a percentage of payroll dollars in each country. Third, many developing host countries currently use tax incentives and subsidies, as well as favored access to credit and restrictions on unions and strikes, as means to attract foreign direct investment. The incentive programs may, in the future, lead home nations to impose countervailing restrictions on host tax inducements. Host countries may, in turn, attempt to avoid these home country retaliatory efforts. Whether developing countries will presently agree to restrict tax inducements appears problematical. Perhaps future home country retaliatory policies may force a more conciliatory approach.[27] National and regional efforts to reduce the effectiveness of transfer pricing techniques may also force multinational firms to perceive the advantages of international tax collaboration schemes. But transnational efforts in the field of taxation appear years away.

Beyond the difficulties inherent in devising principles for assessing the costs and benefits of multinational enterprises, agreeing on the allocation

of costs and benefits among nation-states and corporations, and the act
drafting of technical solutions, other barriers exist to an early adoption
a meaningful code of conduct or a more formal international agreement
transnational enterprises. These additional impediments include the ne
for a periodic assessment of the strengths of respective bargaining positic
and the creation and implementation of an effective enforcement mecl
nism. From the business standpoint, multinational corporations will opp
any meaningful international restrictions as an impingement on their fl
ibility. Transnational regulation, like regional groupings, limits corpo
tions' ability to play one nation off against another. The press
contradictory national regulations may, however, lead multinational fir
to search for transnational uniformity.

Nations differ in their development priorities, national interests, e
nomic, social and political objectives, attitudes and ideological stan
regarding foreign direct investment, levels of governmental sophisticatio
and resource endowments. Industries differ in structure and pattern
behavior; what a corporation deems desirable behavior may vary with
circumstances and therefore be difficult to codify. The interest of labor
developed nations and developing countries must also, of course, be c
sidered. Third World nations, because of the importance of raw materi
in a world facing resources scarcities, believe their bargaining position
improving. Although willing to talk with industrialized nations, spokesm
for the Third World probably will resist entering into compromise arran
ments involving present institutional norms or dispute-resolving mec
nisms as a point of reference, or acceding to a surrender of their respect
national sovereignties. A resolution of the issues through a code of c
duct may evolve by stages; i.e., taking the easy areas first, building up c
abilities and trust, then handling the difficult questions. The Unit
Nations probably constitutes the best arena for dealing with a wide varie
of issues simultaneously and for tapping the disclosure and informati
thrusts undertaken by various UN units.

The dispute-resolving system—including the supervising agency a
enforcement mechanism—is critical in a serious consideration of a tra
national code of conduct. The possibility that a multinational corporati
might pressure the government of its home country led to the creation
the Calvo doctrine, which barred a corporate subsidiary from appeal
to the home government of the parent corporation for protection a
support. "To prevent appeals by aliens to their home governments
diplomatic intervention on behalf of their contract rights, a number
Latin American states, during the latter part of the 19th century, adop
a policy of writing into their contracts with aliens a clause, known as
'Calvo Clause,' the general tenor of which was that the alien agreed th

any disputes that might arise out of the contract were to be decided by the national courts in accordance with national laws and were not to give rise to any international reclamation."[28] A number of Latin American governments currently deny local rights and remedies to any foreign-owned subsidiary if such entity or the parent corporations calls on the home government of the parent (or any foreign government) in a dispute with the host nation. International arbitration tribunals and mixed claims commissions have differed on their interpretations of the Calvo Clause: some have upheld it as a bar to the interposition of the alien's home government; others maintain that the act of an alien cannot restrict the rights of his government under international law.

In the context of a transnational code, developed countries, however, probably will resist the demands of developing countries for vesting exclusive jurisdiction over multinational corporations in host nations. Areas to be resolved in the puzzle include jurisdiction over litigated matters, compensation for nationalization and a prohibition on a home country from interceding in a dispute between a multinational firm and a host government. It is politically unrealistic to think that developed countries will refrain from assisting multinational corporations headquartered in their country at least by diplomatic support and investment guarantees. To promote the acceptance by industrialized headquarter countries of a code of conduct containing the Calvo doctrine, host nations could guarantee economic rights to foreign subsidiaries, provide for nondiscriminatory treatment, establish procedures for compensation following nationalization and devise formulas to determine the level of compensation in the event of the nationalization of a foreign-owned enterprise.

The difficulties entailed in the creation of a transnational supervising agency and enforcement mechanism must be considered. A centralized regulatory agency might be unresponsive to future needs. Regulation by a branch of the United Nations or a newly created international agency might prove too weak. Some critics might predict that a United Nations-based agency would be too inefficient and slow, but developing countries would probably feel more comfortable with an agency within the United Nations system. Multinational corporations and developed countries, on the other hand, might desire a regulatory body not connected with the United Nations. Existing international organizations, such as the United Nations, might resent the intrusion of a new transnational regulatory body. The vested interests of established international organizations combined with the weight of the Third World will lead to pressures for an agency under the United Nations umbrella. Developing nations might find that the international regulatory agency, whether or not under the auspices of the United Nations, would develop a sympathy for the entities regulated, because business ties might supersede the public interest charge of the regulators.

Agreement must also be reached on the functions of an international regulatory agency. Such an agency could perform several possible functions, including: (1) consultation; (2) gathering of information, possibly with the power to compel the production of documents; (3) promulgation of detailed regulations, with the power to enforce such standards; (4) investigation and the making of nonbinding reports; and (5) arbitration of disputes, with nation-states and multinational corporations obligated to effectuate the resultant decisions.[29] As evidenced by the refusal of many developing nations, particularly in Latin America, to sign the Convention on the Settlement of Investment Disputes between States and Nationals of other States, Third World nations remain unwilling to surrender autonomy to a dispute-resolving mechanism that they view as dominated by developed nations.[30] The Convention, formulated by the Executive Directors of the World Bank, which created the International Centre for the Settlement of Investment Disputes, is designed to facilitate the flow of funds to developing countries by providing arbitration and conciliation facilities to deal with investment disputes between the governments of signatory states and the nationals (private investors) of other signatory states. Although the United States and Jamaica are signatories to the Convention, Jamaica has refused to participate in an arbitration proceeding before the Centre involving taxes on bauxite. Jamaica has taken the position that a legal dispute arising directly out of an investment relating to minerals or other natural resources is not subject to the Convention.[31] Likewise, if a dispute-resolving mechanism embodied in a projected code of conduct should be perceived as stacked in favor of the Third World, developed countries will probably manifest intransigence.

Other problem areas involved in setting up an international regulatory agency include: (1) the financing of the agency; (2) the composition of the membership of the agency (for example, should multinational corporations be eligible for membership?); (3) the selection of a voting system (on an equal or weighted basis? and if the latter, what criteria will determine the weight system?); and (4) the collorary question of who will have the controlling voice in the choice of top administrators and what the prior background of the administrators will be.

Third World nations may perceive that an international agreement and the accompanying regulation might only legitimize the activities of multinational corporations, by giving such entities added respectability, without producing any significant benefits beyond national or regional controls.[32] In that case, the Third World might utilize other techniques apart from transnational regulation or, depending on their power position, step up the economic and political confrontation with the Western world

In light of the multitude of problems inherent in devising and implementing meaningful international regulation with respect to the manufacturing activities of multinational corporations and the quandary concerning the transfer of technology, the Third World may rely on national and regional regulation by host countries, on a variety of means to generate more information about global firms, and on the creative use of the United Nations system apart from a transnational code of conduct. Although it is difficult to generalize, since developing nations include the oil-rich, those engaged in manufacturing goods for exportation, countries with a significant infrastructure and technical expertise base, and the poorest of the poor, the Third World should increase its knowledge concerning alternative development paths and goals, the consequences of such paths and goals, and the alternate means of implementation. Technical assistance, which could include such forms as national and regional research and development institutes and advisory, negotiating and mediation services, could strengthen the position of a host nation, lessen dependency and help redress the inequality of knowledge.

A need exists to create and strengthen national research and development institutions that can work on a technology and development policy suitable for local needs and resource capabilities. A national center could perform a multitude of functions: identifying technological needs, providing information on alternate technology sources, analyzing technology suitable for a project, breaking down the package provided by multinational firms and assessing attached costs and conditions, negotiating contracts for the importation of technology, adapting imported technology and developing indigenous technology. Regional or international centers, where developing countries could obtain help on formulating key questions and information on development alternatives, constitute another possibility. Secretary of State Henry A. Kissinger, at the May 1976 UNCTAD IV Conference, proposed the establishment of an international industrialization institute to encourage research and the development of industrial technology appropriate to developing countries, as well as various technical training programs.[33]

The Third World also needs one or more organizations that, drawing on the experience of other host nations, could provide assistance on more specific matters, including the assessment of alternate technologies, the costs and benefits of the involvement of multinational firms, the availability of options and sources of supply for the requisite capital, technology and management, and information about technical, social, and human problems in dealing with a particular firm. The evaluation of various inputs could be based on standardized criteria with the information available from a data bank.

In addition to obtaining outside assistance, developing nations also need help to improve the skills and knowledge of their own officials. A restructuring of a country's educational and training system for development needs may also be required.

Advisory services presently exist, in a nascent state, within the United Nations aimed at improving the knowledge and bargaining position of the Third World. In addition to the United Nations Food and Agriculture Organization in the agribusiness area, of particular interest is the United Nations Industrial Development Organization, which prepares and evaluates projects. The Industrial Inquiry Program of UNIDO provides answers to inquiries from developing nations relating to equipment, technology management and marketing. UNIDO is also building up a referral service on manufactured equipment produced by industrialized nations.[34] The United Nations Centre on Transnational Corporations is setting up training programs and advisory services to strengthen the negotiating ability of the governments of developing countries. The Centre is also establishing a comprehensive information system, preparing profiles on selected multinational corporations, collecting data on contracts between global firms, governments (or governmental agencies) and local enterprises, and conducting research on the political, legal, economic and social effects of the operations and practices of multinational enterprises.[35] The United Nations Conference on Trade and Development could assist developing nations in the formulation of technology policies, the establishment of institutional arrangements for the transfer of technology, and the training of personnel.[36] United Nations units such as the UN Development Program and the Food and Agriculture Organization have also prepared manuals on joint venture negotiations, which build on similar contract situations and lay out alternative choices in specific contract areas.

The possibility of joint venture contract negotiating courses exists, as does more active participation by the United Nations in the negotiations between multinational corporations and Third World countries. The Fishery Division of the FAO, for instance, is indirectly involved in joint venture negotiations by providing technical assistance and legal advisors and by giving written advice to developing nations.

Model contracts, with standardized provisions, could be created to regulate relations between a foreign corporation and a host country. The United Nations could also furnish advisory service to developing countries including the evaluation of the fairness of new private foreign direct investment projects and technical advice on how to handle existing investments. In addition to reviewing a proposed contract and comparing it with other agreements used by a multinational firm (or other corporations in the same industry) in other countries, a unit of the United Nations might act as a broker to assess the benefits offered by each party and, if appropriate, present alternatives to reallocate the costs and benefits more fairly. Such a body could also identify for developing countries the most desirable strategies to use in dealing with multinational corporations. These mechanisms might assist in dispelling mistrust and permit bargaining on the basis of a clearer concept of self-interest and evolve "fair" terms for investments by and operations of multinational enterprises.[37]

A United Nations agency might also offer mediation and conciliation services in the event of disputes between a nation-state and a multinational corporation. It is to be expected that spokesmen for industrialized nations and multinational corporations would resist an expansion of the United Nations' efforts in the areas of negotiation and mediation between a host country and a global firm. For instance, Senator Jacob Javits (R.–New York), a member of the United Nations Group of Eminent Persons, opposed the United Nations acting as a party to adversary negotiations between a host country and a multinational firm. He regarded it as an inappropriate, unrealistic role, considering the wide spectrum of expertise required.[38] But, depending on the bargaining leverage of the corporations vis-à-vis the Third World, the United Nations system may play an expanded role in furthering the national and regional regulation of global firms. Developing nations may also bring pressure for unilateral, bilateral and multilateral steps by home nations. Further efforts may be undertaken to strengthen the transnational position of labor unions to countervail the power of multinational corporations.

12

EFFORTS TO CONTROL MULTINATIONAL FIRMS

This chapter analyzes various steps that home nations sensitized to the problems presented by multinational corporations and the specter of dependency could take to regulate these corporations' conduct and questionable payments and provide additional financial assistance to the Third World. Transnational labor arrangements that may weaken the power of global business firms are also discussed.

HOME NATIONS

A growing awareness of the challenges posed by multinational firms for developed countries as well as the Third World may bring additional unilateral regulation by respective headquarter nations. Some home nations, such as Sweden, have taken the initiative in controlling direct investments abroad. A Swedish firm must, for example, obtain authorization from the Bank of Sweden whenever it wishes to make direct investments abroad or to borrow money in foreign countries to finance investments outside Sweden. Social conditions, including nondiscrimination in employment, promotion and division of work and adequate provisions for training, social security and social welfare, are among the criteria Sweden requires for foreign investment guarantees. These guarantees are made available only for investments that the Swedish government feels will improve the economic development of a host country.

Revelations regarding questionable payments abroad by American multinational corporations have led to a variety of national solutions including increased regulations by the United States Securities and Exchange

Commission under traditional and emerging disclosure standards and by other arms of the executive and legislative branches of the federal government.[2] Working on a three-part premise, the SEC applied the concept of integrity disclosure to force the disclosure of questionable overseas activities by American corporations. Their premise was: (1) the SEC has the duty to enforce United States securities laws, which are designed to protect and inform the investor; (2) in order to fulfill this duty, the Commission must examine those foreign corporate activities that might reasonably affect the decision of a shareholder to buy, sell or hold a security, or affect the decision of a shareholder in deciding how to cast his corporate vote; (3) falsification of corporate books raises questions regarding a company's financial integrity, and linked to a corporation's financial integrity in maintaining its books is the integrity of the corporation's management. The SEC concluded that disclosure of the fact that corporate executives approved foreign payments and that corporate records were falsified—even if the payments were proper under foreign laws—would lead a reasonable investor to question the executives' integrity and their ability to properly discharge their corporate duties. The SEC commissioners also emphasized the potential impact of overseas payments on a company's "quality of earnings." Such payments expose a firm to economic risks, both in the host country and in the United States; for modest initial payments may lead to spiraling demands or, if the payments are uncovered, the corporation may face reprisals overseas, including loss of licenses or other government privileges, or even expropriation of the firm's interests.

The SEC propounded amnesty guidelines, to which a number of corporations responded. A corporation that believed it may have violated the United States securities laws by failing to disclose past foreign payments gained amnesty from the SEC in exchange for a voluntary revelation of questionable payments abroad and the adoption of policies to prohibit such conduct in the future.

A limited disclosure plan under the auspices of the SEC, whether for past or future activities, poses questions of practicality. If a firm disclosed the existence of payments, it might be difficult to keep confidential the specific details. Legislation might be required to prevent disclosure of information by other branches of the federal government that might injure the conduct of American foreign policy. In view of the far-reaching ramifications of disclosure of questionable corporate payments on the American economy and the foreign relations of the United States, primary responsibility lies with Congress and the executive branch to assess the propriety of corporate activities and prohibit corporate conduct by new statutory prohibitions and sanctions.

Senator William Proxmire (D.-Wisconsin) led the congressional response

to the disclosure of questionable corporate activities abroad. Propos
legislation took two basic forms: (1) monitoring the business activities
American firms, and (2) regulating foreign arms sales. Legislation making
a crime for American corporations to engage in activities abroad th
would be illegal if conducted at home (bribery, for example) might be
sented by host nations as American interference in their internal affai.
Also, enforcement of such legislation might require surveillance and i
vestigation of foriegn officials as well as American personnel. But t
United States should, at least, condemn subversive political interventic
by American firms aimed at overthrowing a host country's governme
or at creating situations conducive to such action. Presumably, such leg
lation would be welcomed by host countries as it would signal an offici
policy of noninterference by Americans in foreign internal affairs. In t
matter of multinational firms' engaging in local political controversies
identifying themselves with partisan political activities in host nations,
should be left to the foreign countries to define permissible activiti
and establish sanctions. The application of domestic criminal sanctions
the payment of bribes overseas encounters the further problem that su
actions may not be illegal in a particular foreign country.

Legislation imposing stricter controls over foreign arms deals, includi
congressional approval of arms sales through government channels in e
cess of a fixed dollar amount and the disclosure of commissions, fe
gifts, or political contributions by corporations in connection with su
deals, could create undesirable consequences for the American econom
Foreign military sales have helped provide jobs and have assisted t
United States in bolstering its balance of payments position, particular
with oil-producing nations of the Middle East. Efforts to "purify" t
armaments business may have a negative impact on the American econom

Any national solution to the problem posed by surreptitious corpora
activity abroad suffers from two major shortcomings: (1) consideratio
of the state of the economy and foreign relations present countervaili
factors weighing against the adoption of a strong position by any Weste
nation; and (2) any regulation would reduce the freedom of the corpo
tions of one nation while failing to control the practices of entities inc
porated in other nations.

In the absence of a transnational code of conduct, an adequate respon
may require a unified stance by the governments of the United State
Japan and Western European countries. The Organization for Econom
Cooperation and Development has adopted voluntary guidelines for mul
national corporations located in industrialized nations that are membe
of the OECD.[3]

Another possibility is that corporations, on an individual basis, throu;

national or international trade associations, or on an industrywide basis, either nationally or transnationally, could take the lead in formulating standards of conduct. While a number of corporations have taken the initiative in this area, the delineation of standards for international conduct may not be matched by effective self-imposed enforcement procedures. Standards that embody general concepts are subject to varying interpretations and are, therefore, of limited efficiency, whether devised by corporations or the OECD.

THIRD WORLD FINANCIAL NEEDS

Apart from transnational price and supply arrangements, oil-importing developing nations, facing balance of payments problems and acute capital shortages, are attempting to force developed nations to meet Third World financial needs. The Third World is utilizing three techniques.

LOWERING OR REMOVING TARIFFS AND/OR IMPORT QUOTAS

The developing world is seeking a lowering or removal of tariffs and/or import quotas imposed by industrialized nations on manufactured products from Third World countries. Tariff changes, including a preference for the manufactured goods of developing nations, could not only improve balance of payment positions but also might assist to reduce unemployment in developing countries.[4] Developed nations taking such a step would correspondingly weaken their balance of payments position and increase the competition faced by their domestic manufacturing firms. Developing nations may use their ability to supply raw materials on favorable terms as the lever to gain tariff concessions on manufactured products.

LOANS AND GRANTS TO DEVELOPING COUNTRIES

Third World nations are pressuring existing and new multilateral international financial institutions to make available more funds for loans and grants to developing countries. Responding to these demands, Secretary of State Kissinger in 1975 called for the creation within the International Monetary Fund of a development security fund to provide loans of up to $2.5 billion a year to meet export deficits incurred by developing countries. He also advocated the establishment of an International Fund for Agricultural Development to mobilize capital resources for (1) an international program of research, technical assistance and information exchange and (2) the development of better systems of control, transportation and long-term management. But primary reliance, Secretary Kissinger indicated, should be placed on stimulating the flow of private capital to developing nations. Secretary Kissinger favored an increase in the capital of the World Bank's International Finance Corporation from $100 to $400 million to support private enterprise in developing countries. He proposed the creation of an International Investment Trust to mobilize private capital for investment in local enterprises.[5]

At the UNCTAD IV Conference in May 1976, Secretary Kissinger expanded on his theme that the Third World should rely primarily on private sector investment. He proposed the establishment of an International Resources Bank to aid private investment in developing the resources of Third World nations. The bank would issue bonds to generate capital for the development of a nation's resources. The proposed bank would also guarantee the investor against nationalization. Funds could also be provided for commodity price stabilization.[6] The Third World resisted the Kissinger proposal because of past, unfavorable experiences with private foreign capital.

The Third World has continued to look to multilateral public sector financing. Efforts by the International Monetary Fund and the World Bank include (1) enlarging the availability of credit for underdeveloped member countries experiencing shortfalls, beyond their control, in their export earnings; (2) creating a trust fund, financed by the sale of gold held by the IMF, to make very low interest loans or grants to the poorest countries; and (3) making loans at lower than normal interest rates to credit-worthy nations.[7] But determining the proportion of funds to be advanced by OPEC members and the developed countries (the United States, Western Europe, and Japan) must be resolved before the bail-out of the Fourth World can be undertaken on a massive scale. The Trilateral Commission, a private organization composed of representatives from various business, labor and other groups in the United States, Western Europe and Japan, has advocated that highly liquid OPEC members bear a greater burden of new subsidy programs than industrialized nations that are not currently as liquid.[8]

Developing countries, particularly OPEC member nations, want a greater voice in the running of world monetary organizations in return for their increased financial contributions. OPEC nations want to step up their voting rights in the World Bank and the International Monetary Fund. The United States and other industrialized nations, however, are reluctant to lose control over international financing agencies, especially their ability to veto significant actions. Meaningful participation for OPEC nations may rest on their gaining control of the Executive Board of the World Bank, of which the United States, Western Europe and Japan presently hold majority position.

PUBLIC AID AND INVESTMENT FROM DEVELOPED COUNTRIES

To achieve their development objectives, Third World countries continue to call for more direct bilateral public aid and investment from industrialized nations—unencumbered, it is hoped, by restrictive strings. The official United Nations goal contemplates that development assistance from Western countries will equal 0.7 percent of the gross national product of the respective nations.[9] Sweden has emerged as the first industrial nation to spend .7% of its GNP on foreign aid; the Netherlands and Norway are approaching this figure.[10] The United States, on the other hand, has stressed that the developing world must depend on private loans and investments, not public aid, to meet its capital needs.

As a result of the soaring amounts of borrowing from private and public sources, developing nations have also pressed for a blanket cancellation or reduction of their present indebtedness and for a more rational method for rescheduling the repayment of obligations. Third World nations with adequate credit ratings oppose far-reaching changes that might close their access to private capital. Developed nations have opted for a case-by-case resolution of the debt problem.

TRANSNATIONAL LABOR UNIONS

Labor unions represent a possible force to countervail the power of global firms. According to labor leaders, multinational corporations threaten unions in a variety of ways. A national union's task of influencing management is made more difficult because of the problem of identifying and affecting a decision-making seat outside a nation. A union may also be unfamiliar with the personnel and organizational traits of the management of global firms. A union faces difficulties in obtaining financial data on the profits earned and the wages paid by the total enterprise and each subsidiary. Multinational corporations allegedly possess the ability to shift, temporarily or permanently, production facilities and/or arrange for the use of multiple production facilities, thereby weakening a national union's power. In particular, switching production to developing countries may undermine a union's power. The financial staying power of a multinational corporation with many profit centers enables such an entity to withstand a local strike better than a union with one profit center.[11] Unions also assert that foreign direct investment adversely affects a home country by reducing employment and by redistributing income.

The assertions of union leaders, however, are overstated. Some managements have decentralized responsibility for labor negotiations. Even when decision making over labor matters is centralized, top management ma carefully consider the views of executives located in various subsidiarie The threat of the loss of fixed investment in plant and machinery, and th possible imposition of financial penalties, such as severance pay requir ments, under the laws of a host nation retard the assumed flexibility c multinational corporations to shift operations. A transfer of production c other operations to a plant that lacks geographical proximity or sufficier excess capacity may not prove feasible. The ability of organized worke to stop production in one critical part of a system of vertically integrate operations conducted by a global firm vests considerable bargaining powe in an advantageously located union.[12]

Labor unions have undertaken a three-fold response to the challeng presented by multinational firms. First, they have advocated national legi lation (such as reducing the tax incentives for foreign direct investment) i developed home countries aimed at weakening or undermining the positio of multinational corporations. Secondly, unions representing workers i the same or related industries in different countries collaborate throug international trade union secretariats. International trade union secreta iats engage in research, information and advisory activities. Data such a the collective bargaining contracts for an industry throughout the worl can help a national union in bargaining with the subsidiary of a mult national corporation. Secretariats also sponsor conferences and semina: and establish permanent world councils, composed of representatives c workers from all parts of a corporation or industry, that engage in consu tations with employers. A company council enables worker representativ from a firm's plants throughout the world to meet, exchange informatio and coordinate the activities of unions representing workers in all th countries where a firm operates or on an industrywide basis. A concessio given in one country forms the basis of bargaining everywhere. Example of workers councils include councils for leading auto makers set up by th International Metalworkers Federation and councils in the chemical, ru ber, paper, textile fiber, glass, ceramic and atomic energy industries create by the International Federation of Chemical and General Worker Union.[13] International trade union secretariats also help in organizing an strengthening unions, including encouraging the mergers of nation: unions; bridging religious and ideological differences; training in union pr cedures and techniques; and providing assistance in negotiations.[14]

Thirdly, labor has pursued a variety of international bargaining a proaches. A union in the home country of a firm has supported employe in foreign subsidiaries by bringing pressure on the parent corporatio giving financial assistance for organizing activities, engaging in strikes, bo cotts and demonstrations, refusing to work overtime and holding joir meetings with a multinational firm.[15] For example, a joint confrontation of labor unions in two countries with St. Gobain, a French glass maker, was engineered in 1969 by the International Federation of Chemical and General Workers in support of wage negotiations in which subsidiaries of St. Gobain were engaged. Secretariats have sought to reinforce the position of each national union through coordinated bargaining, which involves putting forth similar demands and seeking, among other things, similar hours of work and common contract termination dates for contracts at all the facilities of a corporation.[16] The ultimate aim of transnational union activity is centralized multinational collective bargaining that will encompass similar wage rates and working conditions.

Serious impediments exist to extensive coordination activities and collective bargaining by transnational unions. These obstacles include the following factors: differences in national bargaining procedures, e.g., industrywide bargaining vis-à-vis enterprise-level bargaining; other national legal provisions governing unions; social, political and historical factors, including the political orientation and ideology of many non-American unions; diverse national systems of social benefits and regulation of business; and differences in the functions and structures of unions and the manner in which a union represents its members. International union arrangements must also overcome the traditional orientation of union leaders to think in national terms. Also, union leaders dislike delegating policy formulation to an international union and may oppose making sacrifices for workers in other countries who may be regarded as competitors for jobs. The attitude of rank-and-file workers to colleagues in other countries is likewise a discouraging factor.[17]

Unions have sought a transnational code of conduct binding corporations and home and host nations. Such a proposed code would create a universal set of fair labor standards to mitigate "substandard" labor conditions in developing countries, including low wages, and to impose similar standards of health and safety in home and host countries. Unions look to the International Labour Organization to promulgate a code of conduct requiring multinational firms to recognize union rights throughout the world; as an alternative, requirements could be imposed on a home nation to insure that multinational corporations under its jurisdiction would adhere to basic labor standards throughout the world.

The quest for universal "fair" labor standards, including wage parity and a harmonization of working conditions, may create an elite local labor force of unionized workers employed by multinational corporations in developing countries. Instead of raising wages for this select group, a transnational code or agreement might require multinational firms to turn over to the governments of developing countries the difference between the going wage rate for similar work in the developing nations and in the country in which the enterprise is headquartered. Such a sum could then be invested in infrastructure improvements that would benefit a wider group of people.[18]

13

AN ASSESSMENT OF THE NEW TRANSNATIONAL ORDER

The widening gap in the standard of living between developed and developing countries during the post-World War II period (marked by an estimated average income level in the rich industrial countries 13 times that in the poorest developing nations) and the desire to overcome the humiliation and feelings of inferiority and insignificance resulting from colonialism and the impact of multinational corporations after independence led Third World countries to engage in national and collective efforts (regional and transnational) and to organize groups of producer nations to redistribute income and improve their status and power. This chapter assesses, from the viewpoints of both developing nations and the West, the prospects for a new transnational order and the possibility for an inward turn of national policies. The means—confrontation, dialogue or unilateral action—used to achieve various ends are also considered.

Building on the experience of the oil cartel organized by petroleum-exporting countries, Third World nations with vital raw materials possess, at least in the short run, considerable negotiating leverage in their dealings with Western nations and global firms. Using this bargaining weight, developing countries may push to strengthen their control over multinational corporations and to secure concessions and reparations from developed nation-states. In a world of growing resource scarcities, major industrial nations and multinational entities will compete for investment outlets and raw material sources, thereby generating friction between such nations and entities and permitting a greater share of the world's wealth to gravitate to developing countries. Economic considerations will probably supplant military power as the decisive factor in transnational relations.

The transnational quest for increasing income, status and power looks to a growing equality of opportunity among nation-states. Little is said about the individual within the new society and the paths of development. The focus rests on Third World governments' reaching compromises with corporate interests and the governments of industrialized nations and de-lineating spheres of exclusive and shared interests among the public and private sectors. Most developing nations apparently wish to live in an interdependent world with Western nations and global firms. The model of economic interdependence, coupled with advances in communications and transportation, envisages a weakening of nation-states. Third World countries are attempting to counter the impact of interdependence and the probable accompanying dependency by seeking, through both respective national actions and collective strength, to tap the benefits of multi-national enterprise (such as managerial skills and technical expertise) yet avoid the costs.

However, it is uncertain whether industrial nations and multinational corporations will co-opt the worldwide movement for equality. The example of concessions given by corporations to workers in the United States during the 1930s, including the recognition of collective bargaining and the provision for social security and higher minimum wages, does not hold much hope that meaningful reform will occur in the transnational system during the last quarter of the twentieth century. For little redistribution of income has occurred on the national level in the West through building the countervailing power of labor. To the contrary, workers have received more because the pie has become larger.

Developing countries may only extract concessions, such as the stabilization or indexation of commodity prices, regulation of the most harmful practices of multinational corporations, freer access for their manufactured products in the markets of developed nations and increased financial assistance, that do not endanger the continued vitality of the world capitalist system. These appear to be the types of concessions the United States is willing to make. Moreover, the agreed-upon measures may only squeeze consumers, including many located in developing countries.

Despite the steps taken and those contemplated, the specter of continued dependency looms for the Third World. Control over the flow of information, not capital, may comprise the key to the future world system. Industrial countries' continued dominance in technology may doom developing countries to a dependency position even if foreign direct investment is controlled or restricted by national, regional or transnational means.

But the assumption of a continued global system of interdependence among industrialized and Third World nations masks two critical questions: (1) What development path should Third World nations pursue? and (2) Should a country turn to greater self-reliance? A nation contemplating breaking free from the existing world system of interdependence based on trade, foreign investment and multinational corporations must first assess the drawbacks of the present global structure. Opposition to world interdependence through trade and investment stems from at least three arguments: (1) free trade in the nineteenth century did not insure peace and prosperity, but resulted in World War I and the Great Depression; (2) the spread of modern technology facilitates the local production of basic needs, which may be thwarted by corporate actions in the fields of trade and/or investment; and (3) the world capitalist system bars national or regional experimentation with alternate forms of social, political and economic organization.

By turning from a system of interdependence, a nation may be avoiding the growing burden of inflation spread through the medium of goods and services exported from developed countries. The inflationary spiral may intensify the inequalities inherent in the present transnational structure. Thus, national self-reliance may serve a variety of goals, such as assisting in overcoming dependency, in removing pervasive poverty, and in focusing on relevant economic, social, and political problems.

A nation wanting to lessen or eliminate its involvement in the world capitalist system faces, however, a number of difficulties. Many nations produce one or two raw materials or commodities and engage to a greater or lesser extent in manufacturing operations for local consumption and for exportation. A rational development plan must rest on an assessment of the value of what a nation produces and the means at the nation's disposal to increase the prices of such goods or services, to increase demand (e.g., by opening new markets), or to reduce the cost of raw materials, commodities or goods, by decreasing wages (an unpalatable alternative) or utilizing new technology. In the short run, it is difficult for a country dependent on the exportation of a single raw material or commodity to curtail such operations and turn to other lines of endeavor. During the transition to greater self-sufficiency, a country may remain part of the interdependent world system even if the ownership and production of the export-oriented resources and the means of production come under state control. A nation may, however, investigate unmet needs, on a national, regional and worldwide basis, and direct the allocation of its capital and manpower to satisfying such needs.

Examples of transitions in a nation's economy do exist. The transformation of the People's Republic of China constitutes the most dramatic shift to self-reliance. Also, during the Great Depression and World War II, when contact was broken with the industrialized West, Latin America, without abandoning reliance on raw material and commodity exports, rapidly industrialized and urbanized.[1]

A nation must consider whether it wishes to merge the road to economic

autarchy with participatory political and work organization structure
Instead of pursuing the consumer rainbow of Western industrial societ
which generally has resulted in depopulated rural areas and unemployme
and underemployment for an uprooted urban multitude concentrated
the ever-growing shantytowns of metropolitan centers, a developing natio
might seek to build a labor-intensive agrarian society based on the use
local resources and appropriate technology. Such a technological altern
tive would consist of small-scale operations using local materials and u
skilled labor. In an environment of capital scarcity, idle labor may
harnessed and work opportunities maximized in countryside work place

As Third World nations turn to self-reliance and/or strive for equali
or even global hegemony to take revenge for their past humiliation a
dependency, developed countries will quite naturally perceive such effo
as tending to destroy the present world capitalist system. Gloomy scenari
rapidly come to mind for an industrialized society already dominated
the machine, characterized by routine in the factory and office and t
ethos of individual consumption. Threats to world peace are posed by t
proliferation of nuclear weapons in Third World hands; and the econom
security of the West is threatened by the potential ability of developi
nations to increase the price for critical raw materials lacking readily ava
able alternative sources of supply or inexpensive substitutes. The prospe
that national, regional or transnational regulation may limit the prof
ability of multinational enterprises raises additional doubts among Weste
business and government leaders, as does the call for the location in t
Third World of an increasing percentage of the world's industrial faciliti

In the midst of these negative prospects, the industrialized world m
resent the aspirations of developing nations for a "fair" share of t
world's income, status and power; or at best, grant only meaningless cc
cessions that will not weaken the position of Western nations or redu
their income levels or growth potentials.

Despite doubts raised as to the ethical validity of a meaningful tra
national redistribution of wealth, status and power,[2] significant benef
would accrue to industrialized nations in meeting the demands of Thi
World nations, above all, a reduction of worldwide tensions. The pri
however, may be too great a burden for the world capitalist system, a
especially for multinational corporations. Can Western market-orient
societies exist without the existence and continued growth of the forei
activities of multinational enterprises?

In analyzing the need for foreign direct investment and corpora
expansion by multinational enterprises, some commentators have stress
the preservation of the global oligopoly advantages enjoyed by Americ
corporations. One observer has concluded:

But there *is* something fundamental to American corporate capitalism—the capitalism of tightly held technology, uncertain information, large economies of scale, and unstable imperfect competition . . . that creates strong pressures for foreign investment. As long as American corporations exercise their virtues of inventiveness and aggressiveness, their government will feel intense, even frantic pressures to create and preserve an international system that facilitates foreign economic expansion.[3]

But there appears no reason that the United States, or other industrialized nations, must continue to build a system at the expense of individuals and nation-states in the Third World and a widening gap between affluent and impoverished areas. The present system opens the West to future blackmail attempts by raw materials cartels and may adversely affect levels of employment and income distribution in the United States and other Western countries. Greater restrictions on foreign investment and the overseas activities of multinational corporations and a redistribution of the world's wealth, power and status, as part of a worldwide welfare system, would not necessarily lead to a collapse of the US economy or the world capitalist system.

The coming era may present a time of promise as well as peril for Western civilization. Curtailment of the wasteful use of raw materials, characterized by profligate individual consumption, may lay the basis for the creation of new values and institutions. The disintegration of the old order may be painful, especially for those possessing status and privilege, but consideration should be directed to the rebirth of Western society, particularly the rationale for vast political and economic organizational apparatuses. In the new environment, self-managed economic institutions may flourish in the Western world as part of a movement for a decentralized, participatory society. Greater use of labor-intensive techniques may alleviate growing concerns regarding unemployment, energy and capital shortages, and the omnipresent danger of pollution. New economic and political institutions may also develop to meet the deep needs for personal fulfillment and concern for others. In short, the emerging transnational order may lay the basis for the liberation of people everywhere and an escape from old, lifeless institutions and values in the West. Thus, the new era may present, over the long term, an unmatched opportunity to transform Western civilization.

In the short run, moreover, a multitude of challenges exists in the United States and in other industrialized nations to tap the expansionist drives of multinational corporations. Perhaps the most pressing is the need to develop the technological and practical possibilities for alternate energy sources, such as solar energy. Attention should be given to the development of synthetic substitutes for raw materials in short supply. Joint public and private efforts could undertake the necessary research and development and implement steps to insure a sufficiency of resources for the new society. America's mounting urban needs, including, housing, mass transportation and waste disposal, also present new dimensions for business and development at home. Demands imposed by the Third World may assist Western governments to channel expertise and capital to areas of social need. A lessening or a cessation of tax incentives offered by home governments for foreign direct investment, when coupled with public sector planning and funds, may prove beneficial over the long run. Public support of technological innovation in the areas of nonmilitary research and development may be especially appropriate.

However, if the United States unilaterally turns inward the danger exists that firms headquartered in such sectors as Western Europe and Japan will fill the void. The American public may be forced to choose between policies that redound primarily to the advantage of United States multinational corporations and those that meet domestic needs and build a more humane society albeit a less competitive one vis-à-vis other industrialized nations. Similar questions must be faced in other developed nations. The greater raw material base of the United States, as well as America's agricultural capabilities, may give the United States more flexibility. A split may, therefore, develop between the United States and less well-endowed industrialized nations.

Critics of capitalism assert that the best way to resolve the problem of dependency is to build socialistic structures in industrialized nations. They argue that a centrally planned economy in a home country would not need foreign markets to compensate for inadequate domestic demand or foreign investments to absorb surplus capital. Goods demanded by consumers in such a society might require fewer imported raw materials. Such countries, therefore, would be less likely to engage in predatory activities. A centrally planned economy operating at a continued high level of industrialization, of course, might still need the same amount of raw materials. The search for outlets for surplus capital does not constitute a prime motivation for overseas corporate expansion. The exploitative behavior of the Soviet Union with reference to its satellite nations does not offer much assurance that a change in economic institutions will solve the efforts of one nation to dominate others.

In addition to unilateral action by any nation, the strivings of the Third World may produce a frightful confrontation, or a new order may emerge by means of a peaceful dialogue. Many developing nations, excluding members of OPEC, seem drifting toward economic stagnation and possible bankruptcy and anarchy over the next five to ten years. Even the Western world seeks to meet the needs of developing countries, the rising expectations may continue to make the remaining inequities intolerable, thus leading to an ever-spiraling list of demands. The desperate position of Fourth World nations and the possible future collapse of the oil cartel may propel Third World countries to turn to ever more authoritarian political regimes and to disruptive actions, including defaulting on their indebtedness, terrorism and nuclear blackmail. Short-term palliatives to stabilize the international order may only postpone, but not avoid, the day of reckoning. Frantz Fanon regarded violence as part of the decolonization process. An individual participating in violent actions could, according to Fanon, expunge himself of inferiority and submission and be transformed psychologically to become capable of creating a new society.[5] The efforts of Third World nations to change from being an object of history to being its subject through liberating acts of violence may destroy Western society and perhaps the entire world. On the other hand, Western spokesmen have contemplated an aggressive military takeover of certain OPEC production and reserve areas in the Persian Gulf to avoid the strangulation of industrialized Western countries and Japan.[6] An escalating specter of confrontation leads to Nkrumah's bleak conclusion: "The danger is now not civil war within individual States provoked by intolerable conditions within those States, but international war provoked ultimately by the misery of the majority of mankind who daily grow poorer and poorer."[7]

The emerging transnational order may, on the other hand, be founded on negotiations between Western nations and the Third World. Because of the power of developing nations over raw materials, industrialized nations and multinational firms will no longer dictate the terms of the economic, political and social order to countries in the periphery of the world capitalist system. Each nation, or more realistically, those possessing a bargaining advantage in the form of raw materials, a competitive manufacturing sector, a large and rapidly growing market, or all three, may freely assess the degree of interdependence with the world capitalist system it deems optimal and the price it is willing to pay for the perceived benefits. Increasingly, a nation may be able to control its developmental goals and its institutional structure based on freely available, meaningful and accurate information. Charting how joint gains will be perceived and shared remains to be worked out as well as the measure of what is equitable regarding the distribution and management of the world's wealth, status and power. The problem of whether there exists an acceptable level of resource transfers that will meet the hopes of poorer nations must be surmounted.

Thus far it has been assumed that gains accruing to developing countries will cause losses for industrialized nations. But the long-run quest for transnational equity, the redistribution of income, power, and status and the development of new institutional arrangements, including commodit stabilization schemes, the control of foreign direct investment and the regulation of multinational enterprises, may produce benefits for developing and developed countries and global firms. One effort to generate mutual benefits, which will be analyzed in Part Four, is the Industry Cooperative Programme of the Food and Agriculture Organization, an affiliate of the United Nations, which attempts to reduce conflict between developing countries and multinational agribusiness corporations. The Industr Cooperative Programme, a business-funded vehicle, acts as a catalyst an provides a supporting framework for dialogue within the United Nation among governments of Third World nations and business entities; this dia logue facilitates an exploration of the reasons for conflicts and attempts t develop remedies that will produce benefits for developing countries an multinational corporations. Although marked by failures as well a successes, the Industry Cooperative Programme may serve as a mod for cooperative government-business endeavors, under the auspices o the United Nations, in other areas.

The shape of the future world order remains difficult to discern. A the Third World emerges from the shadow of dependency, leaders of th developing nations must assess their bargaining advantages and the mo successful techniques to extract concessions from the West. Increase knowledge by the citizenry of industrialized nations regarding the cos and benefits that multinational corporations present for home and ho nations may enable the populace and the leaders of developed nations t propose creative solutions on which a new transnational order may b founded. This new awareness may form the basis for a global dialogue an bargaining on an issue-by-issue basis. Hopefully, this will become th path of the future.

PART FOUR

INDUSTRY COOPERATIVE PROGRAM OF THE FAO

14

TRANSNATIONAL CONFLICT AND THE ORIGINS OF THE I C P

Multinational agribusiness corporations possess a considerable body of expertise, including managerial, technical and marketing skills, as well as capital resources. Third World nations face a variety of critical tasks in feeding their populations, including increasing the output of food (crops, meat and fish) so as to achieve a greater degree of self-sufficiency, fighting crop and animal diseases and reducing the loss and waste of food. In addition to satisfying their food needs and seeking balanced development programs, Third World countries strive to fulfill some or all of the following objectives: increased employment, improved distribution of income and land, reduction (or at least deceleration) of energy consumption, and ecologically sound development paths.

The image (and the reality) of corporate exploitation, the skewing of developmental priorities, and the adversarial confrontation between Third World nations and industrialized countries, characterized by the producing nations' attempt to stabilize or raise the prices of raw materials and commodities, creates a multitude of tensions between developing countries and multinational corporations. The profit-making objectives of multinational corporations have, in the past, conflicted with the developmental goals of Third World countries. A number of "horror" stories abound that illustrate the clash between the profit motive of business and the social goals of Third World nations. The manufacturers of farm inputs, such as tractors and agricultural chemicals, have been primarily interested, as one American corporate executive candidly admitted, in a nation's wealthy agricultural sector. "We benefit," he noted, "the wealthy landlords and the ruling class." Multinational firms skew a country's developmental priorities, such as redistribution of income. In the absence of stringent governmental regulation, small farmers generally fail to bene! from the new technology introduced by multinational agribusiness giant Multinational corporations may also divert crops to the production animal feed, thereby reducing the already scarce supply of protein ava able for human consumption, particularly among a nation's poor. Growi crops for export to the table of the world's elite, as part of a multination contract production scheme, probably will force a developing country expend scarce foreign exchange to import basic foodstuffs—wheat, ri and corn.[1]

Although a number of firms have undertaken small-scale charitab projects in Third World nations out of a concern for the human conditio a sense of social responsibility, and fear of the Third World's wish for vi lent revolution against the established international system, the pro constraint limits the public service activities of multinational agribusine corporations. One of the most laudable efforts of private corporate assi tance to a developing country involved the West German chemical gia Hoëchst A. G. The Indonesian government requested Hoëchst to prote rice against pests. In cooperation with the Indonesian governmer Hoëchst agronomists recommended that farmers be given special seec fertilizers and agrochemicals, training in the proper application (speci cally, spraying techniques) of agrochemicals, and guidance of the use other inputs, including proper watering techniques. Hoëchst advanc the necessary inputs on one-year credit arrangements with Indonesi, farmers, who repaid the loans from the higher profits generated by t larger yields. Although the project involved what Hoëchst officials view as a "modest" expenditure of funds, its success generated good will f the firm and increased sales of its products.[2]

But it is naive to assume that international business firms will enga in wide-scale philanthropic activities in developing nations. A number examples of corporate altruism exist, usually with the same long-run m: keting aims—increased product sales—which may or may not meet nation's social goals. Moreover, the inability to control results may lim corporate participation in charitable ventures. In fulfilling its sense corporate social responsiblity, a chemical corporation, for instance, m benefit another firm in the pesticides industry or a variety of other inp producers, including local suppliers of seed and fertilizer and local man facturers of sprayer equipment. In short, a socially conscious firm m not capture all the benefits flowing from its efforts.

Multiplying the number of corporate "horror" or charity stories not, however, the purpose of this section. Given the objectives of priva business organizations to gather profits and increase sales, can a system created to tap the selfish impulses of business firms, yet yield advantag for the corporations and benefits of a public nature for Third Wor nations? In focusing on the Industry Cooperative Programme of the Food and Agriculture Organization (FAO) of the United Nations as a proto-type catalytic organization operating between multinational agribusiness corporations and developing nations, an assessment is undertaken of the possibility of implementing a synergic[3] institutional system in which an individual or an entity, by pursuing his or its ends, automatically helps other individuals, groups or nations thereby. A structure with high synergy provides for acts that mutually reinforce and benefit two or more sides (or interests). In contrast, in a structure with low social synergy, one side (or interest) becomes victorious over the other side (or interest).

The Industry Cooperative Programme (ICP) originated to make indus-try's expertise and knowledge available to the FAO. When the United Nations placed development work high on its priority list in the early 1950s, at least three groups were looked to for the necessary technological, managerial and financial resources to implement development theories and projects: the World Bank, regional banks, and industry. Public sector organizations preferred to work together, but increasingly the need for implementation became critical. By the mid-1960s, the United Nations Development Program had funneled about 40% of the United Nations' development funds through the FAO. The FAO spent considerable sums of money on "pre-investment" studies to expand agribusiness in develop-ing countries. The failure to implement these feasibility studies resulted in part from the need for follow-up action, in the form of financial, tech-nological, managerial and marketing skills, to turn concepts into realities.

In 1965 Dr. R. B. Sen, the then director-general of the FAO, suggested to the ministers of agriculture of the member nations of FAO that the management ability, technical know-how, scientific experience and capital resources of the leading corporations in Europe and North America should be mobilized to support the FAO's efforts as one of the world's most important development agencies. As described by V. E. Gale,[4] current assistant to the executive secretary of the Industry Cooperative Programme, Dr. Sen felt that a massive expansion of industry related to agriculture production and food distribution deserved the highest priority in the United Nations system. Encouraged by earlier examples of cooperation between its private industry and the FAO in certain fields, such as forestry, fisheries and fertilizer, Dr. Sen proposed to establish a more continuous form of liaison. Instead of contacts with industry, through special panels and various ad hoc advisory committees, Dr. Sen sought a more permanent industry-FAO footing for the implementation of FAO development pro-jects in Third World nations. Consultation by international organizations and developing nations with multinational firms might also help line up equity investors and other forms of financing for UN projects and generally assist the FAO in avoiding pitfalls in its development projects.

Informal discussions with leading agribusiness executives in Western Europe and the United States led to the creation of the Industry Cooperative Programme as a link, through the FAO, between multinational agribusiness firms and developing countries. The Industry Cooperative Programme is thus a unique effort to bring multinational business inside the United Nations system, specifically the FAO, with the primary objective of stimulating agro-industrial expansion in the developing world.

The structure of the Industry Cooperative Programme is simple. The ICP has a secretariat that is part of the FAO's Development Department. The secretariat consists of an executive secretary and four professional officers who are responsible for maintaining liaison services for and between corporate members of the ICP, developing countries and the United Nations system. The ICP also has an office at the United Nations in New York, headed by the deputy executive secretary. The ICP is self financing, sustained by fees to meet the expenses of the secretariat and the program's activities.

The members of the ICP consist of senior executives from multinational agribusiness corporations engaged in on-going operations in the Third World in some sector of agriculture, forestry or fisheries.[5] It was hoped that these senior executives would develop a tradition of business-statesmen and participate directly in the work of the ICP. The ownership of firms i irrelevant, with private corporations, cooperatives, state-owned companie in market economies and firms from centrally planned economies com prising an ICP membership of more than a hundred corporations. Th members meet annually at a session of the general committee of the ICP which elects a chairman and two vice chairmen. An executive committee consisting of the chairman and the two vice chairmen and twelve members meet more frequently, usually on a quarterly basis; this executive com mittee, in cooperation with the director-general of the FAO and th ICP's executive secretary, decides on policy questions and the course c future activities.[6]

The Industry Cooperative Programme has achieved its most notabl successes by acting as a public relations and lobbying organization on b half of multinational agribusiness firms. Specifically, the ICP has enable industry, particularly pesticides manufacturers, to gain access to inte national conferences and the world political system. The ICP has als engaged in training and educational functions. But the ICP has produce few concrete results in the form of factories yielding measurable econom and social benefits for the Third World.

15

ANALYSIS OF GENERAL ACTIVITIES OF THE ICP

To fulfill its function of transferring knowledge from business experts to developing nations, ICP has undertaken both general and specific activities. The general activities include creating a better climate of understanding among multinational agribusiness corporations, leaders of developing countries and the United Nations and acting as a public relations and lobbying organization on behalf of multinational corporations, thereby providing business with access to the world political system. The establishment of a variety of working groups and task forces, sending missions to developing countries and serving as a "marriage broker" comprise the ICP's specific activities. To date, both the general and specific activities of the ICP have redounded to the advantage of corporations rather than aiding the economic and social development of Third World countries.

PROMOTING A BETTER CLIMATE OF UNDERSTANDING

One of the prime functions of the ICP has been to initiate and foster closer links between industry, the United Nations system and developing countries. Many member executives have emphasized the role of the ICP in creating a beneficial climate of opinion and promoting better understanding between business and developing nations, thus facilitating a reduction in the mistrust between multinational corporations and Third World leaders. Bilateral and/or tripartite conversations may emerge from the dialogue process, possibly giving Third World leaders a greater degree of confidence in multinational firms.

As an example of the better climate of understanding fostered by the

ICP, J. F. P. Tate, executive director of Tate and Lyle Ltd. and chairm
of the ICP subcommittee on finance, pointed to the ICP executive co
mittee meeting at the United Nations Industrial Development Organi
tion (UNIDO) headquarters in Vienna in October 1975, at which
members of the executive committee met with UNIDO officials. Af
the initial formal sessions, in which UNIDO officials excoriated mu
national firms, an informal get-together and exchange of views enabled
business executives to show that they were reasonable, responsible in
viduals who headed socially responsible subsidiaries in developing natior
In addition to promoting a better understanding of what multinatio
firms are trying to do, this meeting produced an agreement to expand
cooperation between UNIDO and the ICP and to provide the help of I
members in technical assistance, marketing and investment promot
projects of mutual interest, with UNIDO participating more actively
ICP missions and working groups.

But an improved climate of opinion ultimately serves the interests
business. As Sir George Bishop, the current chairman of the ICP put
by creating a favorable climate of understanding, the ICP lets firms sh
what big corporations can offer developing countries and demonstra
to the UN and governments of the Third World that "increasing agric
tural output and putting new lands into agricultural production is a co
plex process which requires the presence of transnational firms."[2] Aa
Yohalem, executive vice president of CPC International Inc., forthrigh
indicated that better understanding will enable the governments of Th
World countries to see the benefits of multinational corporations so t
leaders will invite firms to come into a nation.[3]

Following improved understanding, the ICP's information intercha
function comes into play. Developing countries lacking knowledge
what they want or to whom they should go, through the ICP, gain inf
mation regarding the technical skills and expertise possessed by mu
national firms. Corporations that view themselves as more socia
responsible may be brought to the attention of Third World nations. Th
the ICP functions as a communications network among corporatio
developing countries and the United Nations system to tell the story
multinational firms, thereby whetting the appetite of host countries,
to tell multinational enterprises about opportunities in developing co
tries, thereby whetting the appetite of transnational firms.

BENEFITS OF MEMBERSHIP IN THE I C P

Digging further into activities of the ICP and the business relations
with the Third World and the United Nations system through the ICF

greater insight may be gained as to why farsighted business executives view the ICP as a form of "self-regarding altruism."[4] In the long run, giving time and expertise to ICP activities, it is hoped, will help the economies of Third World nations and thereby aid global business. Improved world conditions will create a climate favoring the activities of multinational firms. More specific benefits of ICP membership include gaining access to information within the FAO and within the United Nations system generally and using the ICP directly to increase sales and profits. In short, the ICP serves as a "window," one of many, on the world for multinational agribusiness executives. The high-level lobbying functions on behalf of ICP member firms and industries will be analyzed below.

The benefits of better understanding do not always accrue solely to the multinational corporations. Participation in the ICP has sensitized corporate executives to the problems of the Third World. Several of the executives commented on the impact of ICP membership in altering the viewpoint and approaches of corporations toward development. Although it is impossible to document or to isolate the ICP as a causal factor, the ICP has enabled corporations to learn about developing countries and the development needs of the Third World.   -

Many executives stress that their firms have long enjoyed advantages in Third World dealings; their expertise and international prominence have afforded them access to the governments of Third World countries. Such corporations affirm that they do not need the FAO or the United Nations system for introductions to governments, location of projects, or financing.[5]

But more than a few managers admit that the ICP has provided them a variety of benefits. The ICP provides a link for multinational corporations to the United Nations system, thereby permitting members to gain access to the United Nations information network. ICP members may request FAO documents, which are now linked to computer indexing systems coordinated through a documentation center. ICP members have access to the reports of FAO experts. Also, the FAO maintains senior agricultural advisors/country representatives in a number of developing countries; and these experienced agriculturists, in addition to their regular activities, provide advice and assistance to ICP members. For example, Ken MacLean, an FAO staff member located in Nigeria, regularly reports to the FAO on opportunities in the fruit and vegetable processing industries in Nigeria. These reports are made available to members of the ICP without charge, and seemingly without regard to what ICP members do with the reports. Thus, belonging to the ICP can save member firms money on feasibility studies.[6]

In addition to the ICP's function as an information repository, ICP liaison officers facilitate the interpretation of FAO information for

business executives. For instance, while an FAO report may indicate a ze
incidence of an animal disease in a particular country, by talking to FA
experts, ICP staff members may discover that the zero figure came abo
because the country in question lacked the personnel and resources
monitor that disease.

Also, a member firm may use the ICP's access to the FAO to suppc
the firm's activities in a developing country. For instance, a firm may a
the FAO's assistance in requesting a host government to allow free acce
to particular foreigners needed by the corporation.

Some executives have stated that they could gain a similar quanti
and quality of information by working through their national represen
tives to the FAO. But several have noted that their representatives to t
FAO were inadequate, thus generating the need for a service the IC
performs.

At some point the benefits to firms accruing from membership in t
ICP may devalue the program's currency, particularly its linkage to t
United Nations system. Corporations with consulting and/or engineeri
arms may obtain advantages by using the ICP to gain consulting jol
The expenditure of executives' time and corporate funds in ICP endeavo
may quickly rebound to a firm's advantage if a corporation can ha
the ICP staff spread the word to United Nations personnel and developi
country representatives that the firm (or even a group of firms) has e
pertise in a particular area. Enterprises with active research and devel
ment organizations may also gain through expanded contacts; ne
knowledge flowing from the United Nations system may assist in a firn
research and development activities.

THE PUBLIC RELATIONS EFFORTS OF THE I C P

Multinational business uses the ICP as a lobbying organization to ga
access for industry's positions and ideas in the world political system. T
prime focus of this type of activity, which began with the 1972 Unit
Nations Conference on the Human Environment, has been the pesticid
industry. Responsible business spokesmen, building on the respectabili
of the ICP flowing from its link to the FAO and the United Natio
played a constructive role in getting industry's position before internatior
meetings, including the 1974 World Food Conference and the 1975 ∕
Hoc Governmental Consultation on Pesticides in Agriculture and Pub
Health. The World Food Conference marked the first time a major Unit
Nations conference asked industry to participate officially.

The 1972 United Nations Conference on the Human Environment

Stockholm excluded business from direct participation. This bar to access stemmed from a number of factors, including the traditional public sector attitude that business should not be directly represented at a governmental conference and the more specific prejudgment that on environmental matters business constituted a "guilty" party not deserving a hearing.[7] The lack of access and the critical commentary expected from the conference particularly disturbed pesticides members of ICP. Alan J. Maier, of the United Kingdom–based Imperial Chemical Industries Ltd., asked other agrochemical firms at a Pesticides Working Group of the ICP how, under such circumstances, firms could best present their position. Industry felt it could get its viewpoint across through the preparation of a booklet analyzing in detail, from the agrochemical industry's viewpoint, the place of pesticides in the modern world and their impact on the environment and the role of pesticides in the economies of developing nations. Members of the Pesticides Working Group organized a subgroup to prepare the booklet, which took the form of a symposium of separate papers of interest to scientists and lay people.[8]

A more difficult question was what was the best means to get the booklet before the Stockholm conference. At least three routes were available: national trade associations, governmental delegations and the ICP. Brian Cox, of Imperial Chemical Industries Ltd., met with the former ICP executive secretary and secured the ICP secretariat's agreement to permit the Pesticides Working Group to publish the booklet as an ICP Pesticides Working Group project. The booklet, *Pesticides in the Modern World*,[9] was presented to the United Nations Conference on the Human Environment through the auspices of ICP/FAO. The booklet proved a success. Subsequent to the conference it was publicly distributed through the FAO, and international and national pesticides trade association organizations. Thus, prior to the World Food Conference, the ICP provided business a means of access to a United Nations conference.

The success of the pesticides booklet contributed to the growth of the ICP's reputation in the two years after the environment conference, but an even more significant break-through by the ICP, as a spokesman for agri-business, occurred at the November 1974 World Food Conference. The United Nations, not FAO, convened the food conference, so that representatives from the Soviet Union and the People's Republic of China could attend. ICP members and the ICP secretariat wanted industry to have a voice at the World Food Conference, which focused high-level political attention on the food crisis, particularly short-term food aid questions. The leaders of the conference originally had planned to model the World Food Conference after the Stockholm gathering, thereby placing industry on the outside. After Dr. Luigi Desert, then chairman of the ICP, and Sir George Bishop, then a vice chairman, met with Sayed Marei, the secretary general of the World Food Conference, Marei invited the ICP to run a "teach-in" for industry. If business (including both ICP members and nonaffiliated firms) produced something "valid" in the form of specific proposals to increase agricultural output in developing countries, then industry would have an unspecified but continuing role at the World Food Conference. But Marei admonished the ICP, "Don't ask about the big show."[10]

The ICP took Marei's suggestion and organized, under the chairmanship of Sir George Bishop, a conference in Toronto in September 1974, which has become known as the Toronto Consultation. More than 150 senior executives from companies and financing institutions, including non-ICP members, in 28 countries participated in the consultation, as well as members of Marei's staff, including John A. Hannah, deputy secretary general of the World Food Conference and other senior UN officials. The consultation sought to synthesize industry's ideas and proposals for governmental consideration at the World Food Conference. The consultation related its work directly to the World Food Conference's agenda. A number of papers were prepared in advance by industry representatives and by the ICP and served as a springboard for discussions by five separate panels. Leaders of the consultation focused the attention of industry participants on the areas where business expertise could most effectively increase food production and availability in developing countries. By providing markets and profits this approach appealed to business.

The Toronto proceedings naturally stressed certain prerequisites on the part of developing nations for attracting significantly greater agribusiness management and technical expertise to raise food production. Participants recommended that developing nations should make a firm commitment that agriculture would receive the highest priority in developmental plans and the necessary locally available resources. Business also sought arbitration in case of disagreement, encouragement of foreign investment in agriculture by host nations, provision for a fair return to investors, including an equitable repatriation of profits, and protection of intellectual property, including plant breeder's rights. On the international level, the following benefits were proposed to facilitate the transfer of agribusiness expertise: guarantees, such as risk and disaster insurance; access to international research and training facilities in the public and private sectors; and funds for various pre-investment studies and credit on reasonable terms.[11]

John Hannah perceived the Toronto Consultation as indicating industry's innovative response to the challenges and its willingness to become more effectively involved. Hannah relayed this to Marei and, as Walter W

Simons related, the "spirit of Toronto" insured that the ICP would play a role at the World Food Conference.[12] But Marei's position on the ICP apparently jelled only at the last minute. In assessing whether the ICP would have observer or delegate status, Marei, Simons noted, "carefully assessed the strengths of the players at the conference."[13] The developed countries with food supplies held a power position and set the tone for the conference. Cognizant of these realities, Marei accorded the ICP official delegate status in all conference committees. Industry representatives were given delegate status, enabling ICP members to intervene in debates and participate in conference working committees. They could not, however, vote. The Toronto Consultation report became an official World Food Conference document and served as a basic starting point for industry interventions.

The multinational firms set up headquarters in Rome across from the Palazzo dei Congressi—the site of the World Food Conference. Through W. W. Simons, deputy executive secretary of the ICP, the members of ICP established an effective organization, which included lobbying, publicizing and an elaborate monitoring schedule.

From the viewpoint of the pesticides industry, the lumping together of the pesticides and fertilizer questions at the World Food Conference constituted a key problem. During 1974, a world fertilizer shortage and sky-rocketing fertilizer prices excluded many developing countries from the fertilizer market. Fertilizer became an emotionally charged issue. The seemingly rational arguments advanced by the fertilizer industry that less than 15% of the fertilizer sold in the United States went to nonessential uses, that the shortage of fertilizer would be temporary, that fertilizer plants were underutilized (particularly in India, where plants operated at about 50% of capacity) because of lack of maintenance, management and technical expertise and/or inadequacies in a nation's infrastructure (including power), and because of difficulties in transporting and distributing fertilizer in developing countries, fell on the deaf ears of the representatives from the Third World.[14] The pesticides industry representatives complained at the FAO and at the joint pesticides-fertilizer conference committee discussions; they argued that pesticides and fertilizer were different inputs of equal importance and should, therefore, be considered by separate committees.[15] The delegates to the conference ultimately separated the pesticides and fertilizer committees.

At the newly organized pesticides committee, Alan J. Maier and Brian Cox, of Imperial Chemical Industries Ltd., and Walter W. Simons actively participated in discussions. In the committee, government representatives noted the high prices and shortages of pesticides and stressed the need for mounting an internationally coordinated program to insure the availability of pesticides at reasonable prices in developing countries. But, most importantly, the government delegates accepted industry's role and regarded industry as a working partner.[16]

A Pakistani draft resolution laid the basis for the conference's pesticides resolution. Maier, Cox and Simons, along with FAO staff members, assisted governmental delegates from Pakistan, Nigeria and the United Kingdom in redrafting the Pakistani resolution. The key item of discussion in the drafting group was the FAO's suggestion of a further consultation that would include industry.[17] Rather than providing specific action guidelines on pesticides, the Pesticides Resolution of the World Food Conference concluded by calling "on FAO in cooperation with UNEP, WHO and UNIDO to convene on an urgent basis an *ad hoc* consultation, including member governments and industry, to recommend ways and means to give effect to the intentions of this resolution, including the supply-demand information that FAO has been collecting, the investment required in pesticides and equipment supply, the standardization of regulatory procedures and environmental rules, examination of alternative methods of pest control and to take follow-up action."[18]

After the FAO council endorsed the pesticides resolution, Dr. A. H Boerma, then director-general of the FAO, arranged for an Ad Hoc Governmental Consultation on Pesticides in Agriculture and Public Health in April 1975. The FAO extended invitations to member governments of the FAO, the Soviet Union, international organizations, the chemical industry and other interested groups to meet and discuss the specific issues. ICP efforts at the World Food Conference enabled the international trade association of pesticides manufacturers, Groupement International des Associations Nationales des Fabricants de Pesticides (GIFAP), composed of national agricultural chemical associations from the developed world, to attend the Ad Hoc Consultation. W. R. Furtick, of the FAO Plant Protection Service, structured the consultation so that industry representatives chaired two key subcommittess, Pesticide Application and Supply and Demand, and served as a rapporteur of a third subcommittee, Pesticides Production. By sending experts in various fields, industry through ICP/GIFAP coordination, participated in every subcommittee Industry presented a united front at the consultation; all members of th ICP Pesticides Working Group and GIFAP had jointly approved an industr platform carefully prepared in advance of the Ad Hoc Consultation.[1]

One of the most interesting confrontations between industry and de veloping nations at the Ad Hoc Consultation occurred in the subcommitte on pesticides supply and demand. Developing countries, led by India an Bangladesh, pressed for increased corporate disclosure of supply strategie particularly with regard to pesticide availability by region and produc group. Industry, led by subcommittee chairman Alan J. Maier, weathered the developing countries' requests for information. Industry emphasized the importance of commercial confidentiality. Companies representing 90% of the pesticide industry had provided confidential information to the FAO in response to the FAO's Plant Protection Survey, but industry wanted this information to remain confidential and available only to the FAO for use in assessment by the FAO of the world supply/demand situation. Business spokesmen also pointed out that industry, by choice and in certain countries by legal proscription, could not publish information on supplies along the lines sought by Third World countries.[20]

Realizing the power position of pesticides firms, W. R. Furtick of FAO advised representatives from developing countries that if the corporations did not want to disclose their supplies and supply strategy, they simply would not do so. Industry and the developing countries compromised on a supply information system. The resolution adopted by the Ad Hoc Consultation Subcommittee on Information System on Pesticides Supply and Demand concluded by recommending "that FAO, WHO and UNIDO continue their discussions with industry to develop an agreed system for obtaining figures on the supply situation, and for informing governments."[21]

Even more significant, perhaps, than the discussions at the Ad Hoc Consultation and the resolutions emanating therefrom was the continued recognition of industry's role at world public sector and United Nations conferences. The report of the Ad Hoc Consultation, on the initiative of the delegation from the United Kingdom,[22] which has a large stake in pesticides exports, concluded: "The Consultation felt that the presence of representatives of industry, represented by ICP and GIFAP, was a most valuable addition to this meeting and hoped that this practice would continue."[23] This reflected the view of government that industry has a role to play at international conferences. The international system had come a long way from the traditional business-excluded approach of the Stockholm Conference. By maintaining contacts between developing countries and corporations, the ICP probably will participate in future developments, such as an international secretariat for information on the supply/demand for pesticides.

16

ANALYSIS OF SPECIFIC ACTIVITIES OF ICP

ICP working groups, task forces and country missions also enable the knowledge and expertise of multinational agribusiness firms to be made available to developing nations. Of particular interest are the educational projects and training sessions undertaken by the Pesticides Working Group. The activities of the Farm Mechanization, Dairy Industry Development, Fishery Industries Development, and Forestry and Forest Industries working groups will also be discussed in this chapter. The ICP missions to Pakistan, Sri Lanka and Cameroon will then be examined. Finally, the ICP's attempts to match the skills of firms with the needs of Third World countries on specific projects will be assessed.

ICP WORKING GROUPS

The ICP has organized working groups in major agribusiness sectors—dairy, fisheries, forestry, livestock, pesticides and plastics—that focus on policy and technical matters of concern to business, developing countries and the United Nations system. The working groups have undertaken variety of activities, including sponsoring projects and publications and sending out working parties to explore specific field problems.

Because of the importance of markets in developing nations for the agrochemical industry, the Pesticides Working Group has been the most active working group. Facing suspicion on the part of developing countries regarding the safety of pesticides and a lack of knowledge of the conditions under which pesticides can be safely used, the Pesticides Working Group has sought to improve the dissemination of information regarding crop protection products and the conditions beneficial to the use of such products. The members of the working group reached a consensus to focus on the problem of the misuse of pesticides, such as improper selection of equipment and/or pesticides, incorrect field mixing procedures, incorrect volume application per acre, and incorrect time of applications, and to use industry's expertise for educational purposes. The instructional projects stem from industry's belief, as J. I. Hendrie put it, that "on balance the benefits to mankind which have derived from the use of chemicals in reducing crop losses and the spread of insect-borne diseases in the public health sector far outweigh the disadvantages. That disadvantages have arisen as a result of the use of pesticides cannot be denied, but in the vast majority of cases they have resulted from misuse."[1] In short, through the Pesticides Working Group, agrochemical manufacturers have sought to encourage the efficient, safe use of pesticides as part of a total agribusiness input system. Self-interest plays a large role: If an individual is properly trained, he will be a long-term consumer; and long-range sales take precedence over short-term profit gains.

To implement the educational objective, the Pesticides Working Group organized, in collaboration with the FAO Plant Production and Protection Division, a series of training seminars on the safe and efficient use of pesticides in agriculture and public health in developing countries. The success of the first seminar, in Brazil in 1971, resulted in similar meetings in Costa Rica in 1972, Bangkok in 1973, and Nairobi in 1974. At these regional seminars information on pesticides was shared among personnel from ICP members, United Nations staff members, senior-level national governmental officials in plant protection services, and public health representatives responsible for carrying out crop protection and public health programs and developing national legislation regarding pesticides. The seminars reviewed current developments, promoted an exchange of ideas on modern methods and policies, discussed a common approach to the use of pesticides in a region and prepared the participants to improve the coordination and administration of national plant protection and public health programs.

The FAO and ICP members collaborated in running the seminars. Dr. A. V. Adam, of the FAO Plant Protection Service, handled the technical aspects of organizing the seminars and developing programs. FAO technical specialists actively participated in the seminars. ICP members provided financial and technical support, including making corporate experts available to present papers and give demonstrations, paying the travel expenses of national government representatives, preparing and presenting audio-visual materials, and making an airplane available to demonstrate aerial crop-spraying techniques.[2]

The regional seminars probably contributed to improved communication and understanding between the pesticides industry and the governmen of developing nations. The seminars stimulated countries to increas their pesticide programs and seek FAO technical assistance. Nation representatives became more aware of the work done by industry befor marketing a product. Countries arrived at a better appreciation of the nee to reach a balance, appropriate to developmental priorities, between th need for pesticide use and possible environmental dangers. Although i dustry does not oppose the national regulation of pesticides, a key bus ness concern has been the importance of uniformity in pesticides legislatio and in approaches to registration and licensing questions. Industry see the harmonization of national laws because of the high cost of dealin with safety questions, particularly those emanating from diverse nation regulations. A number of the countries involved in the seminars hav adopted the FAO's pesticides specifications.[3]

The FAO and the Pesticides Working Group agreed, in 1976, to shi from regional seminars emphasizing a general orientation and an exchang of views for senior government personnel in the field to practical trainin courses for actively involved low- and medium-level plant protectio supervisors from one nation.[4] The regional seminars were viewed by IC members as involving too many subjects and too many countries, pr ducing a diffuse result, and lacking any follow-up. The first joint FAO/IC national course was held in Pakistan in the fall of 1976, with ICP membe continuing to make contributions in cash and in kind and providin personnel. One ICP member, American Cyanamid, provided a technic expert to serve as input coordinator, with the aim of avoiding the commo pitfalls of national training programs, such as nepotism.

Other ICP working groups vary in effectiveness. Probably the mo active committee after the Pesticides Working Group has been the Dair Industry Development Working Group, which has moved on two front Members of this working group participated in preparing a joint FAO/IC manual for the construction of standardized milk plants in developin countries. This marked a pioneering venture by equipment manufacture in pooling knowledge for the preparation of a manual designed for use i developing countries.

The group also assessed the need for new and special foods to be di tributed in various emergencies. The distribution of surplus products b relief agencies and the UN/FAO's World Food Programme has been rif with problems of waste. For example, people in developing countries ar given bulk amounts of skim milk powder that require further processin The net result of the procedure is that the product may be more costl than if initially distributed in packaged form.

To meet the problem of waste, the working group proposed a segmente relief concept. According to this concept, after a disaster, people should be given products that can be quickly used, even if they are expensive packaged products, such as bread and condensed milk. As individuals are resettled in tents, rice could be made available for cooking. To establish a list of products to meet different needs, depending on the type of calamity, the working group established a subgroup on food and packaging for emergencies, guidance from agencies in the United Nations system and from international relief organizations. Unfortunately, A. A. Bouwes, chairman of the Dairy Industry Development Working Group, noted he had received no response to his inquiries. If guidance were forthcoming, Bouwes reported, multinational firms, the United Nations system and relief agencies "could work together to produce cheaper relief products."[5] Bouwes hoped that other firms could follow the lead of his cooperative, Cooperatieve Condensfabriek "Friesland," which now produces a milk bar for distribution by relief agencies. The milk bar cuts waste and facilitates the calculation of nutritional values.[6]

Education has comprised a prime activity of the sporadically functioning ICP Farm Mechanization Working Group. The group coordinated training efforts for tractor operators by major tractor manufacturers (three ICP members and one nonmember) on the use and maintenance of tractors in the Arab Republic of Yemen. The group arranged for different firms to take turns in providing instructors. Because of a lack of interest among ICP members in the farm mechanization field, the training projects were dropped and the working group entered a period of inactivity.[7]

The ICP secretariat is hopeful that industry will participate in a meaningful way through close ties to the FAO Forestry Department in forestry projects in developing nations. Tapping unexploited forestry resources will not only contribute to a nation's economic growth but also raise food production because of the close linkage between agricultural and silvicultural systems. The Forestry and Forest Industries Working Group was revitalized in 1975 and split into three separate working groups (forestry production and harvesting, mechanical wood processing industries, and pulp and paper industries) and one policy body. Whether the divergent interests of various firms within the new subgroups will stymie activities, as apparently was the case in the old unified group, remains uncertain. Creation of a senior liaison officer post, within the ICP, to service the separate working groups may point the way to more meaningful future activity.

The ICP Working Group on Fishery Industries Development is linked to the FAO Fishery Industries Division, which provides the main servicing for the group. The FAO and ICP members stress fishery joint ventures between multinational corporations and developing countries and industry

assistance to the FAO in implementing projects. The ICP Fishery Industri
Development Working Group has to date accomplished little beyor
holding meetings with the FAO which provide guidance for the FAO c
investment opportunities industry regards as desirable.

I C P MISSIONS

The ICP has attempted to make the knowledge of industry exper
available to developing nations through the ICP country mission progran
The key to the mission concept, as expressed by Sir George Bishop,
the ability of government officials, particularly agricultural ministers, "
discuss their problems and priorities with business leaders."[8] Idealisticall
the ICP emphasizes the helping function provided by the expertise
multinational firms above corporations' use of the mission as a vehic
to find new business opportunities. Industry personnel, it is expecte
bring a sense of realism and use their expertise and insight to pun
holes in projects they deem unfeasible. From the standpoint of the IC
secretariat, missions serve an important objective by involving personal
more ICP members in the program's work. The difficult question remai
of whether members of a mission can be "impartial," that is, not promo
the interests of their own corporation.

To help channel the managerial, technical, scientific and financi
expertise of business, E. Bignami, retired head of Nestlé's worldwi
operations, in 1971 proposed the concept of the ICP Country Mission
A mission, Bignami envisioned, would be composed of a small number
high level representatives from ICP member firms and a member of tl
ICP secretariat who would visit a country at the request of its governmen
A mission seeks to establish a dialogue between government and industr
Through open discussion by decision makers, Bignami reasoned, mutu
long-term interest and the steps necessary to attract business experti
to serve a nation's development needs could be clarified.[9] A mission,
addition to advising and assisting a government on agro-industrial pro
lems, long-range national planning and priorities, would also identi
country-industry partnership possibilities and stimulate new activities l
focusing business resources within the priorities of a government. Tl
prime investment-expertise linkage technique is the preparation and d
semination of a mission report, which is submitted through the IC
secretariat to the government of a developing country, the ICP membe
ship and the United Nations system.

In implementing the mission concept the ICP secretariat faced tw
problems: selection of countries to be visited by missions, and selection

the members for a mission. Once the United Nations system and developing countries became aware of the ICP missions, many nations expressed an interest in the concept. Developing countries either wanted a mission to investigate specific projects from their development plans or sought advice on analyzing priorities in various fields of developments. The ICP executive committee selected countries from among those formally requesting missions on the basis of location in different continents, Asia, Africa and Latin America. Thus, the ICP chose Dahomey, Sri Lanka and Venezuela for its first three missions. Since establishing its mission program, the ICP has also made selections in terms of missions' "effectiveness" in bringing industry's expertise to bear in providing the best business possibilities for multinational firms. Political and strategic considerations, specifically the aim of establishing the program's neutral expertise, probably motivated the choice of Sri Lanka.

To secure industry experts for a mission, the ICP secretariat contacts member firms with commodity or functional expertise or area-country interest and requests volunteers. ICP senior liaison officer, B. Gardner-McTaggart, who was involved in the spring of 1976 in nearly full-time liaison work for an ICP mission to Senegal, produced a sheaf of correspondence that backs up the diligence with which the secretariat conducts its search. The pile of requests to industry also indicates the difficulty the ICP faces in attracting volunteers.

Executives indicate they will not participate in a mission because most missions are not of interest to their firm or because their corporation has priorities in other nations.[10] According to Hector Watts, a participant in the mission to Senegal, the criteria used by the ICP secretariat in the selection process include expertise, availability, language skills, general contacts and knowledge of a country.[11] The FAO may impose an added burden by specifying expertise it wishes industry to make available to a mission. For instance, the FAO insisted on a private sector forestry expert for the mission to Senegal.[12]

A contrast between the ICP missions to Pakistan and Sri Lanka, countries with different ideological attitudes to foreign investment, facilitates the analysis of the operation and impact of missions. In contrast to these efforts, the mission to Cameroon produced limited concrete results in terms of business promotion activities. A request by the Pakistani minister for food and agriculture to the director-general of the FAO culminated in an ICP mission in May 1974. The Pakistani government, which had initiated a program for the establishment of agro-industries in Integrated Rural Development Project areas, invited the mission for two main purposes: "(1) for identification and discussion of government policies regarding foreign participation particularly in agro-allied industrial development, and (2) for providing continuing dialogue on the follow-up actions o project to project basis."[13] Specific Pakistani project ideas, in the dairy fishery and pesticides fields, led to the selection of mission members wit expertise in these areas.

The mission followed the usual pattern of careful preparatory work b the ICP secretariat. The executive secretary of the ICP visited Pakista in September 1973, and the Pakistan delegation to the FAO conferenc met ICP staff personnel in November 1973. The government of Pakista and different government agencies generated information on agro-industrie and agro-industrial requirements in Pakistan for the mission's considera tion. Members of the mission—A. A. Bouwes, mission leader, managin director of Cooperatieve Condensfabriek "Friesland" (Netherlands); J. Hendrie, then head of life sciences, Shell International Chemical Co. Ltc (United Kingdom); E. Kobayashi, area manager for Asia of the Mitsubisl Corporation (Japan); and Dr. A. G. Friedrich, executive secreatry of th ICP—were briefed by FAO divisions having projects in Pakistan. Prior t departing for Pakistan, the members of the mission held discussions wit the ambassador of Pakistan to Italy.[14]

The actual time spent by members of the mission in Pakistan was ver brief. The mission spent three days in Karachi and five days in Islamaba meeting with top level government officials. Only one day was spent i the field, visiting a dam construction area.

The members of the mission, in their discussion with ministers, stresse the need to process agricultural surplus products for export markets. Bot A. A. Bouwes and J. I. Hendrie recalled that their specific export-oriente suggestions were not well received.[15] Both stated that the sale of mea and milk in Pakistan is restricted because limited mass purchasing pow makes higher quality and more sophisticated foodstuffs, such as processe meat with added value, too expensive. The ICP experts suggested tha Pakistan set up a meat exporting business based on the approximatel one million buffalo bull calves that are killed or allowed to die each yea Bouwes suggested that calves be transported to centralized areas for supe vised feeding and that after slaughter the meat be exported, specificall to the Middle East.[16] But the Pakistanis, Hendrie declared, "did not war to export meat."[17]

The mission also analyzed the milk situation. Many FAO-sponsored mil plants were not in operation, as farmers continued to sell milk locally t middlemen, who, after diluting the milk with water, distributed th product. During certain periods of the year milk was wasted, as a resu of either spoilage or insufficient demand. Drawing on his dairy expertis Bouwes recommended that the Pakistani farmers process cheese in sma units on a cooperative basis for export. ICP mission members also suggeste that the FAO milk plants be used to produce cheese for export, but the Pakistanis rejected both of these ideas.[18]

The government of Pakistan emphasized to the members of the mission its desire to encourage foreign direct investment. The government perceived that it had provided "very liberal facilities and incentives for that purpose."[19] Although noting that Pakistan's investment incentives compare favorably with those of most other nations, the mission pointed out that the 1972 Pakistani nationalization program had created apprehension in the minds of foreign investors.[20] In response Pakistan promised to improve its investment climate by not nationalizing new foreign investments.[21] The government of Pakistan implemented this promise in a policy statement towards foreign private investment. As part of a section on compensation guarantees, the policy statement declares, "Government has no intention of nationalizing industries. Should circumstances or an emergency necessitate nationalization in any particular case, just and fair compensation will be paid in the currency of the country of origin."[22]

Although the ICP guidelines for missions place considerable emphasis on follow-up activities, one of the major weaknesses of the ICP mission concept has been a lack of involvement of mission members or other ICP members in on-going endeavors after a mission has reported. To correct this gap, the ICP executive committee appointed Dr. O. Ballarin, chairman of the board of Companhia Industrial e Comercial Brasileira de Produtos Alimentares (Nestlés), special advisor for the preparation and follow-up of ICP missions. As part of his function, Dr. Ballarin visited Pakistan in 1975. He discussed the ICP mission with government officials and also with agencies in the private sector. Ballarin explored new opportunities for the ICP to assist in the assessment of development priorities; he also sought clarification of various points raised by members of the mission and by other ICP members.[23] Despite the work of the mission and the follow-up by Ballarin, the ICP mission to Pakistan apparently has not led directly to any additional investments or other activities by multinational agribusiness corporations in Pakistan.[24]

An earlier ICP mission to Sri Lanka, in September–October 1972, encountered a government less receptive to private foreign investment than that of Pakistan. A June 1972 government White Paper entitled "Policy of the Government of Sri Lanka on Private Foreign Investment" and the general nature of the foreign investment climate in Sri Lanka formed the focal point of the mission. The members of the mission—J. G. Stokes, managing director of Automated Building Components (Aust.) Pty. Ltd. (Australia); A. S. Martowski, deputy general manager of Polimex-Cekop Ltd. (Poland); Dr. J. C. Ramaer, deputy managing director of N. V. Philips' Gloeilampenfabrieken (Netherlands) along with Dr. A. G.

Friedrich, executive secretary of the ICP—sought to clarify the gover ment's policy on cooperation with foreign industry. The mission report that the government would "welcome" foreign investment particularly export-oriented industries.[25]

The mission believed, however, that the government's White Pap required amplification. To implement this suggestion the mission agreed draft, for the Ministry of Planning and Employment, guidelines for t interpretation of the White Paper that would clarify the government intentions regarding foreign industry. Dr. J. C. Ramaer of Philips spe one year subsequent to the mission working on guidelines as an addendu to the White Paper.[26] Although the government of Sri Lanka nationalize foreign-owned plantations in 1975, the government in 1974 had announce sixty specific areas (broadly categorized as industrial and mineral expo industries, agricultural export industries, new agricultural exports, fisheri and tourism) in which foreign enterprises could invest without hindrance. The causal relationship between the mission, the follow-up work of [Ramaer and the subsequent clarifications remain unclear. The governme: of Sri Lanka, however, indicated that the report of the ICP mission had "nil" impact on new legislation relating to foreign direct investments Sri Lanka.[28]

The promotion of business opportunities in Sri Lanka formed a secon ary theme of the mission. The ICP mission in its report delineated secto of the economy where useful foreign cooperation in the form of joi ventures or agreements making available technology, know-how and ma agement and marketing skills would be possible. Among the projects a business possibilities the mission assessed and documented were an int grated sugar industry to reduce sugar imports; better use of inputs in ri production, such as improved rice strains and fertilizer; fishery industri for both local consumption and export; fruit growing and processing; a tourism. But the report apparently has generated no new foreign inve ment or collaboration in Sri Lanka by multinational agribusiness firms.

The ICP mission to Cameroon seemingly produced more, albeit limite concrete results in terms of new business ventures by foreign firms. T 1973 ICP mission to Cameroon—led by Dr. Luigi Desert, president Oltremare S.p.A. (Italy); Ambassador Henry Ingrand, international affa advisor of Charbonnages de France; and Jacques Bertrand, senior liais officer of the ICP, on loan from Sodeteg (France)—undertook, in contra to the ICP missions to Pakistan and Sri Lanka, an extensive field tour Cameroon.[30] The mission focused on businessmen using their experti to assess a variety of short- and long-term projects. Emphasizing the inve ment promotional aspect of the mission, J. Bertrand followed up after t mission and sought to interest corporations, including non-ICP members, in various projects. Bertrand also brought in FAO technical experts, such as Ken MacLean, to study specific problems. Despite infrastructure problems in Cameroon and high wage rates for labor, the mission generated several tangible results, including the involvement of an Italian firm in a tomato concentrate project and a contract for a French group to set up a tomato plant in Cameroon. A consortium of European firms, including Thompson-Houston-Hotchkiss-Brandt, the parent entity of Sodeteg, began work on satellite training, television and audio systems; while Sodeteg undertook an assessment of pig and poultry production in Cameroon.[31]

This review of the missions to Pakistan, Sri Lanka and Cameroon raises several questions. Doubts remain as to the "impartiality" of business members of a mission. An individual may go on a mission because his firm has an interest in a region or a nation and wishes to have an inside track on the most promising opportunities. Bertrand's participation in the Mission to Cameroon probably promoted the interests of his own firm. The ICP secretariat and executive committee must be especially sensitive to this problem. Some members of missions indicated that their participation in the mission enabled their firm to generate high-level contacts in a nation that might prove helpful in the future. Participation in a mission, as well as other ICP activities, may assist corporations in a more subtle manner. Involvement in the mission program may aid a firm's experts in recognizing market and investment opportunities in new areas—even in projects unconnected with a mission.

From the viewpoint of a developing nation, missions may degenerate into tourist jaunts that are costly to governments because the preparation for a mission and the visit by business experts occupy the time of government officials. Also, businessmen may offer advice outside their area of expertise or without proper reflection; increasing the length of time a mission spends in a country may strengthen the effectiveness of the program. Furthermore, although a mission shows industry's goodwill, the superficial platitudes may disappoint a government. A minister's expectations may be further disappointed when nothing happens after a mission. To remedy this problem, a climate must be developed to implement the expert recommendations after the consummation of a mission. To strengthen the follow-up effort, the ICP executive committee, as previously noted, appointed a special advisor on ICP missions to discuss the results of missions with governments and review ideas and possibilities individually with ICP members; whether this follow-up technique will meet the challenge of implementation remains uncertain. Finally, the ICP executive committee must also exercise care in the selection of countries chosen for missions. Rather than going to Brazil or Venezuela, attention probably should be directed to helping countries that lack knowledge regarding planning and the setting of development priorities.

THE I C P SPECIFIC PROJECT—MARRIAGE BROKER FUNCTION

Despite the panoply of ICP activities, a key question remains regarding the worth of catalytic organizations: Has there been any concrete achievement in the form of factories yielding measurable economic and social results? To meet this need the ICP sought to act as a marriage broker on specific projects matching the expertise of multinational corporations with the needs of developing nations. The Industry Cooperative Programme in the late 1960s developed in a project concept. The ICP played a catalytic role and attempted to facilitate official contacts to bring together industry, government and financial partners. The ICP involvement went through two main phases: country-initiated projects and corporate-initiated projects.

The ICP originally brought projects, particularly pre-investment surveys developed by or presented to the development organizations in the United Nations system, to the attention of ICP member firms. This approach suffered from two disadvantages. First, the widespread network of contacts of the most aggressive ICP corporations enabled these firms to be aware of the most promising projects in Third World countries; such companies had their own information system and did not need a catalytic organization to put them in contact with developing countries. Second, the commercial unviability of many of the projects constituted a more serious deficiency in the country-initiated scheme; projects were particularly deficient in marketing analysis.[32]

To remedy the deficiencies of country-initiated projects, the ICP created a system for the promotion of corporate-initiated projects.[33] The ICP devised a general framework for handling corporate initiatives in the developing world. After a firm secured approval of the ICP secretariat for a project that would advance the development of a Third World country, the ICP attempted to gain the consent of the relevant bodies in the UN system and the government of the particular developing nation. The ICP staff worked with the corporation in expediting a project through the various stages, culminating in the government of the developing nation requesting financing from the United Nations Development Programme which then assigned a project to a UN executing agency, generally the FAO. The ICP sought to focus on projects with a multiplier effect: either the project could be repeated elsewhere, or it would stimulate other agribusiness developments in a nation.

The leading illustration of ICP's successful catalytic project role is the promotion of a tomato paste industry in Turkey. However, the role played by the ICP in the project should not be overemphasized. The Turkish government became interested in stimulating agricultural exports, and one of Turkey's leading investors sought ways of entering the food processing industry. The ICP participated in meetings that led to the formation of a mixed private and public Turkish company to build a fruit and vegetable processing plant in Turkey. The most important crop in the project was tomatoes. The project involved bringing together the Turkish group, the FAO and H. J. Heinz, which in looking for a new source of supply for tomato paste had discovered a potential tomato producing region in Turkey.[34] Despite ICP claims that it brought the three elements together, others, including F. E. Agnew, senior vice president of Heinz, minimize the ICP's role and suggest the project would have come together even without the ICP because of the presence of all the elements.[35]

As part of the tripartite project, Heinz sent a tomato agronomist to Turkey for several years and provided technical assistance in the construction and operation of the tomato paste plants. At the same time, an FAO project provided research information on varieties and processing qualities, tested tomatoes and gave advisory services to farms that would supply crops for the project. The factory opened in 1968. Although having no equity interest in the fruit and vegetable processing plant, Heinz secured a preferred position as a buyer.[36] The multiplier effect is apparent. The initial effort spurred an upsurge of interest by investors, both Turkish and foreign, in the processing of fruits and vegetables and stimulated the growth of additional processing plants. Turkey has subsequently become an important tomato paste supplier to the European Economic Community.[37]

The ICP was also involved as a catalytic force, albeit of modest proportions, in a tomato project in Nigeria. The Nigerian government had pressured Cadbury Schweppes Ltd. to seek local tomato supplies for the tomato paste used in the stew that Nigerians avidly consume. Cadbury had previously met its needs by canning imported tomato paste. Cadbury could provide technical assistance and seeds to small farmers who would then sell their tomatoes to the firm. But Cadbury realized it needed an intermediary to deal with the Nigerian government. Cadbury turned to the FAO, which C. E. Gillett, director of Cadbury, recalled was more involved in the project than the ICP.[38] The Nigerian government also requested technical assistance through the FAO for an expert to provide liaison between the local government, Cadbury and small farmers. The FAO expert, Ken MacLean, succeeded in arousing the interest of the farmers in growing tomatoes. He also surmounted farmers' initial skepticism as to whether they could generate profits by raising tomatoes. MacLean also helped farmers to meet the production demands of the Cadbury plant and assured the government that Cadbury was dealing fairly with the farmers. The success of the catalytic work, particularly by the FAO's expert, brought requests from other areas in Nigeria for expertise and processing plants. From Cadbury's viewpoint a lingering problem remains: If the price of tomatoes in the market exceeds the price paid by Cadbury, farmers do not sell their tomatoes to Cadbury; as a result, Cadbury may lack a sufficient supply of tomatoes.

A review of an unsuccessful project involving new technology and the fusing of private sector expertise and public sector funding amplifies the ICP's catalytic role in specific projects. Tate and Lyle's research laboratory developed a technology to convert the sugars in the carob bean, which grows wild through the Mediterranean region, into microbial protein. In 1969, Tate and Lyle's representative to the ICP discussed with the head of the ICP secretariat the possibility of developing this process in the countries bordering the Mediterranean. Tate and Lyle sought a way to close the gap between research, new industries and a method of sharing the risk.[39]

A concept for a joint private industry government–United Nations system pilot plant in Cyprus evolved. The director of the FAO Agricultural Services Division approved participation by the FAO in a pilot plant scheme in Cyprus. The United Nations Development Programme was prepared to set aside allocated funds to cover the costs of the plant's equipment and the FAO's services. Tate and Lyle would provide, free of charge, the technology, know-how and key expertise; the Cyprus government would supply a building and necessary infrastructure.[40]

The project bogged down in 1970. Specialists in the FAO and the UNDP raised a series of technical questions, such as whether the project would cover the total utilization of the carob. The FAO delayed applying for UNDP support, apparently because of indecision on which of three FAO divisions would be responsible for the project. The UNDP backed away from its support of a pilot plant and requested an assessment by another firm. The intra-UN system muddle continued, with the UNDP providing funds for the FAO to subcontract for tests in the Netherlands on the nutritional value and safety of protein from carob for animal feed.[41] The administrator of the UNDP finally concluded in 1970 "[R]esearch has shown that microbial protein grown from carob has proved to be unsatisfactory as feed for chickens, but has reasonably good, although not outstanding, nutritive value for pigs. These findings, in conjunction with the fact that the price of kibbled carob has risen in the intervening period, have cast doubt on the economic validity of the process and it has been decided not to proceed with the construction of the pilot plant."[42]

If the tests had been positive they would have paved the way for a pioneering industrial effort to utilize the carob in several Mediterranean nations. United Nations funds could have helped start a new industrial cycle using a new technology from a member of the ICP. An ignored agricultural resource could have served as the basis for new products in local and export markets.

Although the ICP has continued the project concept, implementation of specific, short-term projects has received a lower priority in the ICP than the more grandiose public relations and political ploys evidenced at the Toronto Consultation and the World Food Conference. Several factors account for the ICP's ordering of priorities. First, the marriage broker function is frustrating, expensive and time consuming for the ICP. With the ICP's eye focused on the image of multinational agribusiness firms, the organization must be especially zealous in sifting proposals and doing projects "right" so as to protect the ICP's reputation as well as the image of corporations. In most instances it is exceedingly difficult for the ICP, as a catalyst, to bring together the requisite elements, unless they are already at least somewhat interested and involved. Secondly, the paucity of industry-generated projects that serve the needs of developing countries limits the ICP's role. Thirdly, suitable projects may be outside the areas of commercial or geographical expertise of ICP staff members who must participate in the implementation function. Finally, it is possible that an intra-FAO conflict between the ICP and the FAO Investment Centre, which identifies and prepares agriculture, forestry and fishery projects for financing by various international banks and financing agencies, may have impeded or blocked the ICP's marriage broker function. Undaunted by these difficulties, the ICP pushed ahead with a project in the nutrition area.

I C P SPECIFIC PROJECT IN NUTRITION

Within the ranks of the ICP membership, a split exists regarding whether the ICP should place greater emphasis on specific projects as a means of tapping the expertise of multinational corporations to meet the food needs of developing nations. In one specific subject area, the ICP attempted to develop low cost, high protein nutritional products. Before considering the ICP effort to combine the resources of government, industry and the UN to provide economical protein foods, we should examine some efforts by industry and government to provide protein-rich foods outside the ICP.

In the 1960s and early 1970s, multinational corporations in the United States attempted to develop and commercially produce and market protein-enriched foods to combat malnutrition in developing countries. Some firms embarked on such ventures on their own initiative. A study of food and pharmaceutical companies operating in India indicated that the became involved in the nutritional effort for several reasons. "Corpora image" was the most important general factor influencing a decision favo ing involvement. General public relations considerations, i.e., use of nutrition project to promote a firm's image to the general public and health and nutritional professionals who influence family food buyin habits, were important. Firms hoped to improve sales. Corporate relation with host governments were considered; multinationals hoped that involv ment on a social issue would be useful in future dealings with a gover ment. Companies also feared being left behind if the field became a maje market. A concern with social responsibility, apparently genuine, als entered into corporate decision making.[43]

Many companies entered the field under the stimulus of various L government programs designed to tap the research and management e pertise, marketing skills and financial capability of American firms produce low cost, nutritious foods. However, governmental program under the sponsorship of the Agency of International Development, i cluding grants to corporations to assess the feasibility of developing ar marketing high protein foods for low income groups, produced disappoin ing results.[44]

Programs under private initiative or a mix of private expertise ar government funding have been most notable for their lack of succes At least four factors hampered efforts to commercially produce and se protein-rich foods to the poor at a price profitable for a company bv affordable for low income groups: (1) the expense of the various forms raw material protein; (2) the cost of processing and packaging to preve: microbiological decay; (3) the need to spur the purchase of processe food through advertising, together with inadequate commercial channe of distribution in rural areas and slow turnover in small fragmented ma kets; and (4) the problem of meeting the taste and texture requiremen of the local community.[45]

In the face of the failure of protein-rich foods to achieve profitab operations or to reach mass groups of consumers, the ICP and the FA created a Joint Task Force on Protein Food Development to establi: viable food industries in developing countries to provide so-called vulne able groups with products they will eat. A viable protein food indust denotes a nutritional orientation aimed at groups with the greatest nee for nutritional products and an economic orientation toward the project bearing its own costs over time. The Joint Task Force was under the c chairmanship of O. Ballarin, chairman of the board of Companhia Industri e Comercial Brasileira de Produtos Alimentares (Nestlé), an ICP membe and M. Ganzin, the director of the Food Policy and Nutrition Division

FAO. The cochairmen hoped that a tripartite collaboration among industry, with its strength in technology and distribution, the governments of developing countries, and the United Nations system, with its nutritional and public health expertise and its ability to provide subsidies, could make a significant impact on the protein deficiency among the more vulnerable groups in one or more developing nations.[46]

The Task Force faced three key problems: (1) devising a unique strategy in the face of failure by individual firms; (2) selecting a country in which to implement the Task Force's concept; and (3) organizing the expertise of industry. The Task Force defined its challenge as developing a high-protein low-cost nutritional product that would lay the basis for a viable food industry from a marketing standpoint. Industry members of the Task Force proposed research to discover consumer needs through an extensive areawide market survey in a nation. Rather than looking to locally grown inputs, the Task Force's strategy proceeded from consumer wishes, which would lead to supplying protein foods to meet these requirements.[47]

The Task Force then turned to selecting a country in which to begin its efforts. The Task Force surveyed ICP members interested in this type of activity to see in what developing countries they would most like to see action taken. The FAO Food Policy and Nutrition Division added several countries to the ICP list. The list was screened and certain countries, viz., India and Brazil, were eliminated because of the complexity of their economic and social environment; others, such as Mexico were excluded because other nations seemed more in need of help.

Five nations—Malaysia, Peru, Sri Lanka, Kenya and Nigeria—were considered in more detail, including personal visits by the cochairmen. Nigeria was finally selected, because of its high occurrence of protein or caloric malnutrition, and because a local awareness of the problem also existed; also Nigeria had an availability of good statistics and a good climate for foreign investment. Three million children were targeted as the vulnerable group.

Five industry members of the ICP agreed to make contributions of $10,000 each, on condition that the United Nations, through the United Nations Development Programme, also commit $50,000. The total of $100,000 would have made possible further research under the management of Unilever, including (1) identifying the problem, (2) consumer marketing, focusing on food people would eat and (3) the testing of food to ascertain whether people would eat it.[48]

The project in Nigeria collapsed, however, when the Nigerian government advised the ICP that Nigeria had decided to go ahead with a product based on the enrichment of a traditional staple food developed by a

Nigerian Industrial Research Organization. As Nigeria did not want to look at other options, the Joint Task Force put the Nigerian market study on the shelf and advised the government of Nigeria that it would be ready to resume the study when the government deemed it proper. To date, the Nigerian product has not been marketed.

The effort of the FAO/ICP Joint Task Force on Protein Food Development is significant in one respect. It marked an attempt by the ICP to implement a concept by drawing on the know-how and expertise of multinational corporations to achieve practical results in the field of nutrition. However, the ICP's implementation focused on a marketing strategy. Five multinational corporations together with the UNDP would have financed a market study. Difficult questions, including the allocation of responsibility between multinational firms and a developing nation over the production and distribution functions, as well as the further contributions of the United Nations system, were never detailed. Still unanswered is the question of whether an operation would have become economically viable, even in social cost terms, within a reasonable period of time. Special emphasis probably should be placed on reaching preschool children, but this approach encounters the difficulty of supplying protein to children who are not in an institutional setting. Distribution through day care and health centers may overcome the high distributional costs of feeding preschool children. In short, the absence of a distribution system poses problems for the delivery of proteins. Uncertainties have also grown from a nutritional standpoint. Doubt exists whether it is preferable to solve the problem of malnutrition through additional protein or calories. Increasingly, it is felt that the protein needs of most people will be taken care of if their calorie requirements are met. But the Task Force did create a model for future tripartite cooperation among industry, government of developing countries and the United Nations system.

17

THE FUTURE OF THE ICP

Before focusing on concrete projects the organization might undertake using business expertise to meet the food and development needs of Third World countries, the ICP must first resolve a series of internal problems. Members are split regarding the aim of ICP. Should the organization only serve to create a better climate of opinion and confidence between multinational agribusiness corporations and developing nations? Should the ICP function by responding to the needs and desires of corporations and Third World nations? Should ICP play a more aggressive role as a project creating and implementing organization? Within the general confines of the emerging FAO policy emphasis on field work, projects and training, what role should be taken by the two main branches of the ICP in delineating policy approaches and priorities? Should the secretariat, instead of executing decisions, be expanded and perhaps take a more active role in formulating concepts? For example, the secretariat could present a project to ICP members and indicate possible results.

Whether the ICP concentrates on its public relations role or stresses projects, two further difficulties must be surmounted. During its first ten years, the ICP has been involved in a multitude of activities. The proliferation of working groups, for instance, expends the limited time of the ICP secretariat. The ICP should resist the centripetal pull of organizing more working groups to cater to the numerous diverse interests of ICP members. Given past practices, this will be difficult. Stated positively, the ICP should direct and focus the energies of the secretariat and member firms on one or two activities. A concentration of effort would not only aid the ICP in the implementation of selected activities but would also help it achieve greater publicity and visibility as a viable organization. However, if the ICP focuses on a particular functional area with the aim of maximizing results in a short time, members who are not involved in that sector may lose interest, temporarily or permanently, in the organization. The need for accomplishment must be balanced against a desire to please ICP members.

Two additional conflicts pervade and weaken the ICP as an organization. First, a gap exists between Western European firms and American corporations. Key ICP members, especially those steeped in a colonial tradition and some individuals on the secretariat, manifest a tendency to look down on American corporations as "pushy, fast buck operators" expanding overseas for short-term gain. Whatever the origins of the fissure within the ICP or the merits of the dispute, which involves questions of moral standards and corporate social responsibility, the split between Western European and American interests, and the accompanying gulf in the ICP secretariat, weakens the ICP as an effective organization. This gap may prevent the ICP from assuming a more activistic stance.

Second, the ICP is also split between giant global firms and more modest-sized corporations. Only a relatively small group of corporate executives, generally from firms in the United Kingdom, play a significant role in establishing ICP policy and implementing ICP efforts. There is a general lack of participation, in part caused by infrequent meetings, the difficulties of communication and a considerable amount of work being done by personal contact, especially among European firms. Besides this situation, executives from smaller firms face additional barriers. Officers of smaller ICP member-firms, who often lack past involvement in transnational politics and business, stand in awe of the giant firms and internationally known experts active in ICP, who have extensive government service and considerable experience in dealing with the Third World food and development problems and with international conferences and reports. The control by a clique and the "clubby" atmosphere may limit the ICP's dynamism.

Smaller firms also complain that the current uniform membership fee of $6,500 per year discourages small corporations from joing the ICP. For a multibillion dollar corporation, a $6,500 annual fee is not excessive, but for smaller firms it may pose an obstacle, although not an insurmountable bar. Diversity of ICP membership in terms of firm size is important for two reasons. First, the expertise and the technology possessed by more modest firms may better permit the ICP to serve the needs of the Third World. Second, intermediate-size firms may function more harmoniously with the FAO, other UN agencies, and public sector finance organizations; dealing with corporate giants may create a sense of uneasiness among international civil servants.

In the interest of involving a variety of firms, the ICP might consider a sliding scale membership fee, based perhaps on a corporation's sales or the number of working groups to which it belongs. However, sound arguments exist in favor of the current fee structure. If the ICP accepts the concept that members join the organization to provide assistance, not to secure benefits (a doubtful assumption, especially for the smaller export-oriented firms), then the fee schedule should remain uniform. A sliding scale fee might only relegate corporations that pay less to a more formal inferior status.

One final possibility in the fee area must be considered: To remove the suggestion that the ICP is a business vehicle, perhaps the FAO should finance the ICP. Increased or complete FAO funding might clarify the issue of the benefits provided by the ICP to the FAO, the United Nations system and Third World versus the benefits derived by multinational agribusiness firms from access to the United Nations system.

Members of the ICP may also want to consider the costs and benefits of membership in the United Nations system, particularly linkage to the FAO. The FAO's structure and bureaucracy may impede a more project-oriented ICP organization. Additional involvement by the ICP in the politics of the United Nations system creates a further bar to project implementation. But the benefits of the United Nations umbrella seem apparent. A private international association of multinational agribusiness corporations could easily be branded as an international association of neo-colonists. Possibly the ICP could accomplish more if linked to another part of the United Nations system, such as the United Nations Industrial Development Organization, or to a more informal liaison with the United Nations system.

Whether catalytic organizations like the Industry Cooperative Programme become more activist or merely respond to crises (such as the World Food Conference), the demands of a single firm or an industry, or the needs of a developing region or nation, two routes appear open to channeling the expertise of multinational agribusiness corporations into projects with social benefits to developing nations. First, private expertise, in fields such as technology, know-how, management and marketing, could be fused with public sector financing capabilities to meet the needs of the Third World. This is the so-called triangulation strategy. Secondly, either apart from or in conjunction with public sector financing, a systems approach to large scale multi-function development projects involving a consortium of firms could be utilized. The systems technique and consortium approach grow out of the awareness that no one corporation may want to or be able to provide all the requisite expertise and handle the implementation of a project by itself. The future possibilities for catalytic

organizations in the area of specific projects rest, in the large measur
on the evolving approach by multinational corporations to foreign dire
investment.

THE TRIANGULAR APROACH

Multinational corporations have grown more flexible in structuri
their activities in Third World countries. In the past firms emphasized tw
strategies: (1) owning large tracts of land, so-called plantations or estate
in developing nations to grow crops for export, primarily to develope
countries; and (2) funneling foreign direct investment, apart from tl
growing of agricultural produce, through wholly owned and controll
subsidiaries in Third World countries. As part of an emerging awarene
by developing nations of the value of their natural resources and an i
creasing availability of information regarding the impact of multinatio
firms engaged in raw material exploitation, including agricultural croj
governments rejected the foreign ownership of plantations. The plantatio
system was perceived as creating economic, social and political obstac
to development.[1] Land came to be regarded as a national patrimony th
should be locally owned—either privately or in the hands of the stat
As a wave of nationalism swept across the Third World, at least with i
gard to land ownership, multinational firms were forced to abandon the
extensive landholdings. Firms were not permitted to own plantation
which in any event, even before nationalization, were regarded as hostag
because of governmental policies that increased wages, fixed selling pric
and controlled export prices.

Sophisticated firms with expertise in tropical crops, such as suga
gained through previous ownership of plantations, turned to a variety
techniques to convert their knowledge into a new corporate profit-maki
center. Leading multinational sugar companies, Booker McConnell, Ta
and Lyle and H.V.A., pursued a similar pattern of establishing consulti
arms, including agricultural, technical and engineering services. In additio
to setting up turnkey sugar estates, managing sugar growing and processi
operations on a contractual basis, these firms engage in a variety of co
sulting activities outside the field of sugar. Booker McConnell and Ta
and Lyle also diversified into the construction of agricultural machinery

Beyond the direct growing of agricultural produce, agribusiness fir
have shifted their approach to structuring ventures involving the proce
ing of agricultural products. Under governmental pressure to increase lo
ownership and management and disassemble the package—that is, separa
the organization, management, technology and access to markets fro

foreign capital—firms responded with a variety of new business arrangements, including joint ventures, minority investments, management and operating contracts, licensing agreements and consulting arrangements. The focus by developing countries on shifting the ownership position held by multinational enterprises may obscure the efforts of global entities to maintain control over foreign ventures in which they participate.

The emerging triangulation strategy links the management, technological and marketing expertise of global firms with third-party financial support. Cognizant of the risks and uncertainties attendant in foreign direct investment, such as nationalization, a limitation on the repatriation of profits, and exchange controls, multinational firms would like to further reduce their risks by fusing their expertise with public sector financing. In contrast to earlier ICP projects, which involved industry "going it alone" in terms of finance and management, increasingly multinational firms will conceive, implement and manage undertakings financed by a variety of public sector financial sources, including the World Bank ("the Bank"), the International Finance Corporation, national organizations in industrialized nations, such as the United Kingdom's Commonwealth Developmental Corporation, regional development sources in the developed world, such as the European Fund for Development, regional development banks, such as the Inter-American Development Bank, financial resources available from OPEC nations and the creation of new organizations, such as the International Fund for Agricultural Development, organized under the auspices of the World Food Council. As part of private industry's triangulation strategy, the ICP may increasingly establish more systematic links to public sector finance groups. Firms may call upon the ICP to explain to these financing agencies the rationale for assuming all or part of the financial risk in connection with agribusiness projects.

The development of linkages by industry, either directly or through intermediary organizations, to the World Bank is particularly significant in view of the Bank's present and projected financial resources and its ability to shape the development policies of other agencies. In emphasizing the economic progress of developing nations, the World Bank makes loans to member governments or to public or private organizations, which obtain the guarantee of the government where the project to be financed is located. After intitially concentrating on the funding economic infrastructure, including power generation and transmission, the Bank has begun to finance social projects in the fields of health, population control, education and development. Except in special circumstances, the Bank lends funds for specific projects based on an analysis consisting of feasibility studies, an appraisal by a Bank staff mission and the use of consultants.

Industry presently enters into the World Bank's project approach by serving as consultants or by supplying goods and/or services for projec Private sector consultants may be retained by the Bank's borrowers connection with a Bank-financed project or by the Bank itself.[3] The latt generally occurs on studies financed by grants made by the Bank or the United Nations Development Programme. Apart from Bank projec firms have been involved in various types of consulting activities. For i stance, after a country nationalizes a foreign-owned enterprise, it m contact the Bank for help in running the operation. The Bank may sugge that the country bring in private expertise, even the former foreign owne on a management contract.

To maintain the support of Western nations, the World Bank general requires borrowers to obtain goods and services for Bank-financed projed through international competitive bidding open to suppliers in the Bank member countries and Switzerland. To stimulate the growth of lo industries, the Bank protects domestic bidders in a borrowing country allowing a margin of preference for local goods or services.[4]

Business executives complain about the Bank's procedures in awardi consulting contracts and the rigidity and bureaucratic mentality of t Bank's staff. Firms with the capability of providing consulting, design a supply functions are particularly critical of the fact that the Bank compi a so-called short list of not more than five firms that it invites to subn proposals for Bank-retained consultants.[5] The bank uses several sourc in compiling a short list, including firms that have expressed interest providing their services, the Bank's file of firms with capabilities in vario fields, and performance evaluations on file in the Bank regarding activit of firms on prior projects in which the Bank was involved. A recipie government or agency may also make deletions or additions to the Bank proposed list. Several executives, especially firms that have recen entered the consulting field, expressed the view that the Bank's "old-bo network of contacts with well-connected firms makes the obtaining o consulting contract nearly impossible.

As the private sector plans to look increasingly to the public sector funding, the Bank's rigid rules, at least as perceived by business executiv constitute a major impediment. A key problem is the Bank's policy agai allowing a firm, if it acts in a consulting or design capacity, to particip in any other capacity on the same project.[6] The rationale seems apparer namely, a corporation may design a project or advise a line of action fav ing goods or services that it can provide. A Bank staff representati reported that the Bank's rules are in fact flexible on this point. If a c poration serves as an engineering or design consultant, it is not au matically disqualified from bidding for the tender of goods and servic Such a corporation will be "looked at carefully" in the subsequent bidd

tages.[7] Despite the rules of the World Bank's Operating Manual, in prac-
ice, corporations apparently have encountered a more automatic dis-
qualification procedure, which they would like ameliorated by the adoption
f "less formalistic awarding procedures."[8]

International businessmen also criticize the traditional approach, the
interminable analyses and prolonged bidding procedures used by the
World Bank in its project conceptualization and analysis. Excessively long
periods, corporate executives think, are required for the implementation
f Bank projects. International funding organizations and agencies gener-
lly have segmented feasibility, design and construction functions into
eparate stages with awards to different organizations. The segmentation
f projects generally results in long intervals between the various stages.
Different responsibilities of contractors and the passage of time lessen the
success of a project. The costs of feasibility studies, which quickly become
bsolete, the changes in conditions and variations from design to construc-
ion stages further spiral the cost of a project. The separation of responsi-
ilities may give rise to unforeseen additional costs stemming from a
esign that may ignore construction processes; or, the execution of a
roject may not consider subsequent operation and maintenance require-
ents.[9]

In several instances, industry has attempted to devise new techniques
in conjunction with more flexible public financing sources to overcome
he negative aspects of the traditional procedures. A most notable example
s the Bakolori project in Nigeria, involving the design and construction of
dam and a supply canal connecting an irrigation and land reclamation
rea. On the Bakolori project the design and construction responsibilities
or land reclamation and irrigation projects are centered in one firm,
mpresit Bakolori (Nigeria) Ltd., a joint venture composed of the two
hareholders, the Federal Government of Nigeria and Impresit S.p.A., a
onsulting-implementing arm of Fiat, thereby avoiding the gap between
esign and construction and the concomitant refusal of any one organiza-
ion, under traditional procedures, to assume overall responsibility. Also,
llowing different stages of the project to overlap in sequencing reduced
he time between conception and construction.[10] Only a relatively
hort period of time, slightly over one year, elapsed from the commence-
ent of feasibility studies to the start of construction of the Bakolori
roject. However, the project relied on an eight-year FAO feasibility study.
Whether the Bank will overcome a tendency to function by traditional
ethods and operating manuals and flexibly respond to private sector
nitiatives and inventiveness is problematic.

Members of the ICP may press for formal linkages bewteen the ICP and
he World Bank so that industry's input can enter into the thinking of the

Bank's top management. The ICP may also fulfill another function overcoming a significant obstacle barring multinational firms from tapp public sector moneys, namely, a lack of knowledge by corporations public sector project preparation and bidding procedures. The ICP its and/or in conjunction with public sector funding sources could tr business executives in the art of bidding.

Instead of using the ICP as a link to the World Bank or other natio and international public funding sources, corporations may choose establish a separate liaison office at the World Bank. Executives may r son that the growing significance of public sector financing requires full-time attention of a liaison unit. As a final, but remote, possibility World Bank or other public financing group might take the initiative a reach out to the private sector in a coordinated joint public-private atta on the problems of food and development in the Third World.

In addition to tapping international public sector funds, business actively used national bilateral foreign assistance by industrialized nati to developing countries as a means of government subsidization a export promotion.[11] Expenditure of bilateral development assistar funds has generally been tied to purchasing goods and services provided the private sector of a donor country. Within the context of meet development needs or other similar donor guidelines, corporations h worked closely with recipient nations. A corporation, under this syste has helped a developing country draw up and present a proposal to corporation's home government, including, of course, products ma factured and/or services provided by the firm. On more than a few oc sions, a firm has also discussed a project with its home government a part of the donor government's decision-making process.[12]

Reacting to criticism that tied development assistance serves the of corporations, not the social goals of developing countries, sev countries in Western Europe, such as the Netherlands, have untied fore aid. But a significant problem still exists. Developing nations lack knowledge and expertise to define their problems. Corporations still as recipient countries in defining problems and suggesting the sale of go and/or services as part of a donor government's new thrust to meet b social problems. A recipient nation presents the project to a donor, wi corporation still getting in on the ground floor. An initial sale of good services forms part of a corporation's long-term aim of selling more phisticated goods and services. By helping a developing country to mee basic needs, firms hope to gain the goodwill and acceptance of a gov ment requisite to the sale of higher profit items.[13]

Within the ICP national subgroups of firms may develop to estab linkages to a national foreign assistance apparatus. Groups of natio firms, perhaps organized on an industry basis, will, as a more likely alternative, evolve to present the viewpoint of farsighted business spokesmen as to how a nation should structure its foreign assistance program to foster, of course, the ends of business.

NEW STRUCTURAL APPROACHES: SYSTEMS ANALYSIS AND CONSORTIUMS

The ICP may serve as a "think tank" allowing business executives to consider innovative structures to facilitate participation by multinational firms in the agribusiness sector of developing countries. Prime examples of possible new techniques are contractual arrangements linked to the achievement of specified development goals and multifirm consortiums.

Corporations may increasingly encounter countries where neither direct foreign equity investment nor the current consulting or management contracts are appropriate; a host government's policies, an inadequate or excessively risky return, or a combination of both may block foreign private direct investment or other forms of involvement. Conversely, the public or private sector of a host nation may regard the agreements for consulting services and/or management, even without any equity investment, as of limited value to the host nation; the nation may feel that a firm will transfer its best technology and management only where it has a financial stake beyond a consulting arrangement.

To utilize the technological, management, production and marketing expertise of multinational firms in such situations, corporations may suggest the use of management contracts linked to the achievement of development goals. Payments under such contracts could be based on the fulfillment of a nation's long-term development objectives as well as the on-going costs of the firm related to the project. A firm would derive revenue from the achievement of interim goals during the contract period; presumably this would act as an incentive for the company to apply its best expertise. Industry would have the time and security to perform properly. A nation would have tangible evidence of a firm's progress toward meeting specified goals. A government might also wish industry to participate in a project through a nonequity investment. Given a contract of sufficient duration, such an arrangement would give evidence of a corporation's financial good faith. One attempt to implement an incentive arrangement, by Ralston Purina International, resulted in failure, however.[14]

The ICP could take the lead in promoting discussions of new techniques among firms and governments of Third World countries or a regional

bloc of nations. These discussions might lead to a dialogue between pub
sector officials and executives of business firms regarding approaches
signed to benefit both sides. The ICP could also create a special gro
to devise new strategies to facilitate the transfer of business experience
meeting the needs of developing countries.

Executives approach agribusiness as a system with numerous co
ponents, requiring the expertise of many firms on a project. A syste
approach "conceives of entities as wholes marked off from the envirc
ment by boundaries and containing subparts whose interactions are cc
ditioned by the presence of the other subparts (subsystems). The acti
of the whole can be understood only by knowledge of the interactic
of all the parts."[15] The systems concept of agribusiness starts from t
premise that the food chain is a seed-to-consumer system linking togeth
actors and actions. The pieces of the system do not exist in isolatic
Actions taken at one point in the system impact on other compone
of the system. For instance, an irrigation system consists of several s
systems: storage, transmission, distribution and the extraction of wat
Analysis must, therefore, focus on the linkages and interdependencies
an agribusiness system.

The commercial applicability of a systems approach to agribusin
leads in turn to the concept of a multicompany consortium that, from t
outset, would be put together to tackle a problem. A vertically in
grated dairy industry project in a developing country might involve t
following inputs from a number of corporations: land cultivation (mach
ery manufacturers), land fertilization (fertilizer corporations), fod
production (seed, pesticide and machinery firms), fodder storage a
processing (equipment and farm building companies), dairy cattle (anin
breeders and producers of animal health products), milking areas (fa
building and milking equipment companies), milk processing (milk pr
essors and container manufacturers), product transportation (transp
manufacturers), and waste disposal (waste processors).[16] The syst
requires, of course, expert coordination for its implementation and ope
tion. Catalytic organizations, such as the ICP, could perceive the int
dependencies, which few corporations are aware of, thereby facilitat
the integration process.

The rationale of a systems approach, namely, that a project may
quire resources beyond the expertise and commitment of any one mu
national firm, regardless of size, ignores a number of problems from
standpoint of both corporations and catalytic organizations. A syste
approach may be easier for a project, such as sugar or pineapple, that ai
at local production and processing for export. American firms with a p
tion in the export (US) market are familiar with the system and

purchase inputs, e.g., fertilizer, at world market prices. However, extending the approach to local agricultural self-sufficiency in basic crops through an integrated package of inputs (seeds, fertilizers, pesticides, equipment and credit) provided by a number of firms may pose many problems. Corporations must overcome unfamiliarity with a non–export-oriented system. Antitrust considerations may also make American corporations hesitant to participate in a consortium. Industry often views consortiums as demanding too much of management time. Finally, legal and financial complexities are too high for the return obtained.

In light of these impediments, from the corporate viewpoint, few successful consortium projects exist. A notable exception is an agricultural venture designed to reclaim a region of Iran from the desert by irrigation and create an integrated complex for the production, processing and distribution of field crops and livestock. The consortium, the International Agribusiness Corporation of Iran, includes American firms (Hawaiian Agronomics Company International, Chase International Investment Corp., and Diamond A Cattle Company) as well as Mitsui and Co. of Japan and Iran enterprises (Ahwaz Beet Sugar Factory and Refinery Company Limited, the Iranian Agricultural Development Bank, and the Khuzestan Water and Power Authority). Hawaiian Agronomics has been the managing partner of the consortium, in which all members are shareholders. Chase and the Agricultural Development Bank of Iran are lenders as well. Areas of functional authority were segmented, with the Khuzestan Water and Power Authority leasing the land and supplying water to the project; the Ahwaz refinery processes all sugar beets produced, Diamond A provides cattle and livestock expertise and Mitsui is both a supplier to and a purchaser of products from the enterprise.[17]

A catalytic organization, such as the ICP, undertaking a consortium arrangement encounters a variety of obstacles. The catalytic group may face two or more companies with different approaches to the system or the supply of any one input. Firms may simply disagree, or corporations may have different objectives. A mechanism would be required to resolve such disputes. Even if two or more firms agree on an approach, the catalytic organization must select the firm to provide a given input. To surmount the obstacles of parceling out a project and bringing in firms to handle slices appropriate to each firm's expertise requires a staff skilled in project implementation and management. Citibank International Development Corp., as a consultant, currently packages multicorporation agribusiness projects in developing countries. To undertake these activities Citibank employs a staff composed of experts in finance (including sources of financing and corporate finance techniques), management consultants to make studies and structure deals and a technical director (a civil engineer) to interface with construction and engineering experts.[18] Catalytic organizations would require additional personnel to put together a consortium involving corporations and public sector financing, thereby increasing an organization's budget. To meet the expertise hurdle, the ICP could engage an outside consultant to implement consortium projects but this would not solve the expense problem. The ICP would also be required to get actively involved in negotiations among the constituent corporations and between the consortium, a developing nation and a possible public sector financing source. All of these problems may incline a catalytic organization to avoid the implementation and management of a consortium project. One final imponderable is whether a significant demand exists for consortium projects in developing nations. If the ICP takes the time to organize a group to tackle a problem in one country will other governments want the consortium to replicate its efforts in their nations?

TWO POSSIBLE SPECIFIC PROJECTS

The viability of the triangular concept linking private expertise, public funds and the resources of developing nations and the possibilities for new structures whereby the skills of multinational agribusiness firms may be transmitted to Third World countries, may cause members of the ICP to ponder with great care the organization's future direction. Beyond facilitating the discussion of these techniques and promoting a better climate of opinion and understanding, what role can and will a catalytic organization play? As J. I. Hendrie pithily stated, "ICP is a concept in search of projects."[19] Although the concept of a more active ICP involved in systems-oriented projects beyond picking up bits and pieces has been vigorously discussed by the members of the ICP, two priority projects seem particularly suited to significantly increasing agricultural production in developing nations thereby meeting the spiraling demand for food, reducing post-harvest crop losses and strengthening national seed industries.

CUTTING POST-HARVEST CROP LOSSES

Prevention of food losses, specifically post-harvest volume and nutrition losses, which occur to food products from the farm (or the fishing craft) to the final consumer, could raise the available supply of food. Estimates indicate that up to one-third of the cereal crop in a developing country can be lost in post-harvest handling, processing and distribution and an even greater proportion of perishable foods such as fruits and vegetables.

The growing awareness of the need for reducing post-harvest food losses culminated in a resolution of the Seventh Special Session of the United Nations General Assembly, which stated, "The further reduction of post-harvest food losses in developing countries should be undertaken as a matter of priority, with a view to reaching at least 50 per cent reduction by 1985."[21] A significant reduction in post-harvest crop losses would increase the available food supplies, thereby making an important contribution to a nation's food supplies. How could private expertise in various segments of the food distribution system, including storage, packaging, refrigeration, preservation, and use of chemicals, be channeled to prevent food losses?

Taking up the challenge, the ICP established a Task Force on Food Loss Prevention. The Task Force narrowed the expansive topic to food losses in food aid programs and commenced cooperating with the FAO's World Food Programme—the arm of the FAO handling food aid. Following up on a concept advanced at a session of the ICP Task Force on Food Loss Prevention for the creation of a modern storage facility that would serve as a regional or subregional center for the training and demonstrating of storage handling and distribution techniques as well as for the better utilization of local materials for storage construction, the World Food Programme pinpointed six priority countries with substantial losses resulting from inadequate storage facilities and a lack of expertise in storage management. The World Food Programme prepared a general proposal for ICP collaboration involving the construction of a warehouse in the Yemen Arab Republic to provide general training for personnel and specific instruction on the use of equipment for control of pests and to serve as a model for other countries in the region. Although expressing support for the project, the members of the Task Force sought additional details with regard to the financial aspects of the building and operational programs, including needed agro-chemicals and the proposed training program for the model warehouse. Even with a detailed program, an attack on the loss problem in the food aid sector involves a delicate interference in local matters by outsiders. A need also exists to demonstrate to farmers that the benefits of a new system outweigh the cost of food loss and waste.[22] The possibilities of rampant corruption in some Third World nations may hamper governments from focusing on cost-benefit equations.

Although joint FAO-ICP demonstration and training projects in the food aid area form a useful starting point, the role industry may play in the broader aspect of post-harvest food losses must also be examined. Experts divide the post-harvest food loss problem into two aspects: on-the-farm losses and off-the-farm losses. Approximately 60–70% of basic food grains (wheat, rice, corn) never leave the farm. Thus, food remaining on the farm offers the greatest possibilities for loss reduction. Pilot farm storage projects have produced dramatic post-harvest crop losses b simple and inexpensive changes in farm storage facilities and the applica tion of small amounts of chemicals. Institutional impediments, howeve may limit the widespread adoption of such pilot projects. Deficiencies i at least four areas work against cutting on-the-farm losses: arrangement for producing the requisite inputs; distribution facilities for the input credit arrangements or purchasing power; and information in the hand of farmers regarding the use of inputs.[23]

Until a nation faces difficult social and economic questions, industry role will be limited to providing training and materials for the constru tion of storage units and for inputs such as pesticides. Thus, increase attention to post-harvest crop losses will promote the sale of storag facilities and chemicals. But multinational firms cannot provide th technology suitable for low-cost, small-scale village industries to produc the chemical, storage and preservation inputs. Concepts like on-the-farm water containers that can be turned into grain storage units will probabl emanate from sources other than global firms.

An arousal of interest in the problem and a desire to cure or alleviat waste must exist among farmers and government officials in developin countries. Few farmers have an accurate picture of losses, which ofte cannot be perceived or are simply accepted. The habits of small farme must be changed. Governments must make a long-term commitment t an on-the-farm food loss reduction program and the rather prosaic nece sary inputs far removed from more glamorous dam and irrigation project In addition to laying the institutional base, governments must condu demonstrations and extension activities and use other methods to persuad farmers to improve farm-level storage. In short, development and accep tance of an integrated program aimed at cutting on-the-farm losses coverin input production and supply, credit mechanisms and extension wi probably be a long, slow process.

Although a larger part of the losses occur in the on-the-farm secto spectacular losses occur off-the-farm as a harvest heads to the consume Improving storage and processing facilities and the staffing of marketin organizations comprise the prime ingredients for reducing off-the-farm losses.[24] Multinational firms could assist in training local technicians i storage, processing, pest control and loss prevention techniques. Like th educational and demonstration activities of the ICP Pesticides Workin Group, these activities would promote, in the long run, sale of product offered by global firms. The Industry Cooperative Programme may facil tate the efforts of business in attacking losses throughout the food chai by working directly with developing nations or by cooperating with th FAO, specifically the FAO Inter-Departmental Sub-Committee o

Reduction of Post-Harvest Food Losses in Developing Countries.

Beyond reduction in the deterioration of harvested crops, significant achievements may be realized in total crop utilization. Research undertaken by multinational firms may increase the food value of many crops by using parts of plants presently discarded. For many years food processors have used only a small portion of a plant, allowing the rest—leaves, roots, and stems—to be wasted. Parts of green plants are regarded as inedible because the residue is indigestible, unpalatable, of low nutritional value, or contains toxins. Greater utilization of those residual materials could produce nutritive food and/or feed. For example, through microbiological conversion of crop wastes, the protein content can be raised and the material used for human and animal feed. By slightly reducing efficiency, high protein foods and feeds may be produced on the village level by using plastic fermenters and a labor-intensive system of culture medium preparation and cell harvesting.[25] Through the ICP, industry's expertise may be made available to developing nations. In addition to inertia and cost factors, the problem of patent protection, however, poses a possible obstacle to the construction of plants to convert whole crops into a food.

STRENGTHENING NATIONAL SEED INDUSTRIES IN DEVELOPING NATIONS

New seeds constitute another key strategy to increasing the agricultural output of Third World nations. In most developing countries the yields of basic food crops, such as rice, wheat, and corn, have remained extremely low and static. Over the past thirty years, private foundations, governments of developing countries, and international research and training institutes have sought to improve agricultural production by breeding plants to give seeds that not only have a higher yield potential but also improve the flexibility of cropping strategies. The Rockefeller Foundation began in 1943 by providing technical assistance to the government of Mexico to develop improved seeds and other technology for Mexico's main food crops and to train technical personnel. The success of the effort led the Rockefeller Foundation to participate in the development of other national research systems in Latin America. The lack of food, crop and animal research in tropical and subtropical areas resulted in the establishment in the 1960s of a network of ten major international agricultural research and training centers, each located in a developing region of the world. These centers, which receive a major proportion of their support from the Consultative Group on International Agricultural Research—a consortium coordinating financial support from national governments, international agencies and foundations (including Rockefeller, Ford and W. K. Kellogg)—

seek to create and perfect the biological components, such as seed varieties and disease and insect control measures, requisite for increasing the yield of each crop in every season, in each region of every developing nation.[26]

The new high-yielding wheat varieties developed by Mexican government and Rockefeller Foundation scientists, first used in Mexico, and similar high-yielding rice varieties from one of the international research centers, the International Rice Research Institute, sparked the so-called Green Revolution. The strategy underpinning the development of new wheat and rice varieties, as Dr. Sterling Wortman observed, rested on the design of crop plants—new biological converters—"capable of converting high levels of applied fertilizers to harvestable product rather than to excessive foliage."[27] Achievement of high crop yields required the melding together of new seed varieties with the availability of a wide range of inputs. The complete package of technology included water and irrigation systems, fertilizers, agro-chemicals, mechanization and credit facilities. In short, the creation of the new seed varieties has expanded the markets in developing nations for a number of the technological inputs supplied by firms in the industrialized world. Thus expensive inputs, such as fertilizers, chemicals, and irrigation, depend on the use of high-quality seeds, a relatively low-cost input, for their feasibility and effectiveness.

In a number of Third World countries major national efforts are underway to accelerate agricultural research and development. The work of the international research centers is adapted and supplemented by national plant breeding institutes. But experts recognize a number of gaps in the seed programs of developing nations. At a 1975 FAO Expert Consultation on Seed Industry Development, which brought together experts mainly from government and academia, participants arrived at a conclusion that numerous academic (9,000) and intermediate-level (35,000 to 40,000) personnel would be required by 1980 to realize the optimal possibilities regarding current cereal seed technology.[28] At the consultation others stated that only a few countries in the Third World have adequate facilities for seed production, quality control and distribution.[29] Insufficient and inefficient seed production and supply acts as a brake on increasing food production.

Inadequate safeguards, from the viewpoint of business, exist for investment in and/or the transfer of knowledge to seed industries in Third World nations. This perception must be contrasted with the situation in developed nations. According to industry experts, the existence of a system for the protection of plant breeders' rights—similar to a patent system—has spurred the efforts of private industry to carry out practical breeding, variety improvement and the development of hybrid seed. Some background on the seed industry may be helpful to analyze industry' insistence on protection. It takes more than ten years (on the average fourteen years) to produce and test a new variety of cereal seed. The process involves a complex system of selection and disease assessment under diverse environmental conditions. After completion of this research and development effort, a competitor who obtains one seed can germinate the new variety; subsequent sales by a competitor would be outside the breeder's control. Thus, industry spokesmen assert that without protection privately financed breeding of new seed types constitutes an economic impossibility.[30]

To provide the requisite protection, a number of developed countries ratified the 1961 International Convention for the Protection of New Varieties of Plants. The convention provides for a system similar to patent licensing, with modifications because of the special nature of plants. Official trials are used to insure that a variety meets the standards of distinctiveness (a new botanical or physiological characteristic), uniformity and stability. The certification system also requires some control over quality. The breeder of a protected variety receives a royalty on the production and sale of seed through a license system. Royalties, however, are not payable on grains for consumption.[31]

In the absence of a system for the protection of plant breeders' rights, in almost all developing nations, the private seed industry manifests a reluctance to make available either capital or, even more importantly, expertise to developing nations with national seed industries. Given such circumstances and the unlikelihood of new protective legislation, how can private industry participate in the production, distribution and usage of high quality seeds for improved crops in Third World countries? These new seeds will generate a demand for a number of other technological inputs—fertilizer, chemicals and tractors.

Third World nations face two critical gaps in moving toward the technological revolution in agriculture so assiduously sought by industry: (1) a lack of trained manpower, and (2) a lack of an organizational structure and the requisite management for multiplying, cleaning, storing and distributing seeds. Industry could provide assistance in training local experts in a number of steps along the seed development system. Instruction could be made available to management and supervisory staff in seed drying and processing, seed harvesting and production supervising, storage, packaging and distribution (including stock control) and in related control systems and procedures. These steps, which are important elements in a seed production program, form part of the daily activities of commercial seed personnel. Industry could also provide help in varietal maintenance, breeding and selection programs and quality control in conjunction with local private or public enterprises. Thus, through training, industry could lay the basis for a sound organizational structure in all phases of the seed industry. The individuals trained by industry could, in succeeding years, themselves train others.

A catalytic organization, such as the Industry Cooperative Programme, could play a significant role in tapping industry's expertise for participation in national seed programs. In contrast with a trade association, such as the International Seed Trade Federation, which lacks contacts with developing nations and an orientation to the UN system, the ICP enables a consensus of the seed industry's opinion to be formulated and funneled through the United Nations. The FAO might compile, by country, a list of major problems and future plans for seed industry development. The ICP could identify firms willing to cooperate together with their areas of expertise. The ICP could also assist in the implementation of a triangulation strategy involving public sector financing. A multinational firm or a consortium of corporations could provide technical experts to develop a new seed variety or hybrid in a country within a given number of years. The firm(s) would enter into an arrangement with a national or international public sector agency to provide funds to cover the out-of-pocket costs of the firm(s) together with a "reasonable" rate of profit. The firm(s) might also agree that in the event the experts failed to develop a seed to meet certain specifications within the prescribed time period, compensation would be waived. Private expertise could be involved in training and transferring know-how for the multiplication of improved varieties for mass distribution to farmers.

At least five problems exist in implementing the triangulation technique in the seed area. First, the activity of international research centers, which employ top people, limits the need for industry to supply expertise in research and development. Secondly, structuring an arrangement to involve industry must take account of the absence of plant breeders' protection legislation in a country, particularly for developments thought significant by the private sector; this would also incline a corporation or a consortium into the area of training and/or seed multiplication and other efforts to spur the distribution of seeds to farmers. Thirdly, a national seed industry in public hands poses special problems for a catalytic organization linking the expertise of multinational enterprises with the needs of developing nations. Even if public funding were available, a seed bureaucracy in country might reject the offer of private industry because national seed employees feel private experts would upstage their efforts (or lack thereof) thereby jeopardizing their jobs. However, if the need is great enough, government officials may reject a national seed bureaucracy's negative attitude toward private outside help; the example of Poland's engaging Massey-Ferguson to expand and modernize its tractor industry may prove helpful. Industry and catalytic organizations might then form alliances with other governmental groups to make the triangulation concept viable. Fourthly, the FAO may, despite the platitudes offered to assuage industry, downgrade the role of industry and the ICP in seed areas; it may try to detour the ICP because the FAO feels it can make direct contacts with the private seed industry, which until recently has not been dominated by global firms. With the acquisition of seed companies by multinational corporations, including ICP members, the FAO may evidence a greater willingness to work with the ICP. Despite the need for education, the FAO still manifests a public sector-to-public sector mentality. The solution to the training quandary offered by the FAO's Expert Consultation on Seed Industry Development, for instance, consisted of a plea for increasing the FAO's staff by three professional officers and one technical assistant.[32] Fifth, just as in the area of on-the-farm crop losses, government and industry face a difficult task of persuading farmers to buy and use new seeds. Mechanisms must be perfected to protect the farmer against the receipt of poor quality seeds. The supply of related inputs and credit, together with extension and demonstration activities, will be required to show that the seeds are more productive and generate a crop of equal value and similar cooking qualities in comparison with traditional seeds.

SECURING PRIVATE SECTOR EXPERTISE

Even if the ICP overcomes its internal problems and defines its function, private sector expertise may be unavailable for ICP projects, thereby limiting the ICP's constructive role. According to W. W. Simons, deputy executive secretary of the ICP, the involvement of industry with developing countries is premised on the assumption that a number of multinational firms wish to involve their expertise if Third World governments give top priority to agriculture.[33] The problem of tapping business expertise must be examined from the viewpoints of both an individual and the organization. Then, possible sources of expertise must be considered. Unfortunately, despite the fond hopes, few businessmen-statesmen exist.

An individual considering spending a protracted time period—six months or one or two years—working on a project for a catalytic organization faces the possibility of being surpassed by his peers in the race up the corporate pyramid. A scientist or an executive might find his career path interrupted or permanently sidetracked. But generativity—the process by which the blooming of an individual's creativity leads to a voluntary commitment to help others—may free more individuals from measuring their worth by profit-and-loss statements.[34] Although not engaged in the generativity business, progressive corporations may build into their pro motional structure increased consideration for individuals who hav gained experience interfacing with international organizations, public sec tor financing institutions and the governments of developing and develope nations. In such cases a corporation may, as part of the firm's long-rang development and management program, encourage individuals to partici pate in ICP projects.

An individual willing to commit his time, however, faces a furthe challenge. Top managers rely on a staff to be effective. Left to himself an executive may be unable to perform a variety of basic level busines functions. Managerial experience in the milieu of a large plant, a skille labor force and capital-intensive technology may be less than usefu in meeting the social needs of developing nations. Individuals may find i difficult to work on ill-defined projects. The impetus of generativity ma outweigh the burden of the organizational division of labor and traditiona modes of operation, but innovative executives or technical personnel wh might transmit and adapt their knowledge in a creative manner may no seek employment in or may be screened out from the upward path i the modern organizational bureaucracies.

A corporation encounters difficulties in making expertise available A lack of commitment on the part of a developing nation's government, a ill-defined project, and hesitancy regarding the setting up of a potentia competitor may dissuade a company. A firm probably will not releas an especially talented person for long time periods. The firm suffers significant (and probably incalculable) loss if an individual, for exampl a scientist, does not devote his time to a project that directly benefit the corporation. An enterprise also experiences problems in planning fo the freeing-up of executives. Corporations want to program the releas of personnel, but the international organizations and developing countrie currently present ad hoc requirements. Future, scheduled ICP project may surmount this obstacle; meanwhile, the ICP secretariat tries to sensi tize ICP members as to the need for expertise to be made available to th UN system, so that a request will not surprise an organization.

A firm must also assess how it will fit an individual who is made avail able to the ICP or the United Nations system back into the organization Although scientists probably will not want to abandon on-going endeavors a corporation can reassign technically oriented personnel to anothe project upon their re-entry in the organization. Middle-level executives particularly those who have reached their plateau in a firm, may also b reslotted to a new assignment. A top manager poses a difficult challenge as another executive must be brought in to fill the vacated position, and it may be difficult to return a top manager to his original post. In a expanding company, managerial talent will, however, probably be accommodated. Uncertainty and the probable reluctance by corporations to make commitments to individuals as to functions assumed on their return to an enterprise, may dampen enthusiasm for volunteer endeavors. Finally, the requisite expertise may no longer be found in private sector firms in industrialized nations. In some areas, tropical agriculture, for example, the expertise accumulated by multinational corporations during the colonial era will diminish as individuals die or retire. Whether public sector programs in developed and developing nations will evolve to replenish this expertise is uncertain.

At least five possible sources of expertise currently exist. First, the ICP could utilize the services of retired individuals, particularly as earlier retirement becomes more commonplace. Second, senior or plateaued executives may arrange for a leave of absence; however, depending on the details of a firm's pension program, specifically, if a pension is tied to salary earned during a fixed period before retirement, an individual may not want to undertake long-term commitments at that stage of his career. Third, recent MBA recipients may be made available after one year of employment. In Europe, personal aides to directors, who are not consolidated within the corporate system, may be released as part of a training program; of course, these individuals may lack the necessary experience. Fourth, expertise from business could be engaged for short-term periods, two to four weeks; conceivably, corporate self-interest, such as the perception of a possible commercial opportunity, would motivate a firm to release top-caliber personnel. Corporations would almost certainly require a long-term interest before making available experts on a consulting basis for projects that required an extended time commitment. Facing these difficulties, catalytic and public sector agencies may turn to consulting organizations or firms with consulting arms.

18

ASSESSMENT OF MULTINATIONAL AGRIBUSINESS CORPORATIONS IN DEVELOPING NATIONS

Even if the ICP can harness the expertise of private firms to solve th[e] food problem in the Third World, which business considers in technic[al] terms—increasing agricultural output—the impact of the technology an[d] expertise transferred by multinational agribusiness firms must be analyze[d]. After assessing the past negative economic and social effects of technolog[y], this chapter will project future consequences. New institutional structure[s] and reforms to harmonize technology to the needs of Third World cou[n]tries will also be examined. An optimistic role for private Western bus[i]nesses rests, in the end, on strengthening the knowledge position [of] developing countries. Possessing sufficient knowledge, a Third Worl[d] country could directly, or through a catalytic organization such as th[e] Industry Cooperative Programme, fuse private sector expertise and publ[ic] sector financing to serve its selected development path.

THE IMPACT OF TECHNOLOGY

In place of the multitude of farmers who currently seek to eke out a[n] existence on tiny landholdings, agribusiness firms wish to spread a resurge[nt] Green Revolution throughout the developing world, bringing about, i[n] the eyes of business executives, a two-fold result. First, expanded ne[w] markets would be created for a variety of inputs, including fertilize[r], pesticides and machinery. Second, the transition from a subsistence to [a] cash economy and the accompanying increase in disposable income woul[d] lay the basis for a consumer society. This society would create a new ma[r]ket for processed food products and a cornucopia of goods and services.

Western corporations would meet this burgeoning consumer demand through trade, foreign-owned subsidiaries, joint ventures or the continued transfer to technology to the Third World. The future stake of sophisticated agribusiness executives in the Third World and catalytic organizations that smooth corporate penetration and the expansion of sales and profits is thus apparent. Through the modernization of agriculture, business foresees the developing world remaining part of a Western-dominated world economic system. This happy scenario, from a business viewpoint, ignores the negative social and economic consequences of the Green Revolution and the transfer of capital-intensive technology to developing nations.

Commentators have generally concluded that the Green Revolution in India in the 1960s had an adverse economic and social impact in terms of employment, income distribution and social stratification.[2] Economic inequality and a polarization of society resulted. Yields no longer depended largely on the inherent qualities of the soil, particularly fertility, and on seeds that had survived the process of natural selection. To effectively use the new high-yield seed varieties, a farmer needed to purchase fertilizer, together with plant protection chemicals, and a wide range of mechanized farm implements; he also had to have access to an irrigation system. The Green Revolution in India occurred where large-scale commercial agriculture existed and on large farms. Easier access to credit and experience in dealing with institutional arrangements and finance enabled large farmers to afford technological inputs. Bigger farmers turned to multiple cropping and a diversification of crops, including profitable commercial produce.

The new inputs favored farmers with political influence and economic resources or access thereto. National and local governments spurred the Green Revolution by financing irrigation facilities, subsidizing various inputs, overvaluing exchange rates (which reduced the cost of imported equipment) and by providing credit. These public efforts further strengthened the advantage of large farmers. As one expert concluded, "Extension agents concentrate on the large farmers; credit agencies concentrate on low risk borrowers. . . . State organizations tend to provide services to those from whom the government seeks approval, and in most instances these are the large landowners."[3] Large-scale agriculture gained at the expense of smaller cultivators.

Poor farmers, with limited capital, restricted access to the credit requisite to using capital-intensive technology and a lack of political connections, could not compete with large-scale commercial agriculture. Although seeds, fertilizer and pesticides are divisible and readily usable on small holdings, irrigation facilities and farm mechanization face economies of scale. These economies of scale may be overcome by cooperative arrangements. Custom-hire services may also provide small farmers with the benefits of mechanization. But the cooperative use of tractors has been expensive, inefficient and unpopular with small farmers.[4] Small farmers may also view cooperative efforts and machinery-hire schemes as a waste of time, particularly with respect to implementation and management. Modern technology generally does not comport with the scale of operatons or the educational levels of small farmers. Moreover, government institutions promoting the new technology adopted policies that were not scale-neutral and favored the large cultivators. The uncertain effectiveness of modern technological inputs and heavy cost burdens also inhibited small farmers. Subsequently, larger farmers purchased the land of smaller cultivators who were unable to use modern inputs to realize the value of their holdings and were squeezed between falling prices and higher costs. In addition to an increase in the concentration of land holdings, land owners hiked rentals and evicted tenants and individual sharecroppers thereby raising the number of landless, unemployed individuals.

Commercial mechanization of large farms, without concern for social consequences, is widely believed to increase rural unemployment, resulting in the massive displacement to shantytowns. The morass of conflicting studies renders impossible a definitive assessment of the impact of modern technology on employment in all countries and all regions. The remark of Arthur T. Olsen, vice president of FMC Corp., downplaying the social consequences of mechanization, characterize the underlying attitude of many, but not all firms. Olsen stated:

Some past attempts to apply mechanization have also found resistance in less developed countries—especially in areas with high unemployment and a seemingly unlimited supply of low cost labor. These have been temporary setbacks, in my opinion, as I feel it inevitable that mechanization will be necessary to gain the dramatic improvement in yields, the lower production costs, and the rigid quality control standards that will be required to be competitive in world market alternatives. These, in turn, overshadow the employment question.[5]

Manufacturers also make the questionable assumption that displaced labor can somehow be absorbed, for example in agricultural processing plants. This remains a doubtful supposition in economies characterized by pervasive unemployment and underemployment.

Farm implement firms, naturally, dispute the correlation between mechanization and unemployment and advocate a policy of selective mechanization to meet the problem of adverse social consequences, particularly labor displacement. Selective mechanization mandates that country in deciding whether or not to mechanize an area (or a specific crop within a region) should balance the costs and benefits of mechanization. Selective mechanization involves "the use of correctly selected machines, combinations of machines and the correct application of machinery to the stages of the farm production cycle."[6] Particular emphasis is placed on mechanization to overcome bottlenecks in an agricultural system, such as seasonal labor shortages, and to support and increase employment opportunities in certain stages of agricultural production and in other activities, such as plowing, cultivation, weeding, seed bed preparation and harvesting. Mechanization may increase yields through greater speed of operation at sowing and harvesting and more thorough cultivation and increase the ability to cultivate harder or economically marginal land; it may also reduce manual toil, lessen harvest losses by more timely harvesting and release land used to meet the food requirements of draft animals for productive crops.

Because no single farm may capture the social benefits accruing from selective mechanization, the concept probably has more validity in public sector agriculture. But few governments evidence the tenacity of purpose required to underpin a selective mechanization policy. Although the possibilities of multicropping a parcel of land may increase the demand for labor, the shift from payments in kind, which insured a minimum food supply, to cash payments probably renders a tenant or a laborer in a mechanized agricultural scheme dependent on the vagaries of the market.

But the long-run social consequences of the system of technological inputs and expertise is most subtle and pervasive. Western control over technological knowledge forms one of the keys to the future activity by multinational agribusiness corporations in the developing world. The genie of technology, which makes it difficult for elites to spurn chemicals and mechanizations, may lock most of the Third World into a continuing system of dependence on multinational firms. Because of a lack of indigenous know-how, research and development, production facilities and technology, as improved by Western minds, must again be transferred in the future. In reality, transfer of technology is a misnomer because developing nations lack absorptive capacity.

The two-strata world of technological dependency characterized by a knowledge-based center and a dependent periphery is most apparent in agro-chemicals. Rapid technological change and continued research and development stimulate a demand for the most modern technology thereby giving multinational pesticides manufacturers a significant advantage. The basis of Western superiority is two-fold. Presently, and for the foreseeable future, giant firms will conduct research and development efforts in laboratories located in industrialized nations. From the vantage point of a corporation, this may be perfectly rational because of the financial savings, the diseconomies resulting from local, decentralized research and develop ment operations, and the desire to facilitate an interchange among a critica mass of scientists and technicians who are concentrated in laboratories industries and universities in the United States, Western Europe and Japan To test the feasibility and appropriateness of products for local conditions firms have established local field screening stations in Third World coun tries. This decentralization strategy improves products and processes fo local markets and may enable a firm to tap specialized, local markets

The manufacture of agro-chemicals perpetuates the dependency origi nating in the research and development stage. Industrialized nations pres ently manufacture the active ingredients for agro-chemicals. Alleged economies of scale require large-size plants.[7] The manufacture of activ ingredients is difficult, if not impossible, in most developing nation because of the lack of a substantial sales volume. A need also exists for a established basic chemical infrastructure, including access to technica knowledge and to the numerous intermediary chemical products employ ing a dyestuff and pharmaceutical base. Because of these requisites, onl a few developing nations with sufficient market clout, such as India and Brazil, have successfully forced the installation of plants for manufactur of active agro-chemical ingredients.

Firms are increasingly decentralizing the formulation process, i.e the dilution of concentrates into end products, in Third World countrie because of the need to tailor products to local conditions and a desire t cut transportation costs. But corporations importing concentrates into developing nation negatively impact that nation's balance of payments The foreign exchange drain may lead to a demand for local production o a cutback in other imports. To meet the problem of a multiplicity o brand names and the selection, by a farmer, of the best one to use, develop ing nations may be relegated to pressuring manufacturers to sell pesticide in generic form. But multinational firms will control the supply of activ ingredients and determine the combination and the prices of inputs sol to developing nations.

In contrast to the pesticide situation, the movement to Third Worl self-sufficiency in fertilizer production has been considerable. Fertilize technology, although complex, is well established and not very fast chang ing. Lack of local feedstocks, high capital equipment costs, and a limited internal market requiring external outlets to dispose of a substantial por tion of the output, however, hinders fertilizer plant construction in Thir World countries. Developing nations, which individually have too smal a demand, could participate in regional (or perhaps international) arrange ments for public sector construction and operation of plants. Such co operative ventures would, of course, involve nations with low-cost feed stocks and/or large domestic markets.[8]

In addition to the specter of dependency, the transfer of technological inputs poses significant future ecological and energy questions. Environmental concerns regarding pesticides in the developed world currently include: (1) direct poisoning of humans by affecting the nervous system and modifying metabolic functions; and (2) the persistence of pesticide residues in the soil, causing a possible contamination of food and a reduction in soil fertility and photosynthesis. Pesticides may also poison the natural enemies of pests or reduce the efficiency of these enemies as pest control agents. Fertilizers used in industrial countries flow, through runoff, into bodies of water, spurring the growth of algae and the depletion of oxygen.[9] But at present, the environmental dangers in developing nations are slight. Only relatively small quantities of pesticides and fertilizer are used. Moreover, the heat and heavy rainfall in many Third World nations facilitate the disappearance of residues.

Future worldwide environmental risks may be lessened by development of chemicals that leave fewer residues. Because of the belief that farmers in developing nations may not be willing to pay higher prices for the new compounds, industry has pursued cautiously the development of environmentally safer pesticides. Multinational firms are also working on new application strategies with reasonably selective effects and the creation of pesticides designed to harm targets more specifically, so as to reduce the use of agro-chemicals and the risk of contamination.

But the long-range doubts linger. Although usage rates of fertilizer and pesticides are low in developing countries, tropical insects develop a resistance to pesticides as fast as or faster than predators in temperate climates.[10] Increased resistance to pesticides presents the need to develop alternate methods to supplement agro-chemicals, including cultivating crops genetically resistant to their enemies and possibly using biological weapons against pests.

An agricultural system and a social system should live within a nation's or a region's resources. The spiraling costs of petroleum and high energy inputs may cause the Third World nations, especially those lacking oil reserves, to reevaluate energy-intensive Western agricultural technology. Energy is omnipresent in the food chain. Petroleum powers farm machinery and transport equipment. Fertilizers and pesticides not only use petroleum feedstocks but also are synthesized in energy-demanding processes. Irrigation systems rely on cheap energy. In short, all links in the food production chain, from chemical and tractor factors to the farm, food processors and consumers, utilize energy. This situation raises serious concern:

In the United States we are currently using an equivalent of 80 gallons of gasoline to produce an acre of corn. With fuel shortages and high prices to come, we wonder if many developing nations will be able to afford the technology of U.S. agriculture.[11]

Alternatives to energy-intensive agriculture exist. Agro-chemicals may be applied by a hand sprayer instead of by a tractor and a sprayer. Biological nitrogen fixation may reduce the dependence on synthetic nitrogen fertilizer, yielding significant energy savings. Animal manure and natural pest killers may be used; alternate crops rotated. Multinational pesticide firms have heralded minimum or zero tillage to reduce the energy expended in operating farm machinery. But the lack of deep plowing in minimum or zero tilling gives insects a greater opportunity to thrive on the crop stubble remaining near the surface, thereby necessitating the use of more pesticides (a not unwelcome result from the viewpoint of an agro-chemical maker).

Unable to face the problem of locking developing nations into an outmoded energy-intensive system and hoping to counter the appeal for low tillage, executives of multinational farm implement firms point to what they perceive as a more basic problem—inadequate maintenance and repair services in Third World nations, which reduce the life of tractors.[12] Repair require a considerable time, during which agricultural machinery is unavailable for productive uses. To increase the utilization of tractors in developing nations, Fiat, for example, has evolved the concept of centralized main repair shops and local repair units. Local shops will handle routine maintenance; if more extensive repairs are required, the local shops will substitute a "loaner" part so that a tractor may continue to be used and send the faulty part to the main repair unit. Other possibilities include sending service trucks to do repairs in the field and developing a multibrand repair and maintenance service center handling a variety of makes. These "solutions" only postpone the eventual need for a developing nation to deal with the prospect of spiraling energy costs and the diminished availability of petroleum. Increased dependence on energy-intensive technology may not constitute a rational long-range strategy for energy-poor Third World nations.

To meet the social consequences of capital- and energy-intensive technology, to reduce social inequities and attempt to solve the food-population-job equation, national governments may intervene more directly and supervise the introduction and spread of the modern technology. The distribution strand of government policy also encompasses national elites and international groups focusing on small farmers and appropriate technology. Labor-intensive agriculture, it is hoped, will provide jobs, meet energy costs and lessen technological dependency. The impact of the modern technological and organizational system on human lives must, however, also be faced.

THE RESPONSE OF THIRD WORLD GOVERNMENTS

In the absence of governmental policies opening the access of knowledge, credit and technological inputs to small farmers, tenants and sharecroppers, a restless rural population facing the prospect of mounting unemployment may look for alternative paths to improved living conditions. The fear of political unrest and instability may incline elites and political leaders to focus on distributional questions. A nation's rural sector may be strengthened by increasing prices paid for agricultural products. These price hikes need not be passed on to consumers. With the help of outside loans and grants, a government may undertake an integrated rural development program, including funds for infrastructure improvements and a credit system, opening modern technology to small cultivators. Support may also be provided in extension, marketing, health and education. Finally, a land reform program, including redistribution or limitation on landholdings and/or control of land tenure arrangements and rental terms, may be devised. Through land reform a government can attempt to give more individuals a stake in society and provide incentives to keep people in rural areas.

Redistribution policies comprising a broad economic and social development program, when coupled with an availability of birth control devices, will probably lessen population growth. Large families traditionally served as production units; parents enjoyed the labor of their offspring, who also provided a source of old age insurance. Improved income levels, more equitable income distribution, greater employment opportunities, better education and health conditions, declining infant mortality and the emerging role of women in the work force and society will contribute to a reduction in birth rates. A sound economic base permitting personal and social fulfillment and security may enable people to turn away from regarding children as a form of old age insurance and may create an interest in limiting reproduction.

The distribution thrust affects multinational firms. Governments of Third World countries may emphasize appropriate technology and small farms in an attempt to evolve a better fit of agricultural technology with the way of life of farmers. But Western firms are reluctant to invest funds and engineering time to alter product designs to meet conditions in developing nations. Farm implement makers have transferred standardized capital-intensive products based on an existing technology that is suitable for Western economic and social conditions.[13] From the standpoint of multinational firms this may be rational, as there is no domestic market to build volume and spread the costs of smaller tractors. Each nation wants to locally manufacture its own tractors, using local materials, thereby impeding the development of a large enough market. A prime exception, the seven-horsepower, two-wheeled, walk-behind tractor developed by the Ford Motor Company, never became commercially viable. Three factors, according to Ford spokesmen, caused the demise of the project: credit programs for small farmers failed to function effectively; local content requirements would have priced the tractor out of the reach of the farmers for whom it was intended; and government agencies favored large cooperatives using bigger farm machinery.[14] Lacking support from individual governments of Third World nations and facing competition from Japanese manufacturers of small tractors, multinational firms have manifested a greater interest in marketing tractors and devising other new products originally suited to Western markets.

The concept of alternative technology has evolved to meet the technological juggernaut of multinational corporations. Labor-intensive, small-scale technology would neither be so simple that it is tied to low production nor so complex that it is beyond the capabilities of local people. The new technology, based on idle labor power, would reduce labor in busy seasons by overcoming bottlenecks in harvesting, but not so much as to create more unemployment. In short, appropriate technology would serve people's needs, be resource-conserving and environmentally sound and simple enough to be used and maintained in areas with low income and skill levels.[15]

Appropriate technology may encounter a significant obstacle. The elites of developing nations want the best, the most modern technology, not what is viewed as second-rate. Reasoning that their nation is as good as any Western nation, they must have the latest technology. This line of thinking overlooks the potential negative economic and social consequences of modern agricultural technology. In addition to the cost, the sophistication of technology and the use of manpower, end product suitability must also be considered. For example, with respect to flour milling, a country could use a hammer mill, which involves a lesser capital investment and is labor-intensive but yields a variable quality product with limited shelf life Or a nation could install a high-cost flour mill that yields a substantially higher output of consistent quality, marketable flour.

What may emerge among rational elites is an assessment of the most appropriate technology for each industry in various regions. Several appropriate technology approaches may also be combined to use more labor and raise farm output. For instance, rather than spraying the field as is done in the West, a farmer with a knapsack sprayer could apply herbicides on weeds, which would cause less damaging erosion than tilling Growing lima beans and legumes, which capture nitrogen from the air reduces the need for chemical fertilizers, because the rotting of bean root in the ground enriches the nitrogen in the soil. Growing a variety of crops together can help lessen soil erosion, cut destruction by pests and diseases and increase yields; also, the diversity of multi-cropping offers security against total failure. Soil acidity may be controlled by mulching fields with leaves from certain trees and shrubs instead of using lime.[16]

It is doubtful that multinational firms could actively participate in small village agribusinesses using appropriate technology concepts. At least three possibilities exist. Multinational firms, or more likely individuals within global giants, could, through a catalytic organization, work with national, regional or transnational research centers, United Nations units or nongovernmental bodies to assess the most appropriate forms of technology for a developing nation. Possibly the ICP could seek out smaller firms (or perhaps organize a group of smaller firms) capable of providing socially relevant technology and involve such firms in the technology transfer process. Because the possibility of co-optation exists, the developing world may spurn offers of outside assistance. Multinational firms would seemingly have little to contribute to appropriate technology programs or to an analysis of alternate development paths. The ICP could strive to involve more Third World public or private enterprises in its programs. Local elites, who may be closely linked to global firms, often dominate these Third World multinationals; thus the interests of Third World firms might parallel those of the global corporations. The ICP could establish closer ties to appropriate technology groups to increase the range of expertise available under one umbrella to developing nations. However, because of the antipathy of multinational firms to concepts other than the latest, most modern technology (i.e., their own products), the possibility of fusing the ICP and appropriate technology organizations seems remote. As the ICP Mission to Pakistan concluded, "This type of industry [small agro-industry in rural areas] is unlikely to attract the international investor whose experience and equipment does not usually cater for small unit operation."[17]

THE HUMAN DILEMMA

Even if agricultural output is increased, income better distributed and labor mobilized through intensive use, how will individuals lead their lives and participate in the decision-making process in the agribusiness system? Farm production and processing units may be organized along a variety of lines: individual ownership of land, cooperatives with or without individual land ownership, communal ownership and operation, or state-owned farms or collectives. In addition to the best means of providing access to financial and production inputs, market outlets and technical knowledge, a number of difficult questions must be faced: the ownership of the means of production, the efficiency of units of various sizes, the extent of government intervention in farm management, the choice of individual or social incentives, and the problem of the elites and hierarchical patterns. These questions relate to the institutions for production of agricultural inputs and the marketing or produce. A nation must also decide whether it should export agricultural crops to pay for imports of food, capital goods and military hardware or rather, strive for self-sufficiency in basic foodstuffs despite possible diseconomies attendant on such a policy.

Self-sufficiency to reduce food imports, gain independence from foreign breadbaskets and lessen dependency on the vagaries of world food markets and the risk of high prices or unattainable supplies is linked to mobilizing the populace—small farmers—to increase output, create employment in rural areas and improve the standard of living for rural citizens. The small farmer strategy is based on the rationale that the output per acre is higher because of more intensive labor utilization on small farms than on large farms.[18] Increased productivity and production on small farms, in turn, rest on financial support (the availability of infrastructure, credit and inputs when and where needed and at reasonable prices), organizational guidance (extension personnel to demonstrate the proper mix of inputs and convince farmers of the profitability of using technological inputs) and an outlet that yields farmers a reasonable price for their harvest.

From the standpoint of global firms, involving small cultivators in modern agricultural production centers on linking a nucleus estate with small growers. Satellite farming will provide a channel to bring inputs to small farmers, including technology, credit and supervisory services, and an outlet for processing and marketing their crops. In commenting on the use of satellite farming to strengthen family farms in developing nations, Orville Freeman, former US secretary of agriculture and currently president of Business International Corporation, stated, "This could be a kind of contract farming, which has come to be almost universal in producing fruits, vegetables and exotic agricultural commodities."[19]

But the satellite concept and contract farming have proved a mixed blessing in the Third World. Grouping smaller farmers around a nucleus estate to date, has been used for export crops, such as sugar. A prototype smallholder scheme involving a nucleus estate with processing facilities is the Mumias project in Kenya. The government of Kenya and the Commonwealth Development Corporation have jointly financed the Mumia Outgrowers Co. Ltd. to represent the small farmers in dealing with the

Mumias Sugar Co. and to provide technical and financial assistance.[20] But the linking of Third World nations to the industrialized world perpetuates dependency. Although the exportation of luxury items, such as fruits and flowers, may generate needed foreign exchange, provide some jobs and lessen a nation's reliance on one or two traditional agricultural exports, an export-oriented policy reduces the land, people and financial resources capable of meeting a nation's basic food needs. Fewer local food resources may go to feed local people.

A contract system may not benefit small farmers. Through production contracts a processor can link input suppliers (which may include a vertically integrated processor), growers, wholesalers and retailers. A farmer agrees to grow and harvest specified crops for delivery to a processor. In return for surrendering some management prerogatives, a grower receives a guaranteed market, an assured return on labor and investment and some price stability. The processor, as contractor, sets crop and agricultural planning specifications, such as delivery dates, thereby modernizing farm management, and judges whether the growers have achieved produce specifications. Requirements that crops be grown to the standards of multinational firms enables such crops to be sold in export markets. Processors generally assist and supervise farmers in using up-to-date technological inputs. Processors may also provide financing for growers.[21]

The negatives emanate from the superior bargaining position of the processors. In one of the few studies of the economic and social impact of contract farming, the US Department of Agriculture's Packers and Stockyard Administration concluded that the earnings of contract broiler chicken growers in the southern United States did not keep pace with those of broiler growers in other areas or for all United States farmers. The study discovered less desirable practices on the part of vertically integrated contracting firms with their own hatchery, feed mill and processing units, including a failure to supply growers with adequate information during delivery or at settlement time and charging "inflated prices" for feed and chicks, which worked against growers when they bargained for new contracts.[22] The lack of bargaining power on the part of small farmers led one expert to conclude that contract farming as practiced in the United States "would not appear too practical for small farmers in other nations because of economic exploitation by larger, well-financed and knowledgeable entrepreneurs."[23]

A nation may organize (or encourage farmers to organize) cooperatives for the purpose of bargaining and signing contracts, thereby attempting to countervail the power of multinational firms. Government-sponsored cooperatives, with the active support of rural elites, probably will not prove viable. Cooperatives, which require sufficient infrastructure, a sound political and economic base and the commitment of individual members to work together, are especially vulnerable to capture by local elites and large landlords when organized by outside agencies or governmental units.

The involvement of a nation's lower income and status sectors in a development process is limited by a range of factors: economic and political power, social structures and attitudes, and administrative capabilities. Massive redistribution of wealth, status and power, although idealistically desirable, will probably founder if the reforms threaten a nation's economic, social or political status quo. The governmental, agricultural, and business elites of a country may collaborate with multinational firms to subvert policies aimed at redistribution and focusing on the small farmer. Concessions may be given only grudgingly to prevent mass uprisings. A policy of reducing inequalities in income distribution may only further increase the demand for food, especially if the population spiral does not abate.

A democratic, decentralized society focusing on labor-intensive small-scale agriculture and industry using appropriate technology, with a cooperatively organized participatory management system, encounters the problem of keeping people in rural areas. Propelled by advances in transportation and communication, the restlessness in the countryside may not lessen the flood of the mass urban migration. Future generations may resist being tied to the land and the brutal, physically demanding drudgery of farming, a low status, seasonal occupation. "The noble peasant is a rich man's delusion. People infected with rising expectations prefer almost anything to farming, and history equates progress with a decline, not a rise, in agricultural employment."[24]

If the demise of the rural sector as a source of jobs materializes, alternative policies can only dimly be perceived. The continuing lack of jobs and the urban migration of untrained, unemployable individuals erode the social fabric of a society. But the problem of unemployment and underemployment may be met by individuals involved in the production process. Massive public works programs and industrial projects using labor-intensive methods could provide employment. Individuals with a stake in society, through individual or social incentives, might be more interested in participating in public works projects. Decentralized industrial operations could create jobs for the people outside a few big cities. Large farms using capital-intensive technology could produce most of a nation's agricultural requirements. New energy sources, such as solar and wind power, might assist in laying the basis for the more diversified, decentralized society.

But will nations have the capital to generate alternative forms of employment? In addition to significant increases in outside assistance, world tax system might provide funds for labor-intensive projects and widespread social services and cultural amenities. Of course, even if financing were available, the requisite organizational capacity might not be present. As a last resort, state intervention, in the form of compulsory population control and settlement policies, might be necessary.

As nations face the prospect of emerging from subsistence agriculture, governments must assess whether they wish a Western consumer society (or a pale imitation thereof) to flourish in their nation. Multinational firms hope Third World nations will shift from subsistence farming to a money economy based on commercial agriculture and modern technology. The business executive perceives that improved conditions in the Third World will turn the citizens of developing countries into better consumers as more individuals join a money economy system. Orville Freeman noted, "These small cultivators could, given the requisite help, transform their own misery into relative well-being; they could create in that process a vast new market for industry and services, thus stimulating broad-based economic development. . . ."[25] A desire to increase sales and profits would lead business to stimulate consumer demand. Producers would seek to create wants by promoting the consumption of superfluous goods. Advertising, especially on television, would be used to spur consumption, thereby diverting income from basic nutritional items.

It is easy to say people should lead less gadget-ridden lives or that individuals should not toil merely to buy new energy-using automobiles every three years; but how will nations gravitate to commercial agriculture, yet avoid a consumer society? Resource scarcities might lead governments to restrict consumption. Taxes could be imposed on goods considered socially undesirable. Through either voluntary or government regulation of consumption, it might be possible to develop a subsistence standard including a minimum level of food, clothing, housing and health care for all individuals in a country.

If individuals turn away from consumption, whether voluntarily or by government fiat, smaller organizations could meet the diminished industrial production requirements. Smaller economic and political communities, a reduction in the size of urban centers and a decentralization of industry and administration could facilitate a greater degree of individual participation in all areas of life. These more humane communities would meet human needs in a variety of ways. Smaller economic units would enable workers to be more informed and to assume responsibility for the social consequences of an enterprise. Workers could participate in a wide range of managerial decisions. A return to craftsmanship in an individual's daily toil might also result, as the motivation for work would become intrinsic.

The development of these renewable alternate energy sources, such as solar and wind power, can open possibilities for smaller, decentralized more comprehensive economic and political units. Energy and technology smaller in scale, could form the bases for new communities. People could regain power over aspects of everyday life, and develop a realization and sense of community.

The benefits to be derived from decentralization must, however, be assessed. The repeated discussion of "small" issues may not result in creative and efficient process. The interest and span of attention of individuals is likely to lessen as the novelty of participation decreases. Inability to make decisions, particularly on distribution questions, may destroy participatory structures or at least create obstacles to the achievement of speedy decisions. In a non-homogeneous community, participation may highlight differences and increase conflict. Speculators and traders who seek personal gain by operating in the interstices of the economic and political system, may flourish. Finally, within each community or region, an elite group may perpetuate itself. The "Iron Law of Oligarchy" rests on the need to develop authority in large groups, creating a gulf between the leaders and the masses. Elitist theorists posit that every institution develops an oligarchy because the rank-and-file, through incompetence and apathy, cannot and do not desire involvement in decision-making. From the mass springs a minority which raises itself to the rank of a governing class that is elitist by virtue of education, cultural superiority, and lust for power. The end result is that a minority of leaders dominate a majority of directed people, in a condition of tutelage.

The response to this attack turns on a new value orientation. Individuals looking to both self-fulfillment and a concern for others may create and operate institutions so as to meet the challenge of a new social era. Instead of a narcissistic vision of personal growth, a consensus may develop that individual development can only occur within a social context. Diffusing economic, political and social power through participation may be accompanied by a focus on distributional questions, specifically a limitation of income levels and wealth holdings.

No definitive or final solution exists to the range of problems that have been considered in this book. An urgent need exists to explore the possibilities for a reorientation of institutions and a community orientation to foster a political-economic system which may more adequately serve both present and long-range human needs, and the full development of individuals who are not alienated, status-minded, or subordinated to authority. This book has sought to encourage a rethinking of such difficult social questions, specifically a transnational social order based on multinational corporations.

CHAPTER 1: THE ECONOMIC SIGNIFICANCE OF M N Cs

1. Richard J. Barber, *The American Corporation: Its Power, Its Money, Its Politics* (New York: Dutton, 1970), p. 264; Robert L. Heilbroner, "The Multinational Corporation and the Nation-State," *New York Review of Books* 16 (11 February 1971): 24.

2. Judd Polk, "American Labor and the U.S. Multinational Enterprise in an Emerging World Economy," in *American Labor and the Multinational Corporation,* ed. Duane Kujawa, with a foreword by Robert G. Hawkins (New York: Praeger, 1973), p. 280.

3. United Nations, Department of Economic and Social Affairs, *Multinational Corporations in World Development* (ST/ECA/190), 1973), p. 13.

4. Ibid., pp. 13–14.

5. Richard J. Barnet and Ronald E. Müller, *Global Reach: The Power of the Multinational Corporations* (New York: Simon & Schuster, 1974).

6. U.N., Department of Economic and Social Affairs, *Multinational Corporations,* p. 7.

7. Mira Wilkins, *The Maturing of Multinational Enterprise: American Business Abroad from 1914 to 1970* (Cambridge: Harvard University Press, 1974), p. 329, Table XIII; "U.S. Firms Increase Direct Investment in Foreign Affiliates," *Wall Street Journal,* 26 August 1976, p. 7; Robert L. Heilbroner, "None of Your Business," *New York Review of Books* 22 (20 March 1975): 6.

8. U. S. Department of Commerce, Bureau of International Commerce, *The Multinational Corporation: Studies on U.S. Foreign Investment* 1 (March 1972): 12; U.S. Congress, Senate, Committee on Finance, *The Implications of Multinational Firms for World Trade and Investment and for U.S. Trade and Labor,* by United States Tariff Commission, T. C. Pubn. 537 (Washington, D.C., 1973), 1: 104–105.

9. U.N., Department of Economic and Social Affairs, *Multinational Corporations,* pp. 8–9, 1968–1969 figures, and tables 11 and 12, pp. 147–148.

10. Ibid.; see J. N. Freidlan and L. A. Lupo, "U.S. Direct Investment Abroad in 1973," *Survey of Current Business* 54 (August 1974) pt. 2, pp. 16–29, tables 9–10.

11. U.S. Department of Commerce, *Multinational Corporations: Studies,* 1 1972); 6–7.

12. Senate, Committee on Finance, *Implications of Multinational Firms,* 2: 96–98,

101–103; Raymond Vernon, *Sovereignty at Bay: The Multinational Spread of U*
Enterprises (New York: Basic Books, 1971), p. 62; United Nations, Department
Economic and Social Affairs, *The Impact of Multinational Corporations on Develo*
ment and on International Relations (E/5500/Rev./ST/ESA/6), 1974, p. 133, sta
ment of J. Irwin Miller.

13.   Richard B. DuBoff, "Communications: Transferring Wealth from Und
developed to Developed Countries Via Direct Foreign Investment: Commen
Southern Economic Journal 38 (July 1971): 119.

14.   C. Fred Bergsten, "The Threat from the Third World," *Foreign Policy* Summ
1973, p. 113; see Peter F. Drucker, "Multinationals and Developing Countri
Myths and Realities," *Foreign Affairs* 53 (October 1974): 121, for a view t
developing nations are not important as sales or profit sources.

15.   Ned G. Howenstine, "Property, Plant and Equipment Expenditures by Majori
Owned Foreign Affiliates of U.S. Companies," *Survey of Current Business* 55 (S
tember 1975): 29.

16.   Wilkins, *Maturing of Multinational Enterprise*, p. 375; Abdul A. Said a
Luis R. Simmons, "The Politics of Transition," in *The New Sovereigns: Multinatio*
Corporations as World Powers, Abdul A. Said and Luis R. Simmons, ed. (Englewo
Cliffs, N.J.: Prentice-Hall, 1975), p. 12, Table 1.

17.   Barnet and Müller, *Global Reach*, pp. 445–446; U.S. Congress, Senate, Co
mittee on Finance, *The Multinational Corporation and the World Economy*, Co
mittee Print (Washington, D.C.: Government Printing Office, 1973), pp. 14–1
Table 3; see "U.S. Companies that Made Most of Their Money Abroad," *Fortune*
(November 1974): 175, for a list of twenty-five firms from the *Fortune* F
hundred industrial corporations which earned more than 50% of their net pro
overseas in 1973.

18.   "Banking: Foreign Operations: The Swinging Days are Over Overseas," *Bu*
ness Week no. 2377 (21 April 1975): 99.

19.   U.N. Department of Economic and Social Affairs, *Multinational Corporatio*
pp. 8, 10–12, 46, Table 10; Charles Levinson, *Capital, Inflation, and the Mu*
nationals (London: Allen and Unwin, 1971), pp. 76–92; International Labour Offi
Multinational Enterprise and Social Policy (Geneva: International Labour Offi
1973), pp. 7–8.

20.   U.N., Department of Economic and Social Affairs, *Multinational Corpo*
tions, pp. 10–12, 151, table 15; Said and Simmons, "Politics of Transition," p. 2
Yoshi Tsurumi, "Japanese Multinational Firms," *Journal of World Trade Law*
(January–February 1973), p. 74; Neil A. Martin, "Yen for a Change: Soaring F
Costs Spur Japanese to Diversity," *Barron's,* 11 August 1975, p. 24.

21.   See Brendan Jones, "Issue and Debate: Should U.S. Curb Investing by F
eigners?" *New York Times,* 7 April 1975, p. 49; Sanford Rose, "The Misguid
Furor about Investments from Abroad," *Fortune* 91 (May 1975): 175; Charles
Stabler, "Infusion Confusion: Foreign Capital, a Key to Rise of Early U.S., N
Stirs Misgivings," *Wall Street Journal,* 5 March 1975, p. 1.

22.   Felix G. Rohatyn, "Getting Foreign Cash," *New York Times,* 6 April 19
p. 19.

23.   "West Germany is Studying Law to Curb Foreign Take-Overs," *New Yo*
Times, 1 April 1975, p. 53.

24.   Levinson, *Capital,* pp. 113–119; Thomas A. Wolf, *East-West Economic Re*
tion and the Multinational Corporation, Occasional Paper no. 5 (Washington, D.
Center for Multinational Studies, 1973), pp. 51–52.

25.   "Direct U.S. Investment by Foreigners Rose in 1975," *Wall Street Journal,*
August 1976, p. 4; "Why Foreign Companies are Betting on the U.S.," *Busin*
Week no. 2427 (12 April 1976): 50–51; Steven Rattner, "Foreign Industries I
panding in U.S.: Investments from Overseas are Seen Continuing at Increased Rate
New York Times, 26 July 1976, p. 33; "The New Immigration," *Forbes* 116 (1 N
vember 1975): 29, 32–33; Robert B. Leftwick, "Foreign Direct Investment in t
United States in 1973," *Survey of Current Business* 54 (August 1974) pt. 2, p.

CHAPTER 2: THE CONCEPT OF THE MULTINATIONAL BUSINESS ENTERPRISE

1.   Alfred D. Chandler, *Strategy and Structure: Chapters in the History of the Industrial Enterprise* (Cambridge: M.I.T. Press, 1962); Alfred D. Chandler and Fritz Redlich, "Recent Developments in American Business Administration and their Conceptualization," *Business History Review* 35 (Spring 1961): 103.

2.   Stephen Hymer, "The Multinational Corporation and the Law of Uneven Development," in *Economics and World Order from the 1970's to 1990's*, ed. Jagdish N. Bhagiwati (New York: MacMillan, 1972), pp. 117–121; Stephen Hymer, "The Efficiency (Contradictions) of Multinational Corporations," *American Economic Review* 60 (June 1970): 441; John Fayerweather, "The Internationalization of Business," *The Annals of the American Academy of Political and Social Science* 403 (September 1972): 4–5.

3.   "Special Report: Multinational Companies," *Business Week* no. 1755 (20 April 1963): 80.

4.   Michael Z. Brooke and H. Lee Remmers, *The Strategy of the Multinational Enterprise: Organization and Finance* (New York: American Elsevier, 1970), p. 234; Stephen Guisenger, "The Rise of the Multinational Corporation and U.S. Trade Policy," *Social Science Quarterly* 54 (December 1973): 555–557; Christopher Tugendhat, *The Multinationals* (London: Eyre and Spottiswoode, 1971), ch. 8; Sanford Rose, "The Rewarding Strategies of Multinationalism," *Fortune* 78 (15 September 1968): 101.

5.   United Nations, Department of Economic and Social Affairs, *The Impact of Multinational Corporations on Development and on International Relations* (E/5500/Rev./ST/ESA/6), 1974, p. 154, statement of Hans Schaffner.

6.   Sidney M. Robbins and Robert B. Stobaugh, *Money in the Multinational Enterprise: A Study of Financial Policy* (New York: Basic Books, 1973), pp. 26–27, 60–62.

7.   Raymond Vernon, *Sovereignty at Bay: The Multinational Spread of U.S. Enterprises* (New York: Basic Books, 1971), p. 108.

8.   United Nations, Department of Economic and Social Affairs, *Multinational Corporations in World Development* (ST/ECA/190), 1973, pp. 33–34; Brooke and Remmers, *Strategy of Multinational Enterprise*, ch. 3–4; Jack N. Behrman, *Some Patterns in the Rise of Multinational Enterprise* (Chapel Hill: University of North Carolina Press, 1969), pp. 74–82.

9.   Robbins and Stobaugh, *Money in the Multinational Enterprise*, pp. 49–74.

10.   Robert J. Alsegg, *Control Relationships Between American Corporations and Their European Subsidiaries* (New York: American Management Association, 1971), pp. 88–93.

11.   A. E. Safarian, *Foreign Ownership of Canadian Industry* (Toronto: McGraw-Hill of Canada, 1966), pp. 88–93.

12.   Behrman, *Some Patterns*, pp. 13–14.

13.   Tom Houston, "Dimensions of U.K. Transnational Business," ed. S. Prakash Sethi and Richard H. Holton, *Management of the Multinationals: Policies, Operations, and Research* (New York: The Free Press, 1974), pp. 47–74.

CHAPTER 3: THE RATIONALE FOR FOREIGN DIRECT INVESTMENT

1.   International Labour Office, *Multinational Enterprise and Social Policy* (Geneva: International Labour Office, 1973).

2.   Burton Teague, "Multinational Corporations: Profiles and Prospects," *Conference Board Record* 8 (September 1971): 23.

3.   Stephen Hymer and Robert Rowthorn, "Multinational Corporations and International Oligopoly: The Non-American Challenge," in *The International Corporation: A Symposium*, ed. Charles P. Kindleberger, (Cambridge: M.I.T. Press, 1970), pp. 57–

91; Jack N. Behrman, *Some Patterns in the Rise of Multinational Enterprise* (Cha
Hill: University of North Carolina Press, 1969).

4.   Mira Wilkins, *The Maturing of Multinational Enterprise: American Busin
Abroad from 1914 to 1970* (Cambridge: Harvard University Press, 1974); Willi
Gruber, Dileep Nehta, and Raymond Vernon, "The R & D Factor in Internatio
Trade and International Investment of the U.S. Industries," *Journal of Politi
Economy* 75 (February 1967): pp. 20-37.

5.   Richard E. Caves, "International Corporations: The Industrial Economics
Foreign Investment," *Economica* 38 (new series, February 1971): 8.

6.   Raymond Vernon, "Competition Policy Toward Multinational Corporation
American Economic Review 64 (May 1974): 278.

7.   Herbert I. Schiller, "Madison Avenue Imperialism," *Transaction* 52 (Mar
April 1971): 52-58; Stuart W. Robinson, *Multinational Banking: A Study of Cerr
Legal and Financial Aspects of the Postwar Operations of the U.S. Branch Bank
Western Europe* (Leiden: A. W. Sijthoff, 1972); Julien-Pierre Koszul, "Ameri
Banks in Europe," in *The International Corporation: A Symposium,* ed. Charle:
Kindleberger (Cambridge: M.I.T. Press, 1970), pp. 275-279; Martin Meyer, 1
Bankers (New York: Weybright and Talley, 1974), pp. 457-458; Jeremy Ma
"The First Real International Bankers," *Fortune* 76 (December 1967): 143; R
Wolff, "The Foreign Expansion of U.S. Banks," *Monthly Review: An Independ
Socialist Magazine* 23 (May 1971): 17.

8.   "Bank Vulnerability to Oil Riches Eyed: Senate Panel is Assessing Imp
of Shift in Wealth to Producers of Petroleum on U.S. Financing," *New York Tim
26 August 1975, pp. 39.

9.   Michael von Clemm, "The Rise of Consortium Banking," *Harvard Busir
Review* 49 (May-June 1971): 125; Bowen Northrup, "Working Together: C
sortiums of Banks Multiply in Europe; Some U.S. Banks Join, Others Shy Awa
Wall Street Journal, 25 May 1973, pp. 28; Charles Levinson, *Capital Inflations
the Multinationals* (London: Allen and Unwin, 1971), pp. 102-103.

10. George W. Mitchell, "How the Fed Sees Multinational Bank Regulatio
The Banker 124 (July 1974): 759; "Finance: The Edge is Off the Edge Act Bank
Business Week no. 2375 (7 April 1975): 42.

11. Edward P. Foldessy, "Branching Out: U.S. Banks Find Money in Off
Abroad: Foreign Profit Gains Outpace Home Results," *Wall Street Journal,*
May 1972, pp. 22; Harry Magdoff, *The Age of Imperialism* (New York: Mont
Review Press, 1969), pp. 72-80.

12. David T. Cook, "U.S. Banking Abroad: Cautious Optimism: Emphasis Sh
from Growth to Profitability as Federal Scrutiny of Foreign Operations Increase
Christian Science Monitor, 30 April 1976, pp. 11; "Finance: U.S. Banks Cool T
Go-Go Style Abroad," *Business Week* no. 2398 (15 September 1975): 74; "Ba
ing: Foreign Operations: The Swinging Days are Over Overseas," *Business We
no. 2377 (21 April 1975): 99.

13. Raymond Vernon, *Sovereignty at Bay: The Multinational Spread in U
Enterprise* (New York: Basic Books, 1971), p. 66.

14. Raymond Vernon, "International Investment and International Trade in
Product Cycle," *Quarterly Journal of Economics* 80 (May 1966): 196; Verr
Sovereignty at Bay, pp. 65-77; Louis T. Wells, "International Trade: The Prod
Life Cycle Approach," in *The Product Life Cycle and International Trade,*
Louis T. Wells, (Cambridge: Harvard University Press, 1972), pp. 11-15.

15. John K. Galbraith, *Economics and the Public Purpose* (Boston: Hough
Mifflin, 1973); Richard D. Robinson, "The Developing Countries, Developm
and the Multinational Corporation," *The Annals of the American Academy
Political and Social Science* 403 (September 1972): 71; Vernon, *Sovereignty
Bay,* p. 117.

16. Vernon, *Sovereignty at Bay,* p. 117.

17. U.S. Congress, Senate, Committee on Labor and Public Welfare, *The M
national Corporation and the National Interest,* by Robert Gilpin, Committee P

(Washington, D.C.: Government Printing Office, 1973); U.S. Congress, Senate, Committee on Finance, *The Implications of Multinational Firms for World Trade and Investment and for U.S. Trade and Labor,* by United States Tarriff Commission, T.C. Pubn. 537 (Washington, D.C.; 1973) 2: 119–122; Michael Z. Brooke and H. Lee Remmers, *The Strategy of the Multinational Enterprise: Organization and Finance* (New York: American Elsevier, 1970), p. 237; "The World Economy: Tension with Host Nations: New Era for Multinationals," *Business Week* no. 2338 (6 July 1974): 73–74.

18.   Judd Polk, Irene W. Meister, and Lawrence A. Veit, *U.S. Production Abroad and the Balance of Payments: A Survey of Corporate Investment Experience* (New York: National Industrial Conference Board, 1966), pp. 42, 59–61; Wilkins, *The Maturing of Multinational Enterprise,* pp. 324, 376–377, 379; Senate, Committee on Finance, *Implications of Multinational Firms* 2: 111–113; Endel J. Kolde, *The Multinational Company: Behavioral and Managerial Analysis* (Lexington, Mass.: Lexington Books, 1974); pp. 31–33; Sanford Rose, "The Rewarding Strategies of Multinationalism," *Fortune* 78 (15 September 1968): 101.

19.   Chamber of Commerce of the United States, *United States Multinational Enterprise: Report on a Multinational Enterprise,* with a preface by Arch N. Booth (Washington, D.C.: Chamber of Commerce, 1972), pp. 23, 54.

20.   U.S. Congress, Senate, Committee on Finance, *Multinational Corporations, A Compendium of Papers Submitted to the Subcommittee on International Trade,* Committee Print (Washington, D.C.: Government Printing Office, 1973), p. 73.

21.   Kolde, *The Multinational Company,* pp. 26–29.

22.   Senate, Committee on Finance, *Implications on Multinational Firms,* 2: 108–110; Wilkins, *Maturing of Multinational Enterprise,* pp. 304–308, 324, 387, 391; Raymond Vernon, "Foreign Enterprises and Developing Nations in Raw Materials Industries," *American Economic Review* 60 (May 1970): 122; Gabriel Kolko, *The Roots of American Foreign Policy: An Analysis of Power and Purpose* (Boston: Beacon Press, 1969), pp. 50–58, 84–85; Heather Dean, "Scarce Resources: The Dynamic of American Imperialism," in *Readings in U.S. Imperialism,* ed. K. T. Fann and Donald C. Hodges (Boston: P. Sargent, Extending Horizons Book, 1971), p. 139.

23.   Senate, Committee on Finance, *Multinational Corporations,* p. 733.

24.   Kolko, *Roots of American Foreign Policy,* p. 53.

25.   Magdoff, *Age of Imperialism,* p. 46.

26.   See Council on International Economic Policy, *Special Report: Critical Raw Materials* (Washington, D.C.: U.S. Government Printing Office, 1974), pp. 4–5, 24; Magdoff, *Age of Imperialism,* pp. 45–54; Kolko, *Roots of American Foreign Policy,* ch. 3, for analyses of the dependence of the American economy on the importation of raw materials.

27.   Vernon, *Sovereignty at Bay,* pp. 30, 34, 75; Brooke and Remmers, *The Strategy of Multinational Enterprise,* pp. 232–233; Caves, "International Corporations," pp. 10–11.

28.   Wilkins, *Maturing of Multinational Enterprise,* pp. 285–289, 331–341; Marina von Neuman Whitman, *Government Risk-Sharing in Foreign Investment* (Princeton, N.J.: Princeton University Press, 1965); see Magdoff, *Age of Imperialism,* ch. 4, for an analysis of the intertwining of U.S. business and American foreign aid.

29.   U.S. Congress, House, Committee on Ways and Means, *General Tax Reform (Testimony from Administration and Public Witnesses),* 93rd Cong., 1st sess., 1973, pt. 12, p. 4920.

30.   Senate, Committee on Finance, *Multinational Corporations,* pp. 758–759; U.S. Department of Commerce, Bureau of International Commerce, *The Multinational Corporation: Studies on U.S. Foreign Investment,* (March 1972) 1:15–16; Brooke and Remmers, *Strategy of Multinational Enterprise,* 230–234, 227–229, table 9.1.

31.   Senate, Committee on Finance, *Implications of Multinational Firms* 2: 114;

Christopher Tugendgart, *The Multinationals* (London: Eyre and Spottiswoode, 1971), pp. 175, 178.

32.   Senate, Committee on Finance, *Implications of Multinational Firms* 2: 122–125; Behrman, *Some Patterns*, pp. 17–20; Lawrence B. Krause, *European Economic Integration and the United States* (Washington, D.C.: Brookings Institution, 1968), ch. 4.

33.   Paul Streeten, "Costs and Benefits of Multinational Enterprises in Less-Developed Countries," in *The Multinational Enterprise*, ed. John H. Dunning, (London: Allen and Unwin, 1971), p. 247, citing a study by the Institute of Development Studies and Queen Elizabeth House; Yair Aharoni, *The Foreign Investment Decision Process* (Boston: Harvard University Press, 1966), p. 171.

34.   "Belgium: A Multinational Bleat Over 5% Tax," *Business Week* no. 2400 (29 September 1975): 38.

35.   Dale R. Weigel, "Multinational Approaches to Multinational Corporations," *Finance and Development* 11 (September 1974): 42.

36.   Harold O. Walker, "Border Industries with a Mexican Accent," *Columbia Journal of World Business* 4 (January–February 1969): 25–32.

37.   Gyorgy Adam, "Some Implications and Concomitants of Worldwide Sourcing," *Acta Oeconomica* 8 (1972): 309–322; Gyorgy Adam, "New Trends in International Business: Worldwide Sourcing and Dedomiciling," *Acta Oeconomica* 7 (1971) 349–366; James Leontiades, "International Sourcing in the LDSs," *Columbia Journal of World Business* 6 (November–December 1971) 19–26; United Nations, Department of Economic and Social Affairs, *Multinational Corporations in World Development* (ST/ECA/190), 1973; G. K. Helleiner, "Manufactured Exports from Less Developed Countries and Multinational Firms," *The Economic Journal* 83 (March 1973): 21–47.

38.   U.S. Congress, Joint Economic Committee, *A Foreign Economic Policy for the 1970's*, pt. 4, 91st Cong., 2d sess., 1970, pp. 813–816, statement by Paul Jennings.

39.   U.S. Congress, Senate, Committee of Finance, *The Multinational Corporation and the World Economy*, Committee Print (Washington, D.C.: Government Printing Office, 1973), p. 5.

40.   U.S. Congress, Senate, Committee on Finance, Subcommittee on International Trade, 93d Congress, 1st Session, 1973, p. 105, statement by Donald M. Kendall.

41.   Wilkins, *Maturing of Multinational Enterprise*, p. 414.

42.   See "Big Money Shifts to Some Developing Countries," *Business Week* no. 2394 (18 August 1975), 118, for an analysis of the continued shift of manufacturing investment to developing countries. But compare George H. Hildebrand, "Problems and Policies Affecting Labor's Interests," *American Economic Review* 64 (May 1974): 284–287; James E. McLinden, "World Outlook for Electronics, *Columbia Journal of World Business* 7 (May–June 1972): 65–71.

43.   Aharoni, *Foreign Investment Decision Process*, pp. 58–61, 132–138.

44.   Vladimir I. Lenin, *Imperialism: The Highest Stage of Capitalism, A Popular Outline* (New York: International Publishers, 1939), pp. 107–108.

45.   John A. Hobson, *Imperialism: A Study*, with an introduction by Philip Siegman (Ann Arbor: University of Michigan Press, 1965), pp. 71–93.

46.   Paul A. Baran and Paul M. Sweezy, *Monopoly Capital: An Essay on the American Economic and Social Order* (New York: Monthly Review Press, 1966), pp. 71–77, 104–111; "surplus" for Baran and Sweezy is apparently the difference between what a society produces and the costs of producing it.

47.   Harold Wincott, "Labour's Policies: Strange Meeting of Minds," (London Financial Times, 23 June 1964, n.p., quoted in Brooke and Remmers, *Strategy Multinational Enterprise*, p. 234; see Senate, Committee on Finance, *Implications of Multinational Firms* 2:119, which notes that mature American corporations may have surplus funds and management capability and foresees only marginal domestic opportunities.

48.   U.S. Department of Commerce, Office of Foreign Direct Investments, *Foreign Affiliate Financial Survey, 1966-1969,* cited in Sidney M. Robbins and Robert B. Stobaugh, *Money in the Multinational Enterprise: A Study of Financial Policy* (New York: Basic Books, 1973), pp. 71-72.

49.   Magdoff, *Age of Imperialism,* pp. 154-155; Senate, Committee on Finance, *Multinational Corporations,* pp. 555, 764; Robbins and Stobaugh, *Money in Multinational Enterprise,* pp. 49-74; Vernon, *Sovereignty at Bay,* pp. 131-133.

50.   Eli Schwartz and J. Richard Aronson, "Communications: The Corporate Sector: A Net Exporter of Funds," *Southern Economic Journal* 33 (October 1966): 252-257.

51.   Robert Stobaugh, "Financing Foreign Subsidiaries of U.S.-controlled Multinational Enterprises," *Journal of International Business Studies,* Summer 1970, p. 43.

52.   Robbins and Stobaugh, *Money in Multinational Enterprise,* pp. 63-66; Endel J. Kolde, *The Multinational Corporation: Behavioral and Mangerial Analysis* (Lexington, Mass: Lexington Books, 1974), pp. 54-56; Wilkins, *Maturing of Multinational Enterprise,* pp. 335-336.

CHAPTER 4: ANALYSIS OF THE ECONOMIC CONSEQUENCES OF M N Cs

1.   Ronald Müller, "A Qualifying and Dissenting View of the Multinational Corporation," in *Global Companies: The Political Economy of World Business,* ed. George W. Ball, (Englewood Cliffs, N.J.: Prentice-Hall, 1975) pp. 21-41; Charles Levinson, *Capital, Inflation and the Multinationals* (London: Allen and Unwin, 1971), ch. 8.

2.   Lawrence Krause, "Private International Finance," in *Transnational Relations and World Politics,* ed. Robert O. Keohane and Joseph S. Nye, Jr., (Cambridge, Mass.: Harvard University Press, 1973), pp. 173-190; Jane S. Little, *Eurodollars: The Money-Market Gypsies* (New York: Harper & Row, 1975), p. 6.

3.   Joseph S. Nye, Jr., "Multinational Corporations in World Politics," *Foreign Affairs* 53 (October 1974): 160-161.

4.   Abdul A. Said and Luiz R. Simmons, "The Politics of Transition," *The New Sovereigns: Multinational Corporations as World Powers* (Englewood Cliffs, N.J.: Prentice-Hall, 1975), p. 11.

5.   United Nations, Department of Economic and Social Affairs, *Multinational Corporations in World Development* (ST/ECA/190), 1973, p. 65.

6.   U.S. Congress, Senate, Committee on Finance, *Implications of Multinational Firms for World Trade and Investment and for U.S. Trade and Labor,* by United States Tariff Commission, T.C. Pubn. 537 (Washington, D.C.: 1973), 2: 539.

7.   Ibid.

8.   Benjamin Klein, *The Role of U.S. Multinational Corporations in Recent Exchange Crises* (Washington, D.C.: Center for Multinational Studies, 1974), p. 3.

9.   United Nations Department of Economic and Social Affairs, *Multinational Corporations,* p. 62.

10.   United Nations, Department of Economic and Social Affairs, *Summary of Hearings Before the Group of Eminent Persons to Study the Impact of Multinational Corporations on Development and on International Relations* (ST/ESA/15, 1974), pp. 12-15; Klein, *Role of U.S. Multinational Corporations,* p. 14.

11.   United Nations, Department of Economic and Social Affairs, *Summary of Hearings,* pp. 12-15.

12.   U.S. Congress, Senate, Committee on Finance, *Multinational Corporations: Hearings before the Subcommittee on International Trade,* 93d Cong. 1st sess., 1973, p. 18.

13.   Charles N. Stabler, "Keystone of New IMF Accord Presenting Broad Changes in Language, Philosophy," *Wall Street Journal,* 12 January 1976, p. 14.

14.   Ann Crittenden, "Floating Rates Burden Business: Deals Abroad are Harder Under Current Exchange System, Survey Finds," *New York Times,* 13 December 1975, p. 37.

15.   Peggy B. Musgrave, *United States Taxation of Foreign Investment Income* (Cambridge: Harvard University Press, 1969), pp. 44–48.

16.   Compare U.S. Congress, Joint Economic Committee, *The Economics of Federal Subsidy Programs: A Compendium of Papers,* Joint Committee Print (Washington, D.C.: Government Printing Office, 1972), pt. 2, p. 213; Susan B. Foster "Impact of Direct Investment Abroad by United States Multinational Companies on the Balance of Payments," *Federal Reserve Bank of New York, Monthly Review* 54 (July 1972): 166–177.

17.   Senate, Committee on Finance, *Implications of Multinational Firms,* 2:172 174, 180, 184, 187–189, 351–352.

18.   U.S. Department of Commerce, Bureau of International Commerce, Office of International Investment, *The Multinational Corporation Studies on U.S. Foreign Investment* 1 (March 1972); Robert B. Stobaugh, Piero Telesio, and Jose de la Torre *The Effect of U.S. Foreign Direct Investment in Manufacturing on the U.S. Balance of Payments, U.S. Employment and Changes in Skill Composition of Employment* (Washington: Center for Multinational Studies, 1973), p. 8; Foster, "Impact of Direct Investment," pp. 166–177.

19.   U.S. Department of Commerce, *Multinational Corporations* 1 (March 1972) 36–37.

20.   Organization for Economic Co-operation and Development, "Interim Report of the Industry Committee on International Enterprises," March, 1974, p. 41 John H. Dunning, "Foreign Investment in the United Kingdom," in *Foreign Investment: The Experience of Host Countries,* ed. Isaiah Litvak and Christopher Maule (New York: Praeger, Special Studies in International Economies and Development 1970), pp. 232, 238; Canada, *Foreign Direct Investment in Canada* (Ottawa: Information Canada, 1972), ch. 6.

21.   Jack N. Behrman, *National Interest Over the Multinational Enterprise: Tensions Among the North Atlantic Countries* (Englewood Cliffs, N.J.: Prentice Hall 1970), p. 23.

22.   Martin Mayer, *The Bankers* (New York: Weybright and Talley, 1974) pp. 440–441.

23.   Charles N. Stabler, "Eurocurrency Market Problems Remain, But Bankers Say the Outlook is Improved," *Wall Street Journal,* 13 June 1975, p. 7; Charles N Stabler, "U.S. Banks' Foreign Activities Will Face More Federal Control, Official Predict," *Wall Street Journal,* 9 April 1975, p. 4; Frederick R. Dahl, "International Operations of U.S. Banks: Growth and Public Policy Implications," *Law and Contemporary Problems* 32 (Winter 1967): 100; Stuart W. Robinson, *Multinational Banking: A Study of Certain Legal and Financial Aspects of the Postwar Operation of the U.S. Branch Banks in Western Europe* (Leiden: A. W. Sythoff, 1972), pp. 3: 42, 46–48.

24.   Lewis Berman, "How It All Came Apart in the Eurodollar Market," *Fortune* 91 (February 1975): 175; Stabler, "Eurocurrency Market," p. 7; Richard F. Janssen "Cautious Consortium: International Bank Group Now Stress Safety Above A Polish Up Their Image," *Wall Street Journal,* 31 March 1975, p. 15.

25.   Little, *Eurodollars;* Fritz Machlup, *Eurodollar Creation: A Mystery Story* Reprints in International Finance no. 16 (Princeton, N.J.: Princeton University Press, 1970); Milton Friedman, "The Euro-Dollar Market: Some First Principles' *Morgan Guaranty Survey,* October 1969, p. 4; Paul Einzig, *The Euro-Dollar System Practice and Theory of International Interest Rates* (New York: St. Martin's Press 1973, 5th ed.).

26.   Little, *Eurodollars,* ch. 3; Berman, "How It All Came Apart," p. 85.

27.   U.S. Department of Commerce, *Multinational Corporations* 1:44, 46; Yoon S. Park, *The Euro-Bond Market: Function and Structure* (New York: Praeger, 1974); Robert Prinsky, "Billion-Dollar Baby: Young Eurobond Market Leads New York as Main Source of International Financing," *Wall Street Journal*, 25 November 1975, p. 44.
28.   Neil McInnes, "Talking Money: Threat of Inflation: It Remains, Warns Jacques Rueff, as Virulent as Ever," *Barron's*, 4 August 1975, p. 3; Friedman, "Euro-dollar Market," pp. 4–14; Milton Friedman, "Letters: Two Economists Side with Secretary Simon: Six Fallacies," *Wall Street Journal*, 30 June 1975, p. 9; "Economics: Sowing the Seeds of World Inflation," *Business Week* no. 2397 (8 September 1975): 66, 68; Arthur B. Laffer, "Global Money: Growth and Inflation," *Wall Street Journal*, 23 September 1975, p. 26.
29.   Little, *Eurodollars*, pp. 168–169; see "Euromoney and Inflation—Guilt by Association?" *First National City Bank of New York, Monthly Economic Letter*, February 1976, p. 9.
30.   Little, *Eurodollars*, p. 192; Fred H. Klopstock, "Impact of Euromarkets on the United States Balance of Payments," *Law and Contemporary Problems* 34 (Winter 1969), pp. 157–171.
31.   Andrew F. Brimmer, "Multinational Banks and the Management of Monetary Policy in the United States," *Journal of Finance* 28 (May 1973), pp. 443, 446.
32.   Little, *Eurodollars*, pp. 167, 233, 235, 238.
33.   Alvin Toffler, *The Eco-Spasm Report* (New York: Bantam Books, 1975), p. 11.
34.   Robert M. Smith, "Oil-Land Deposits 5% at Six Top Banks," *New York Times*, 12 March 1976, p. 45; David T. Cook, "Oil Nations Putting Funds into U.S. Banks," *Christian Science Monitor*, 21 June 1976, p. 16; "Bank Vulnerability to Oil Riches Eyed," *New York Times*, 24 August 1975, p. 39; Einzig, *Eurodollar System*, ch. 18.
35.   "Why the Debt Time-Bomb Won't Go Off," *First National City Bank of New York, Monthly Economic Letter*, June 1976, p. 14; Fred B. Ruckdeschel, "Risk in Foreign and Domestic Lending Activities of U.S. Banks," *International Finance Discussion Paper No. 66*, 1 May 1975.
36.   Emma Rothschild, "Banks: The Coming Crises," *New York Review of Books* 23 (27 May 1976): 16; Emma Rothschild, "Banks: The Politics of Debt," *New York Review of Books* 23 (24 June 1976), p. 25.
37.   Mayer, *Bankers*, pp. 4–63; see "Money and Credit: What Went Wrong at Herstatt," *Business Week* no. 2342 (3 August 1974): 13–14; Berman, "How It All Came Apart," pp. 85, 87.
38.   Stabler, "Eurocurrency Market Problems Remain," p. 7; Berman, "How It All Came Apart," pp. 85, 175.
39.   Stabler, "Eurocurrency Problems Remain," p. 7; Richard A. Debs, "International Banking," *Federal Bank of New York Monthly Review*, June 1975, pp. 122–129.
40.   Stabler, "Eurocurrency Market Problems Remain," p. 7; Richard F. Janssen, "Global Report: Taiwan Spurs Nuclear-Plant Building; Central Bankers Move to Consult More," *Wall Street Journal*, 9 February 1976, p. 6.
41.   Eugene V. Rostow, "The Multinational Corporations and the Future of the World Economy," in *Global Companies: The Political Economy of World Business*, ed. George W. Ball, (Englewood Cliffs, N.J.: Prentice-Hall, 1975), pp. 118–121.
42.   "IMF Should Become World Central Bank, Its Chief Says, Offering 'Workable' Plan," *Wall Street Journal*, 29 October 1975, p. 21.
43.   William M. Carley, "Profits Probes: Investigations Beset Multinational Firms, with Stress on Pricing," *Wall Street Journal*, 19 December 1974, p. 1; Sanjaya Lall, "Transfer-Pricing by Multinational Manufacturing Firms," *Oxford Bulletin of Economics and Statistics* 35 (August 1973), pp. 173–195.
44.   Task Force on the Structure of Canadian Industry, *Foreign Ownership and the Structure of Canadian Industry* (Ottawa: Information Canada, 1970), pp. 122–131,

149; Canada, *Foreign Direct Investment*, pp. 16–22; Isaiah Litzak and Christopher Maule, "Foreign Investment in Canada," *Foreign Investment: The Experience of Host Countries* (New York: Praeger, Special Studies in International Economics and Development, 1970), p. 89.

45.   Raymond Vernon, *Sovereignty at Bay: The Multinational Spread of U.S. Enterprise,* (New York: Basic Books, 1971), pp. 21–24; Jean Jacques Servan-Schreiber, *The American Challenge,* trans. Ronald Steel, with a foreword by Arthur Schlesinger, Jr., (New York: Atheneum, 1968), pp. 12–14; United Nations, Department of Economic and Social Affairs, *Multinational Corporations in World Development* (ST/ECA/190), p. 17, 164, 169, table 23.

46.   International Labour Office, *Multinational Enterprises and Social Policy* (Geneva: International Labour Office, 1973), p. 16; "The World Economy: Tension with Host Nations: New Era for Multinationals," *Business Week* no. 2338 (6 July 1974): 73.

47.   Organization for Economic Co-operation and Development, "Interim Report," p. 41.

48.   G. Rosenbluth, "The Relation Between Foreign Control and Concentration in Canadian Industry," *Canadian Journal of Economics* 3 (February 1970): 14–38.

49.   U.S. Congress, Joint Economic Committee, *A Foreign Economic Policy for the 1970's,* pt. 4, 91st Cong., 2d sess., 1970, p. 916, statement by Melville H. Watkins.

50.   Robert Gilpin, *France in the Age of the Scientific State* (Princeton, N.J.: Princeton University Press, 1968), pp. 12, 451–452; Behrman, *National Interest and the Multinational Enterprise,* ch. 14.

51.   Behrman, *National Interest and the Multinational Enterprise,* ch. 10.

52.   Ibid., pp. 55–69.

53.   John H. Dunning, "The Multinational Enterprise: The Background," in *The Multinational Enterprise,* ed John H. Dunning, (London: Allen and Unwin, 1971) p. 45; "World Economy: Tension With Host Nations," p. 73.

CHAPTER 5: THE CHALLENGE OF M N Cs TO LABOR AND TO THE CONCEPT OF DECENTRALIZED PARTICIPATORY WORK STRUCTURES

1.   AFL-CIO Economic Policy Committee, "World Trade in the 1970's," *American Federationist* 80 (April 1973): 16–24; Paul M. Goldfinger, "An American Trade Union View of International Trade and Investment," in *American Labor and the Multinational Corporation,* ed. Duane Kujawa, with a foreword by Robert F Hawkins (New York: Praeger, [1973]), pp. 34–38.

2.   International Labour Office, *Multinational Enterprises and Social Policy* (Geneva: International Labour Office, 1973), p. 28.

3.   Robert H. Frank and Richard T. Freeman, "Multinational Corporations and Domestic Employment," (Ithaca, New York: n.d.), p. 22, table 2.

4.   U.S. Department of Commerce, Bureau of International Commerce, *The Multinational Corporation Studies on U.S. Foreign Investment* 1 (March 1972) 19–21.

5.   U.S. Department of Commerce, *Multinational Corporations,* p. 28.

6.   Robert G. Hawkins, *Job Displacement and the Multinational Firm: A Methodological Review,* Occasional Paper No. 3 (Washington, D.C.: Center for Multinational Studies, 1972), pp. 21–22.

7.   U.S. Department of Commerce, *Multinational Corporations,* 1:30; Robert Stobaugh, Piero Telesio, Jose de la Torre, *The Effects of U.S. Foreign Direct Investment in Manufacturing on the U.S. Balance of Payments, U.S. Employment and Changes in Skill Composition of Employment* (Washington, D.C.: Center of Multinational Studies, 1973).

8.   U.S. Congress, Senate, Committee on Finance, *Multinational Corporations: A Compendium of Papers Submitted to the Subcommittee on International Trade,* Committee Print (Washington, D.C.: Government Printing Office, 1973), p. 5; National Foreign Trade Council, *The Impact of U.S. Foreign Direct Investment on U.S. Employment and Trade: An Assessment of Critical Claims and Legislative Proposals* (New York: National Foreign Trade Council, 1971), pp. 4, 10.

9.   Hawkins, *Job Displacement and the Multinational Firm,* p. 26.

10.   U.S. Congress, Senate, Committee on Finance, *The Implications of Multinational Firms for World Trade and Investment and for U.S. Trade and Labor,* by U.S. Tariff Commission, T.C. Pubn. 537 (Washington, D.C.: 1973) 2: 331.

11.   U.S. Department of Commerce, *Multinational Corporations,* 29, 31; Senate, Committee on Finance, *Implications of Multinational Firms* 3: 688.

12.   Jose de la Torre, Robert Stobaugh, Piero Telesio, "U.S. Multinational Enterprises and Changes in the Skill Composition of U.S. Employment," in *American Labor and the Multinational Corporation,* ed. Duane Kujawa, with a foreword by Robert G. Hawkins (New York: Praeger, 1973), p. 137.

13.   Sanford Rose, "The Misguided Furor about Investments from Abroad," *Fortune* 91 (May 1975): 292.

14.   U.S. Congress, Senate, Committee on Labor and Public Welfare, *The Multinational Corporation and the National Interest,* by Robert Gilpin, Committee Print (Washington, D.C.: Government Printing Office, 1973), pp. 18, 36, 71; U.S. Congress, Joint Economic Committee, *The Economics of Federal Subsidy Programs: A Compedium of Papers,* Joint Economic Print (Washington, D.C.: Government Printing Office, 1972), pt. 2, pp. 209, 211.

15.   Joint Economic Committee, *Economics of Federal Subsidy Programs,* pp. 207–208.

16.   Ibid., pp. 177, 207–208.

17.   U.S. Congress, House, Committee on Foreign Affairs, *The Multinationals: Functions and Future,* Committee Print (Washington, D.C.: Government Printing Office, 1975), p. 67.

18.   Brendan Jones, "Issue and Debate: Should Multinational Companies' Taxes Be Raised?" *New York Times,* 13 August 1975, p. 45.

19.   U.S. Congress, Senate, Senator Hartke, speaking for the Foreign Trade and Investment Act of 1973, S. 151, 93d Cong., 1st sess., 9 January 1973, *Congressional Record* 119:S. 365–370.

20.   National Foreign Trade Council, *Economic Implications of Proposed Changes in the Taxation of U.S. Investments Abroad,* with an introduction by Senator Vance Hartke (New York: National Foreign Trade Council, 1972), pp. 12–22; U.S. Congress, House, Committee on Ways and Means, *General Tax Reform (Testimony from Administration and Public Witnesses),* 93d Cong., 1st sess., 1973, pt. 12, p. 4920; Richard P. Caro, "The Burke-Hartke Bill: A Critical Analysis of the Proposal to Curtail U.S. Foreign Direct Investments," in *Management of the Multinationals: Politics, Operations, and Research,* ed. S. Prakash Sethi and Richard H. Holton (New York: The Free Press, 1974), pp. 117–133.

21.   Howard V. Perlmutter, "A View of the Future," in *The New Sovereigns: Multinational Corporations as World Powers,* ed. Abdul A. Said and Luiz R. Simmons (Englewood Cliffs, N.J.: Prentice-Hall, 1975), p. 173.

22.   Trade Act of 1974, 19 U.S.C. § 2101 et seq.

23.   Nat Weinberg, "The Multinational Corporation and Labor," in *The New Sovereigns: Multinational Corporations as World Powers,* ed. Abdul A. Said and Luiz R. Simmons (Englewood Cliffs, N.J.: Prentice-Hall, 1975), pp. 91–107.

24.   Raymond Vernon, *Sovereignty at Bay: The Multinational Spread of U.S. Enterprises* (New York: Basic Books, 1971), p. 145.

25.   Kenneth Simmonds, "Multinational? Well, Not Quite," *Columbia Journal of World Business* 1 (Fall 1966): 115; Vernon, *Sovereignty at Bay,* pp. 145–150.

26.   Lawrence G. Franko, "Who Manages Multinational Enterprise?" *Columbia Journal of World Business* 8 (Summer 1973): 38–39.

27.   Vernon, *Sovereignty at Bay*, p. 149; Michael Z. Brooke and H. Lee Remmers, *The Strategy of the Multinational Enterprise: Organization and Finance* (New York: American Elsevier, 1970), p. 141; International Chamber of Commerce, *Realities: Multinational Enterprises Respond on Basic Issues,* with an introduction by Wilfrid S. Baumgartner (Paris: International Chamber of Commerce, 1974), pp. 88–96.

28.   Peter F. Drucker, "Multinationals and Developing Countries: Myths and Realities," *Foreign Affairs* 53 (October 1974): 129.

29.   Franko, "Who Manages Multinational Enterprise?" p. 39.

30.   Howard V. Perlmutter, "A Drama in Three Acts—The Tortuous Evolution of the Multinational Corporation," *Columbia Journal of World Business* 4 (January–February 1969): 9–18; Howard V. Perlmutter and David A. Heenan, "How Multinational Should Your Top Managers Be?" *Harvard Business Review* 52 (November–December 1974): 121–132.

31.   See Lewis D. Solomon, *Humanizing the Corporation: An Experiment in Social Planning* (Cambridge, Mass.: Schenkman, 1977).

CHAPTER 6: THE IMPACT OF M N Cs ON THE POLITICAL PROCESS OF DEVELOPED NATIONS

1.   See William Appleman Williams, *The Tragedy of American Diplomacy* (New York: World Publishing, Prometheus Books, 1969); Walter LaFeber, *The New Empire: An Interpretation of American Expansion 1860–1898* (Ithaca, N.Y.: Cornell University Press, 1963); Richard J. Barnet, *Roots of War* (Baltimore: Penguin Books, 1972) pp. 146–148, 152–155, 217, 222; Gabriel Kolko, *The Roots of American Foreign Policy: An Analysis of Power and Purpose* (Boston: Beacon Press, [1969]), ch. 3 Harry Magdoff, *The Age of Imperialism: The Economics of U.S. Foreign Policy* (New York: Monthly Review Press, 1969), ch. 1, 5; Heather Dean, "Scarce Resources The Dynamic of American Imperialism" in *Readings in U.S. Imperialism,* ed. K.T Fann and Donald C. Hodges, pp. 139–154, for analyses of the historic pattern of the American government basing its foreign policy on an "Open Door" for American business.

2.   See C. Wright Mills, *The Power Elite* (New York: Oxford University Press Galaxy Book, 1956); C. Wright Mills, "The Power Elite: Comment on Criticism, *Dissent* 5 (Winter 1957): 22–34; G. William Domhoff, *Who Rules America?* (Englewood Cliffs, N.J.: Prentice-Hall, 1967); G. William Domhoff, *The Higher Circles The Governing Class in America* (New York: Random House, 1970); G. William Domhoff, *The Bohemian Grove and Other Retreats: A Study in Ruling-Class Cohesiveness* (New York: Harper & Row, 1974); Richard J. Barnet, *Roots of War* (Baltimore: Penguin Books, 1972) chs. 3, 5, 7; Kolko, *Roots of American Foreign Policy,* ch. 1; G. William Domhoff, "Who Made American Foreign Policy, 1845 1963?" in *Corporations and the Cold War,* ed. David Horowitz, (New York: Monthly Review Press, 1969), pp. 25–69; David S. McLellan and Charles E. Woodhouse "Businessman in Foreign Policy," *Southwestern Social Science Quarterly* 39 (Ma 1959): 285; Lawrence H. Shoup, "Shaping the Postwar World: The Council o Foreign Relations and the United States War Aims During World War Two," *Insurgen Sociologist* 5 (Spring, 1975): 9–52.

3.   William Domhoff, "State Ruling Class in Corporate America," *Insurgen Sociologist* 4 (Spring, 1974): 9–10.

4.   Dennis M. Ray, "Corporations and American Foreign Relations," *Annals o the American Academy of Political and Social Science* 403 (September 1972): 91.

5.   Kolko, *Roots of American Foreign Policy,* pp. 64, 70; Magdoff, *Age of Im perialism,* ch. 4; Teresa Hayter, *Aid as Imperialism* (Baltimore: Penguin Books, 1971 but compare Raymond Vernon, *Sovereignty at Bay: The Multinational Spread o U.S. Enterprises.* (New York: Basic Books, 1971), p. 212.

6.   James R. Kurth, "Testing Theories of Economic Imperialism," in *Testin*

Theories of Economic Imperialism, ed. Steven J. Rosen and James R. Kurth (Lexington, Mass.: D. C. Heath, 1974), pp. 3–14; Steven J. Rosen, "The Open Door Imperative and U. S. Foreign Policy," in *Testing Theories of Economic Imperialism,* ed. Steven J. Rosen and James R. Kurth, (Lexington, Mass.: D. C. Heath, 1974), pp. 117–142; Richard J. Barnet and Ronald E. Müller, *Global Reach: The Power of the Multinational Corporations* (New York: Simon & Schuster, 1974), pp. 78–79.

7.   James R. Kurth, "Testing Theories of Economic Imperialism," pp. 9–13; Kolko, *Roots of American Foreign Policy,* pp. 85–89; Barnet and Müller, *Global Reach,* pp. 79–80.

8.   Jerry Landauer, "Big Oil Firms Tried to Shape U.S. Policy in Mideast at Arabs' Behest, Memos Show," *Wall Street Journal,* 7 August 1974, p. 6; U.S. Congress, Senate, Committee on Foreign Relations, *Multinational Oil Corporations and U.S. Foreign Policy,* Committee Print (Washington, D.C.: Government Printing Office, 1975), pp. 121–163; Sarah Jackson, "Oil MNCs: Are They in the National Interest?" *Columbia Journal of World Business* 9 (Fall 1974): 26.

9.   United Nations, Department of Economic and Social Affairs, *Multinational Corporations in World Development* (ST/ECA/190), 1973, p. 43.

10.   Lewis D. Solomon and Leslie G. Linville, "Transnational Conduct of American Multinational Corporations: Questionable Payments Abroad," *Boston College Industrial and Commercial Law Review* 17 (March 1976): 303–309.

11.   See Anthony Sampson, *The Sovereign State of ITT* (Greenwich, Conn.: Fawcett, 1973), pp. 259–288.

CHAPTER 7: MNCs, THE THIRD WORLD AND DEPENDENCY

1.   Johan Galtung, "A Structural Theory of Imperialism," *Journal of Peace Research* 13 (1971): 81; Andre G. Frank, *Capitalism and Underdevelopment in Latin America: Historical Studies of Chile and Brazil* (New York: Monthly Review Press, 1967); Paul Baran, *The Political Economy of Growth* (New York: Modern Reader Paperbacks, [1968]), chs. 5–7; Theontonio Dos Santos, "The Structure of Dependence," *American Economic Review* 60 (May 1970): 231–236; Oswaldo Sunkel, "Big Business and 'Dependencia': A Latin American View," *Foreign Affairs* 50 (April 1972): 517–531; Thomas E. Weisskopf, "Capitalism, Underdevelopment and the Future of the Poor Countries," in *Economics and World Order from the 1970's to the 1990's,* ed. Jagdish N. Bhagwati (New York: Macmillan, 1972); pp. 43–75; but see David Ray, "The Dependency Model of Latin American Underdevelopment: Three Basic Fallacies," *Journal of Interamerican Studies and World Affairs* 15 (February 1973): 4–20.

2.   Steven Rosen, "The Open Door Imperative and U.S. Foreign Policy," in *Testing Theories of Economic Imperialism,* ed. Steven Rosen and James R. Kurth (Lexington, Mass.: D. C. Heath, 1974), p. 125.

3.   Stephen Hymer, "The Efficiency (Contradictions) of Multinational Corporations," *American Economic Review* 60 (May 1970): 441–448; Stephen Hymer, "The Mulitnational Corporation and the Law of Uneven Development," in *Economics and World Order from the 1970's to the 1990's,* ed. Jagdish N. Bhagwati (New York: Macmillan, 1972), pp. 124–126, 129.

4.   Raúl Prebisch, "International Trade and Payments in an Era of Co-existence: Commercial Policy in the Underdeveloped Countries," *American Economic Review* 49 (May 1970): 251–273; Luis E. Di Marco, "The Evolution of Prebisch's Economic Thought," in *International Economics and Development: Essays in Honor of Raúl Prebisch,* ed. Luis E. Di Marco (New York: Academic Press, 1972), pp. 3–13.

5.   P. T. Ellsworth, "The Terms of Trade between Primary Producing and Industrial Countries," *Interamerican Economic Affairs* 9 (Summer 1956): 47–65; Gottfried Haberler, "Terms of Trade and Economic Development," in *Economic Development for Latin America,* ed. Howard Ellis (New York: St. Martin's Press, 1961), pp. 275–307.

6. United Nations, Conference on Trade and Development, Secretariat, *Terms of Trade of Developing Countries: Note by the UNCTAD Secretariat* (UNCTAD/CD Misc. 60, GE, 75-46608), n.d., p. 6.

7. Ibid., p. 14.

8. Edwin L. Dale, "Idea of Growing Disparity in World Prices Disputed," *New York Times,* 25 May 1975, sec. 1, p. 1; see United Nations, Press Section, Office of Public Information, Note no. 3916, 27 May 1975.

9. Jonathan Power, "Of Raw Materials, Raw Statistics and Raw Deals," *New York Times,* 31 August 1975, sec. 4, p. 15.

10. Robert B. Stobaugh, "Systematic Bias and the Terms of Trade," *Review of Economics and Statistics* 49 (November 1967): 617–619.

11. Baran, *Political Economy of Growth,* p. 197; Peter B. Evans, "National Autonomy and Economic Development: Critical Perspectives on Multinational Corporations in Poor Countries," in *Transnational Relations and World Politics,* ed. Robert O. Keohane and Joseph S. Nye (Cambridge, Mass.: Harvard University Press, 1973), pp. 325–342.

12. Raymond F. Mikesell, "The Contribution of Petroleum and Mineral Resources to Economic Development," in *Foreign Investment in the Petroleum and Mineral Industries: Case Studies of Investor-Host Country Relations,* ed. Raymond F. Mikesell, and others (Baltimore: Johns Hopkins Press, published for Resources for the Future 1971), pp. 3–28; Raymond Vernon, "Foreign Enterprises and Developing Nations in Raw Materials Industries," *American Economic Review* 60 (May 1970): 122.

13. International Chamber of Commerce, *Multinational Enterprises and Their Role in Economic Development* (Paris: International Chamber of Commerce, Doc. 191/83 1974), p. 13; James E. Zinser, "Alternative Means of Meeting Argentina Petroleum Requirements," in *Foreign Investment in the Petroleum and Mineral Industries,* ed. Mikesell et al., pp. 189–215.

14. Michael Tanzer, *The Political Economy of International Oil and the Underdeveloped Countries* (Boston: Beacon Press, 1969), ch. 22.

15. Sidney M. Robbins and Robert B. Stobaugh, *Money in the Multinational Enterprise: A Study of Financial Policy* (New York: Basic Books, 1973), p. 91; Sanjaya Lall, "Transfer-Pricing by Multinational Manufacturing Firms," *Oxford Bulletin of Economics and Statistics* 35 (August 1973), pp. 173–195.

16. United Nations, Conference on Trade and Development, Board of the Cartagena Agreement, *Policies Relating to Technology of the Countries of the Andean Pact: Their Foundations* (TD/107), 29 December 1971, pp. 128–129; Ronald Müller, "The Multinational Corporation and the Underdevelopment of the Third World," in *The Political Economy of Development and Underdevelopment,* ed. Charles K. Wilber (New York: Random House, 1973), pp. 143–144, table 4.

17. United Nations, Conference on Trade and Development, *Policies Relating to Technology of the Countries of the Andean Pact: Their Foundations* (TD/107, Corr. 1), 21 March 1972, para. 128–129.

18. U.N., Conference on Trade and Development, *Policies Relating to Technology* (TD/107), pp. 128–129.

19. Ronald Müller and Richard Morgenstern, "Multinational Corporations and Balance of Payments Impacts on LDCs: An Economic Analysis of Export Pricing Behavior," *KYKLOS* 27 (1974): 304–321.

20. Raymond Vernon, *Sovereignty at Bay: The Multinational Spread of U.S. Enterprises* (New York: Basic Books, 1971), p. 139.

21. Jacques E. Maisonrouge, "The Mythology of Multinationalism," *Columbia Journal of World Business* 9 (Spring 1974): 7, 11; U.S. Congress, Senate, Committee on Finance, *Multinational Corporations: A Compendium of Papers Submitted to the Subcommittee on International Trade,* Committee Print (Washington, D.C.: Government Printing Office, 1973), pp. 283–295.

22.   James H. Greene and Michael Duerr, *Intercompany Transactions in the Multinational Firm: A Survey* (New York: National Industrial Conference Board, Managing International Business no. 6, 1970), pp. 21–22.

23.   Christopher Tugendhat, *The Multinationals* (London: Eyre and Spottiswoode, 1971), pp. 145–148.

24.   Fernand Braun, "International Control from the Standpoint of the European Economic Community," in *International Control of Investment: The Düsseldorf Conference on Multinational Corporations,* ed. Don Wallace (New York: Praeger, 1974), p. 54.

25.   William M. Carley, "Profit Probes: Investigations Beset Multinational Firms with Stress on Pricing," *Wall Street Journal,* 19 December 1974, p. 6.

26.   United Nations, Department of Economic and Social Affairs, *The Impact of Multinational Corporations on Development and on International Relations* (E/5500/Rev. 1, ST/ESA/6), 1974, p. 88.

27.   Ibid.

28.   Compare Richard J. Barnet and Ronald E. Müller, *Global Reach: The Power of the Multinational Corporations* (New York: Simon & Schuster, 1974), pp. 266–267 and Anthony M. Solomon, "International Control of Investment in the Trade Sector," in *International Control of Investment: The Düsseldorf Conference on Multinational Corporations,* ed. Don Wallace, (New York: Praeger, 1974), pp. 16–18.

29.   Robert B. Stobaugh, "The Multinational Corporation: Measuring the Consequences," *Columbia Journal of World Business* 6 (January–February 1971): 59–64.

30.   Robbins and Stobaugh, *Money in the Multinational Enterprise,* pp. 91–92.

31.   Stobaugh, "Multinational Corporation," p. 59.

32.   George W. Ball, "The Relations of the Multinational Corporation to the 'Host' State," in *Global Companies: The Political Economy of World Business,* ed. George W. Ball, (Englewood Cliffs, N.J.: Prentice-Hall, American Assembly, 1975), p. 65.

33.   Jack Baranson, *Automotive Industries in Developing Countries* (Washington, D.C.: International Bank for Reconstruction Development, [1969]).

34.   David Belli, "Sales of Foreign Affiliates of U.S. Firms, 1961–65, 1967 and 1968," *Survey of Current Business* 50 (October 1970): 18–20.

35.   U.N. Conference on Trade and Development, *Policies Relating to Technology* (TD/107) and (TD/107/Corr. 1) para. 128–129.

36.   United Nations, Conference on Trade and Development, *Restrictions on Exports in Foreign Collaboration Agreements in India* (TD/B/389), 1971.

37.   United Nations, Conference on Trade and Development, *Restrictions on Exports in Foreign Collaboration Agreements in the Republic of the Philippines* (TD/B/388), 1972; United Nations, Conference on Trade and Development, Secretariat, *Restrictive Business Practices* (TD/122/Supp. 1), 7 January 1972, pp. 38–49; United Nations Conference on Trade and Development, *Restrictive Business Practices in Relation to the Trade and Development of Developing Countries* (TD/B/C.2/119), 1973.

38.   Harry G. Johnson, "The Multinational Corporations as a Development Agent," *Columbia Journal of World Business* 5 (May–June, 1970), pp. 25, 29.

39.   International Chamber of Commerce, *Multinational Enterprises,* p. 32.

40.   International Chamber of Commerce, *Realities: Multinational Enterprises Respond on Basic Issues,* with an introduction by Wilfrid S. Baumgartner (Paris: International Chamber of Commerce, 1974), pp. 44–45.

41.   · United Nations, Department of Economic and Social Affairs, *Multinational Corporations in World Development* (ST/ECA/190), 1973, p. 52.

42.   United Nations, Department of Economic and Social Affairs, *Summary of the Hearings Before the Group of Eminent Persons to Study the Impact of Multinational Corporations on Development and on International Relations* (ST/ESA/15), 1974, pp. 397–404; Raúl Prebisch, *Change and Development–Latin America's Great Task* (New York: Praeger, [1971], pp. 30–31, 233; Müller, "The Multinational Corporation and the Underdevelopment," pp. 132–135.

43. Müller, "The Multinational Corporation and the Underdevelopment," p. 133.

44. U.N., Department of Economic and Social Affairs, *Multinational Corporations*, p. 52; Charles P. Hyson and Dale R. Weigel, "Investment in the LDCs: The Unresolved Debate," *Columbia Journal of World Business* 5 (January–February 1970): 36–37; Keith Pavitt, "The Multinational Enterprise and the Transfer of Technology," in *The Multinational Enterprise,* ed. John H. Dunning (London: Allen and Unwin, 1971), pp. 74–79; compare International Labour Organization, *Multinational Enterprises and Social Policy* (Geneva: International Labour Office, 1973), pp. 59, 62.

45. U.N., Department of Economic and Social Affairs, *Multinational Corporations*, p. 52; U.N., Department of Economic and Social Affairs, *Impact of Multinational Corporations*, p. 76; International Labour Organization, *Multinational Enterprises*, pp. 55–58, 73.

46. Susumu Watanebe, "International Subcontracting, Employment and Skill Promotion," *International Labour Review* 105 (May 1972): 425.

47. Organization of American States, Executive Secretariat for Economic and Social Affairs, *Sectoral Study of Transnational Enterprises in Latin America: The Automotive Industry* (SG/Ser. G. 42/3), 1974, pp. 16–17, 20; U.N., Department of Economic and Social Affairs, *Summary of Hearings*, p. 87.

48. United Nations, Department of Economic and Social Affairs, *The Acquisition of Technology from Multinational Corporations by Developing Countries* (ST/ESA/12), 1974, p. 21.

49. Louis T. Wells, "Economic Man and Engineering Man: Choice and Technology in a Low-Wage Country," *Public Policy* 21 (Summer, 1973): 319–342; U.N., Department of Economic and Social Affairs, *Acquisition of Technology*, pp. 12–13.

50. U.N., Department of Economic and Social Affairs, *Acquisition of Technology*, pp. 12–14.

51. United Nations, Institute for Training and Research, *The Transfer of Technology and the Factor Proportions Problem: The Philippines and Mexico* (UNITAR Research Report no. 10), 1971; R. Hal Mason, "Some Observations on the Choice of Technology by Multinational Firms in Developing Countries," *Review of Economics and Statistics* 60 (August 1973): 349.

52. United Nations, Institute for Training and Research, *The International Transfer of Commercial Technology to Developing Countries* (UNITAR Research Report no. 13), 1971, pp. 25–26.

53. Wells, "Economic Man," pp. 319–342.

54. Exxon Corporation, Public Affairs Department, "The Role of Technology in Development," January 1974, p. 10; Michael G. Duerr, *R & D in the Multinational Company; A Survey* (New York: National Industrial Conference Board, Managing International Business no. 8, 1970).

55. U.N., Conference on Trade and Development, *Policies Relating to Technology* (TD/107/Corr. 1) para. 132.

56. Ibid., para. 132–133.

57. U.N., Department of the Economic and Social Affairs, *Multinational Corporations*, pp. 20–21; Müller, "The Multinational Corporation and the Underdevelopment," p. 130; Jonathan Kandell, "Brazilians Voice Growing Fear of Dominance by Multinationals," *New York Times*, 26 January 1976, p. 35.

58. Stephen Hymer, "The Efficiency (Contradictions) of Multinational Corporations," *American Economic Review* 60 (May 1970): 443.

59. Louis Turner, *Multinational Companies and the Third World* (New York: Hill and Wang, 1973), p. 49–50; Carlos F. Diaz Alejandro, "Direct Foreign Investment in Latin America," in *The International Corporation, a Symposium*, ed. Charles P. Kindleberger (Cambridge: M.I.T. Press, 1970), p. 331.

60. Constantino Vaitsos, "Comment," in *International Control of Investment The Düsseldorf Conference on Multinational Corporations*, ed. Don Wallace (New York: Praeger, [1974]), p. 129.

61. Claes Brundenius, "The Anatomy of Imperialism: The Case of Multinational Mining Corporations in Peru," *Journal of Peace Research* 9 (1972): 189, 199.

62. Müller, "The Multinational Corporations and the Underdevelopment," pp. 147–148.

63. Barnet and Müller, *Global Reach*, p. 160.

64. Ibid., pp. 153–154.

65. United Nations, Conference on Trade and Development, *Transfer of Technology* (TD/106), 10 November 1971.

66. Dos Santos, "Structure of Dependence," p. 234.

67. U.N., Department of Economic and Social Affairs, *Multinational Corporations*, p. 54.

68. Ibid.

69. U.N., Conference on Trade and Development, *Restrictive Business Practices*, pp. 19–20; Charles T. Nisbet, "Transferring Wealth from Underdeveloped to Developed Countries Via Direct Foreign Investment: A Marxist Claim Reconsidered," *Southern Economic Journal* 37 (July 1970): 93–96.

70. Barnet and Müller, *Global Reach*, pp. 140–141; Müller, "The Multinational Corporation and the Underdevelopment," pp. 136–138.

71. Evans, "National Autonomy and Economic Development," pp. 332–335; Barnet and Müller, *Global Reach*, pp. 172–184.

72. Robert J. Ledogar, *U.S. Food and Drug Multinationals in Latin America: Hungry for Profits*, with an introduction by Ralph Nader (New York: IDOC/North America, 1975), ch. 9; D. B. Jelliffe, "Commerciogenic Malnutrition?" *Nutrition Reviews* 30 (September 1972): 199–205.

73. Mike Muller, *The Baby Killer* (London: War on Want, 2d ed., 1975).

74. Herbert Schiller, *Mass Communication and Americans* (New York: A. M. Kelley, 1969); Alan Wells, *Picture-Tube Imperialism: The Impact of U.S. Television on Latin America* (Maryknoll, N.Y.: Orbis Books, 1972).

75. Herbert Schiller, "Madison Avenue Imperialism," *Transaction*, March–April 1971, 55; James A. Field, "Transnationalism and the New Tribe," *International Organization* 25 (Summer 1971): 353; David Osterberg and Fouad Ajami, "The Multinational Corporation: Expanding the Frontiers of World Politics," *Journal of Conflict Resolution* 15 (December 1971): 457–468.

76. Abdul A. Said and Luiz R. Simmons, "The Politics of Transition," in *The New Sovereigns: Multinational Corporations as World Powers*, ed. Abdul A. Said and Luiz R. Simmons, (Englewood Cliffs, N.J.: Prentice-Hall, 1975), p. 27.

77. Andre G. Frank, *Capitalism and Underdevelopment in Latin America* (New York: Monthly Review Press, 1967), pp. 281–318; Paul Baran, *The Political Economy of Growth* (New York: Modern Reader Paperbacks, [1968]), p. 153; Evans, "National Autonomy and Economic Development," pp. 339–340.

78. Theodore H. Moran, *Multinational Corporations and the Politics of Dependence: Copper in Chile* (Princeton, N.J.: Princeton University Press [1974]), pp. 172–215; Theodore H. Moran, "The Alliance for Progress and The Foreign Copper Companies and their Local Conservative Allies in Chile 1955–1970," *Interamerican Economic Affairs* 25 (Spring 1972): 3–24.

79. Vernon, *Sovereignty at Bay*, pp. 197–200.

80. U.N., Department of Economic and Social Affairs, *Impact of Multinational Corporations* pp. 45–46; "Kissinger Called Chile Strategist: He Is Said to Have Directed Economic Fight against Allende Personally," *New York Times*, 15 September 1974, pp. 1, 19.

CHAPTER 8: THIRD WORLD EFFORTS TO BREAK FREE FROM THE GRASP OF DEPENDENCY

1. "Interview with Venezuela's President Carlos Andres Perez: What the Third World Wants," *Business Week* no. 2402 (13 October 1975): 56.

2.   United Nations, Department of Economic and Social Affairs, *The Impact of Multinational Corporations on Development and on International Relations* (E/5500/Rev. 1, ST/Est/6), 1974, p. 32; Theodore H. Moran, "The Theory of International Exploitation in Large Natural Resource Investments," in *Testing Theories of Economic Imperialism,* ed. Steven J. Rosen and James R. Kurth (Lexington, Mass.: D. C. Heath, 1974), pp. 168–169.

3.   Paul Streeten, "Costs and Benefits of Multinational Enterprises in Less-developed Countries," in *The Multinational Enterprise,* ed. John H. Dunning (London: Allen and Unwin, 1971), p. 248.

4.   Raymond Vernon, *Sovereignty at Bay: The Multinational Spread of U.S. Enterprise* (New York: Basic Books, 1971), p. 106.

5.   M. Y. Yoshino, "Japan as Host to the International Corporation," in *The International Corporation: A Symposium,* ed. Charles P. Kindleberger (Cambridge: M.I.T. Press, 1970), pp. 345–369; Noritake Kobayoshi, "Foreign Investment in Japan," in *Foreign Investment: The Experience of Host Countries,* ed. Isaiah Litvak and Christopher Maule (New York: Praeger, Special Studies in International Economics and Development, 1970), pp. 123–160; Allan R. Pearl, "Liberalization of Capital in Japan," *Harvard International Law Journal* 13 (Winter 1972): 59.

6.   "The World Economy: Tension with Host Nations: New Era for Multinationals," *Business Week* no. 2338 (6 July 1974): 73–74; "Multinationals Find the Going Rougher," *Business Week* no. 2389 (14 July 1975): 64.

7.   *In Mexico The Best Investment: Law to Promote Mexican Investment and to Regulate Foreign Investment,* 1974, ch. 1, arts. 5, 8; Rosemary Werrett, "Mexico: Drawing in the Reins of Foreign Investment," *Columbia Journal of World Business* 9 (Spring 1974): 88–97.

8.   United Nations, Department of Economic and Social Affairs, *Summary of the Hearings Before the Group of Eminent Persons to Study the Impact of Multinational Corporations on Development and on International Relations* (ST/ESA/15), 1974, pp. 25, 31.

9.   Phiroze B. Medhora, "Foreign Investment in India," in *Foreign Investment: The Experience of Host Countries,* ed. Isaiah Litvak and Christopher Maule (New York: Praeger, Special Studies in International Economics and Development, 1970) pp. 280–302.

10.   John Fayerweather, "Canadian Foreign Investment Policy," *California Management Review* 17 (Spring 1975): 74–83, Thomas M. Franck and K. Scott Gudgeon, "Canada's Foreign Investment Control Experiment: The Law, the Context and the Practice," *New York University Law Review* 50 (April 1975): 76–146; "Canada Slates October for Phase 2 of Review of Foreign Investment," *Wall Street Journal,* 21 July 1975, p. 8.

11.   *Mexico: Best Investment,* art. 7; Werrett, "Mexico: Drawing in the Reins," p. 94; "Licensing: A Revolt Against 'Exorbitant Fees,'" *Business Week* no. 2389 (14 July 1975): 68.

12.   Raymond Vernon, "Future of the Multinational Enterprise," in *The International Corporation: A Symposium,* ed. Charles P. Kindleberger (Cambridge: M.I.T. Press, 1970), pp. 391–392; U.N., Department of Economic and Social Affairs, *Summary of Hearings,* p. 162.

13.   United Nations, Department of Economic and Social Affairs, *Multinational Corporations in World Development* (ST/ECA/190), 1973, pp. 85–86.

14.   Council of the Americas, *The Andean Pact: Definition, Design, and Analysis* (New York: Council of the Americas, 1973); Ralph A. Diaz, "The Andean Common Market: Challenge to Foreign Investors," *Columbia Journal of World Business* (July–August 1971): 22–28; William P. Avery and James D. Cochrane, "Innovation in Latin American Regionalism: The Andean Common Market," *International Organization* 27 (Spring 1973): 181–223.

15.   U.N., Department of Economic and Social Affairs, *Multinational Corporations* p. 85; U.N., Department of Economic and Social Affairs, *Summary of Hearings,* p. 136

16. John Helliwell and Julian Broadbent, "How Much Does Foreign Capital Matter?" *National Economic Issues: The View from the West Coast,* BC Studies Special Issue no. 13, Spring 1972, pp. 38–39.

CHAPTER 9: THE RESPONSE OF M N C s TO THIRD WORLD REGULATORY EFFORTS

1. Wolfgang Friedman and Jean-Pierre Beguin, *Joint International Business Ventures in Developing Countries* (New York: Columbia University Press, 1971).
2. Thomas A. Wolf, *East-West Economic Relations and the Multinational Corporation,* Occasional Paper No. 5 (Washington, D.C.: Center for Multinational Studies, 1973), pp. 74–76; John B. Holt, "New Roles for Western Multinationals in Eastern Europe," *Columbia Journal of World Business* 8 (Fall 1973): 131–139; Peter P. Gabriel, "Adaptation: The Name of the Multinational Corporation's Game," *Columbia Journal of World Business* 7 (November–December 1972): 7–14; Miodrag Sukijasovic, "Foreign Investment in Yugoslavia," in *Foreign Investment: The Experience of Host Countries,* ed. Isaiah Litvak and Christopher Maule (New York: Praeger, Special Studies in International Economics and Development, 1970), pp. 385–406.
3. Friedman and Beguin, *Joint International Business Ventures,* p. 383; John M. Stopford and Louis T. Wells, *Managing Multinational Enterprise: Organization of the Firm and Ownership of the Subsidiaries* (New York: Basic Books, [1972]), pp. 152–153.
4. Friedman and Beguin, *Joint International Business Ventures,* pp. 385–386.
5. Ibid., p. 386.
6. United Nations, Department of Economic and Social Affairs, *The Impact of Multinational Corporations on Development and on International Relations* (E/5500/ Rev. 1, ST/ESA/6), 1974, pp. 60–61.
7. Stopford and Wells, *Managing Multinational Enterprise,* pp. 152–153, 159–66; United Nations, Department of Economic and Social Affairs, *The Acquisition of Technology from Multinational Corporations by Developing Countries* (ST/ESA/12), 1974, pp. 29–30; Bernard Bonin, "The Multinational Firm as a Vehicle for the International Transmission of Technology," in *The Multinational Firm and the Nation State,* ed. Giles Paquet ([Don Mills, Ontario]: Collier-Macmillan, 1972) p. 119.
8. Friedman and Beguin, *Joint International Business Ventures,* pp. 213–219.
9. United Nations, Department of Economic and Social Affairs, *Multinational Corporations in World Development* (ST/ECA/190), 1973, p. 39; Peter P. Gabriel, "Multinational Corporations in the Third World: Is Conflict Unavoidable?" *Harvard Business Review* 50 (July–August 1972): 93–102; Richard D. Robinson, "The Developing Countries, Development, and the Multinational Corporation," *Annals of the American Academy of Political and Social Science* 403 (September 1972): 77.
10. Wolf, *East-West Economic Relations,* pp. 66–69.
11. Jack Baranson, "Technology Transfer Through the International Firm," *American Economic Review* 60 (May 1970): 435–440.
12. Albert O. Herschman, "How to Divest in Latin America, and Why," *Essays in International Finance* no. 76 (Princeton, N.J.: Princeton University, International Finance Section, 1969); compare Jack N. Behrman, "International Divestment: Panacea or Pitfall?" *Looking Ahead* 18 (November–December 1970): 7.
13. U.N., Department of Economic and Social Affairs, *Impact of Multinational Corporations,* p. 135.
14. Guy B. Meeker, "Fade-Out Joint Ventures: Can It Work for Latin America?" *Interamerican Economic Affairs* 24 (Spring 1971): 29–32.
15. Behrman, "International Divestment," pp. 1–4; International Chamber of Commerce, *Multinational Enterprises and Their Role in Economic Development* (Paris: International Chamber of Commerce, Doc. 191/83/1974), p. 5; U.N., Department of Economic and Social Affairs, *Impact of Multinational Corporations,* p. 121.

CHAPTER 10: THE RAW MATERIALS LEVER

1.   Raymond Vernon, *Sovereignty at Bay: The Multinational Spread of U.S. Enterprises* (New York: Basic Books, 1971), ch. 2; Theodore H. Moran, "The Theory of International Exploitation in Large Natural Resource Investments," in *Testing Theories of Economic Imperialism,* ed. Steven J. Rosen and James R. Kurth (Lexington, Mass.: D. C. Heath, Lexington Books, 1974), pp. 163–181.

2.   "Peru Seizes Iron-Ore Firm Largely Held by Cyprus Mines and Utah International," *Wall Street Journal* 28 July 1975, pp. 11.

3.   Theodore H. Moran, "New Deal or Raw Deal in Raw Materials," in *A Reordered World: Emerging International Economic Problems,* ed. Richard N. Cooper (Washington, D.C.: Potomac Associates, 1973), pp. 168–181.

4.   H. J. Maidenberg, "Venezuela, Its Oil within Grasp, Needs Foreign Concerns' Refining Technology," *New York Times,* 3 November 1975, p. 57.

5.   Theodore H. Moran, "Transnational Strategies of Protection and Defense by Multinational Corporations: Spreading the Risk and Raising the Cost for Nationalization in Natural Resources," *International Organization* 28 (Spring 1973): 273–287.

6.   Geoffrey Barraclough, "The Great World Crisis," *New York Review of Books* 22 (23 January 1975): 22.

7.   Morris A. Adelman, *The World Petroleum Market* (Baltimore: Johns Hopkins University Press, 1972); Anthony Sampson, *The Seven Sisters: The Great Oil Companies and the World They Made* (New York: Viking Press, 1975).

8.   International Economic Policy Association and the IEPA Advisory Committee on Natural Resources, *Petroleum and Foreign Economic Policy* (Washington, D.C.: International Economic Policy Association, 1975), pp. 3–4; Paul Lewis, "Getting Even," *New York Times Magazine,* 15 December 1974, pp. 78.

9.   "Why OPEC's Rocket Will Lose Its Thrust," *First National City Bank Monthly Economic Letter,* June 1975, pp. 11–15; "Brookings Study Expects West to Adjust to Oil Rises," *New York Times,* 25 November 1975, p. 51; "Economist Differs with Banks on Oil," *New York Times,* 17 June 1975, p. 43; "Money and Credit: The Oil Nations Go on a Borrowing Spree," *Business Week* no. 2391 (28 July 1975): 26; International Economic Policy Association, *Petroleum and Foreign Economic Policy,* pp. 7–10.

10.   Richard N. Cooper, "The Invasion of the Petrodollar," *Saturday Review* 1 (25 January 1975): 10–13; Hollis B. Chenery, "Restructuring the World Economy," *Foreign Affairs* 53 (January 1975): 242, 257.

11.   "5 to 15% Price Rise in Oil Seen by Iran, Envoy Bars Link to Cartel 'Extremists,' " *New York Times,* 19 September 1975, p. 51.

12.   International Economic Policy Association, *Petroleum and Foreign Economic Policy,* p. 8; Irving S. Friedman, "The New World of the Rich-Poor and the Poor-Rich," *Fortune* 91 (May 1975): 247; Juan de Onis, "Arab Oil Nations Will Aid Others," *New York Times,* 5 May 1975, p. 49; H. J. Maidenberg, "Venezuela is Aiding Poor Nations on Oil," *New York Times,* 15 September 1975, p. 27; H. J. Maidenberg, "Venezuela Asserts Her Oil Power," *New York Times,* 27 April 1975, sec. 3, p. 2.

13.   Benjamin B. Wallace and Lynn R. Edminster, *International Control of Raw Materials* (Washington, D.C.: Brookings Institution, 1930); John W. F. Rowe, *Primary Commodities in International Trade* (Cambridge, England: Cambridge University Press, 1965); Alton D. Law, *International Commodity Agreements: Setting, Performance and Prospects* (Lexington, Mass.: D. C. Heath, Lexington Books, 1974) chs. 2–3.

14.   "Cartel Wheel: Bauxite Official Finds Organizing's No Cinch for 10-Nation Group," *Wall Street Journal,* 23 April 1975, p. 1; Ian Stewart, "Asians, Studying OPEC, Consider Plans for Cartels," *New York Times,* 26 January 1975, sec. 3, pt. 2 p. 47; James N. Goodsell, "Sugar, Other Cartels Seek to Keep Prices High," *Christian Science Monitor,* 6 January 1976, p. 2; Paul Lewis, "Raw Materials: New Effort at Stable Prices," *New York Times,* 18 May 1975, sec. 3, p. 6.

15.   Stephen D. Krasner, "Oil is the Exception," *Foreign Policy* 14 (Spring 1974): 68–84; Hans H. Landsberg, "Assessing the Materials Threat," *Resources for the Future,* September 1974, p. 1; Raymond F. Mikesell, "More Third World Cartels Ahead?" *Challenge* 17 (November–December 1974): 24; John E. Tilton, "Cartels in Metal Industries," *Earth and Mineral Sciences* 44 (March 1975): 41; C. Fred Bergsten, "The Threat is Real," *Foreign Policy* 14 (Spring 1974): 84–90; C. Fred Bergsten, "New Era in World Commodity Markets," *Challenge* 17 (September–October 1974): 34–42.

16.   John O. Ward and F. E. Wagner, "Commodity Cartels, Economic Rent, and the United States," *Journal of Economics* (Missouri Valley Economic Association) 1975, p. 144; Bergstein, "New Era in World Commodity Markets," pp. 34–42.

CHAPTER 11: TRANSNATIONAL APPROACHES AND THE THRUST TOWARD A NEW WORLD ORDER

1.   United Nations, Conference on Trade and Development, *An Integrated Programme for Commodities: Compensatory Financing of Export Fluctuations in Commodity Trade* (TD/B/C.1/166/Supp. 4), 13 December 1974.

2.   United Nations, Conference on Trade and Development, *An Integrated Programme for Commodities* (TD/B/C.1/166), 9 December 1974; United Nations, Conference on Trade and Development, *An Integrated Programme for Commodities: The Role of International Commodity Stocks* (TD/B/C.1/166/Supp. 1), 12 December 1974; United Nations, Conference on Trade and Development, *An Integrated Programme for Commodities: The Role of International Commodity Stocks* (TD/B/C.1/ 166/Supp. 1/Add. 1); United Nations, Conference on Trade and Development, *An Integrated Programme for Commodities: A Common Fund for the Financing of Commodity Stocks* (TD/B/C.1/166/Supp. 2); Ursula Wasserman, "Commodities: An Integrated Approach," *Journal of World Trade Law* 9 (1975): 584; Ursula Wasserman, "Multi-Commodity Approach to International Agreements," *Journal of World Trade Law* 9 (1975): 463.

3.   Edwin Cowan, "U.S. Strategy to Tempt OPEC Members to Cut Oil Prices Urged by Professor," *New York Times,* 15 September 1975, p. 27; "House Takes Up Energy Tax Bill, Backs Import Quota and Rejects Buying Agency," *Wall Street Journal,* 11 June 1975, p. 2.

4.   Bernard Gwertzman, "Kissinger Unveils U.S. Plan to Spur New Fuel Sources," *New York Times,* 4 February 1975, p. 1; Anthony J. Parisi, "Commentary/Energy: The Case Against a Price Floor for Oil," *Business Week* no. 2376 (14 April 1975): 51.

5.   Neil Ulman, "Algeria Suggests the Oil Conference Hold 'Parallel' Talks on Other Raw Materials," *Wall Street Journal,* 9 April 1975, p. 7; "Paris Energy Talks at Impasse; U.S. and Algeria Lead Factions," *New York Times,* 15 April 1975, 46.

6.   "Excerpts From Kissinger's Address to the U.N. Assembly by Moynihan," *New York Times,* 2 September 1975, p. 20; "U.S. to Ask Nations for Grain Reserve," *New York Times,* 25 September 1975, p. 51.

7.   "Preamble and Excerpts from U.N. Summary of Development Text," *New York Times,* 17 September 1975, p. 10.

8.   Clyde H. Farnsworth, "France Invites 27 Lands to Meet on Economic Ills," *New York Times,* 16 September 1975, p. 1.

9.   Barrington Moore, Jr., *Reflections on the Causes of Human Misery and Upon Certain Proposals to Eliminate Them* (Boston: Beacon Press, 1970), p. 53.

10.   Richard F. Janssen, "Commodity Cushion: Common Market Devises Plan to Stabilize Developing Countries' Export Revenues," *Wall Street Journal,* 24 March 1976, p. 36.

11.   United Nations, Department of Economic and Social Affairs, *The Impact of Multinational Corporations on Development and on International Relations* (E/5500/ Rev. 1, ST/ESA/6), 1974, pp. 52–54.

12. United Nations, Economic and Social Council, Commission on Transnational Corporations: *Report on the First Session (17–28 March 1975), Supplement no. 12* (E/5655/E/C.10/6), 1975, p. 1.

13. United Nations, Department of Economic and Social Affairs, *Multinational Corporations in World Development* (ST/ECA/190), 1973, p. 87; United Nations, Department of Economic and Social Affairs, *Summary of the Hearings Before the Group of Eminent Persons to Study the Impact of Multinational Corporations on Development and on International Relations* (ST/ESA/15), 1974, p. 93.

14. George W. Ball, "Cosmocorp: The Importance of Being Stateless," *Columbia Journal of Business* 2 (November–December 1967): 25–30; George W. Ball, "The Need for International Arrangements: G. W. B. : Proposal for an International Charter," in *Global Companies: The Political Economy of World Business,* ed. George W. Ball (Englewood Cliffs, N.J.: Prentice-Hall, American Assembly, 1975), pp. 170–171.

15. Seymour J. Rubin, "Corporations and Society: The Remedy of Federal and International Incorporation," *American University Law Review* 23 (Winter 1973): 295–300.

16. Paul M. Goldberg and Charles P. Kindleberger, "Toward a GATT for Investment: A Proposal for Supervision of the International Corporation," *Law and Policy in International Business* 2 (Summer 1970): 318.

17. Richard D. Robinson, "The Developing Countries, Development and the Multinational Corporation," *Annals of the American Academy of Political and Social Science* 403 (September 1972): 78–79.

18. Eugene V. Rostow, "The Need for International Arrangements: E. V. R.: The Need for a Treaty," in *Global Companies: The Political Economy of World Business,* ed. George W. Ball (Englewood Cliffs, N.J.: Prentice-Hall, American Assembly, 1975), pp. 160–161.

19. U.N., Economic and Social Council, *Report on the First Session,* pp. 9–10, 18–22.

20. U.N., Department of Economic and Social Affairs, *Summary of Hearings,* pp. 174–175.

21. Anthony M. Solomon, "International Control of Investment in the Trade Sector," in *International Control of Investment: The Düsseldorf Conference on Multinational Corporations,* ed. Don Wallace (New York: Praeger, 1974), p. 20; U.N., Department of Economic and Social Affairs, *Impact of Multinational Corporations,* pp. 86–87.

22. U.N., Department of Economic and Social Affairs, *Impact of Multinational Corporations,* pp. 56, 89; Constanino Vaitsos, "Comment," in *International Control of Investment: The Düsseldorf Conference on Multinational Corporations,* ed. Don Wallace (New York: Praeger, [1974]), pp. 127–128.

23. United Nations, Conference on Trade and Development, *An International Code of Conduct on Transfer of Technology* (TD/B/C.6/AC.1/2/Supp. 1/Rev. 1), 1975.

24. United Nations, Conference on Trade and Development, Trade and Development Board, Committee on Transfer of Technology, *Report of the Intergovernmental Group of Experts on a Code of Conduct on Transfer Technology on its Resumed Session* (TD/B/C.6/14), 8 January 1976.

25. U.N., Department of Economic and Social Affairs, *Impact of Multinational Corporations,* p. 56; United Nations, Department of Economic and Social Affairs, *The Acquisition of Technology from Multinational Corporations by Developing Countries* (ST/ESA/12, 1974), p. 45.

26. United Nations, Department of Economic and Social Affairs, *Impact of Multinational Corporations on Development and on International Relations: Technical Papers: Taxation* (ST/ESA/11), 1974; Vernon, *Sovereignty at Bay,* p. 276

27. C. Fred Bergsten, "Coming Investment Wars?" *Foreign Affairs* 53 (October 1974): 141–142.

28.   U.N., Department of Economic and Social Affairs, *Multinational Corporations*, p. 81, n. 15; Lionel M. Summers, "The Calvo Clause," *Virginia Law Review* 19 (March 1933): 459–484.

29.   Detlev Vagts, "Formal and Structural Problems of International Organization for Control of Investment," in *International Control of Investment: The Düsseldorf Conference on Multinational Corporations,* ed. Don Wallace (New York: Praeger, [1974]), pp. 235–245.

30.   International Centre for Settlement of Investment Disputes, International Bank for Reconstruction and Development, *Convention on the Settlement of Investment Disputes between States and Nationals of Other States* (ICSID/2), 14 October 1966; Paul C. Szasz, "The Investment Disputes and Latin America," *Virginia Journal of International Law* 11 (1971): 256–265.

31.   "Bauxite Tax Testing Arbitration Unit," *New York Times,* 2 October 1975, p. 61.

32.   Vaitsos, "Comment," pp. 127–128, 130.

33.   "Excerpts from Kissinger Address to U.N. Conference on Trade and Development," *New York Times,* 7 May 1976, p. A12.

34.   United Nations, Conference on Trade and Development, Secretariat, *Transfer of Technology Action to Strengthen the Technological Capacity of Developing Countries: Policy and Institutions* (TD/190/Supp. 1), May 1976, pp. 37–38.

35.   United Nations, Economic and Social Council, Commission on Transnational Corporations, *Report on the Second Session (1–12 March 1976), Supplement no. 5* (E/5782, E/C.10/16), 1976; United Nations, Economic and Social Council, Commission on Transnational Corporations, Secretariat, *Information on Transnational Corporations, Preliminary Report* (E/C.10/11), 23 January 1976.

36.   U.N., Conference on Trade and Development, *Transfer of Technology* (TD/190/Supp. 1), p. 42.

37.   U.N., Department of Economic and Social Affairs, *Impact of Multinational Corporations,* p. 74.

38.   Ibid., p. 107; Organization for Economic Cooperation and Development (OECD), USA–Business and Industry Advisory Committee, Committee on International Investment and Multinational Enterprise, "Review of the Report of the Group of Eminent Persons to Study the Role of the Multinational Corporations on Development and on International Relations," November 1974, pp. 18–19, 25–26.

CHAPTER 12: EFFORTS TO CONTROL MULTINATIONAL FIRMS

1.   Working Party for Multinational Firms, "Multinational Firms–Swedish Viewpoints," *Current Sweden* no. 80 (July 1975): 2; Sven Ersman and Torsten Garlund, "In Sweden, Investment Abroad Is a Moral Issue," *Columbia Journal of World Business* 5 (January–February 1970): 26–32.

2.   Lewis D. Solomon and Leslie G. Linville, "Transnational Conduct of American Multinational Corporations: Questionable Payments Abroad," *Boston College Industrial and Commercial Law Review* 17 (March 1976): 303; Edwin L. Dale, "Ford Seeking to Require Report of Payouts Abroad," *New York Times,* 4 August 1976, p. 1.

3.   "OECD Plans Tougher Code on Bribery for Multinationals Than Stated Earlier," *Wall Street Journal,* 27 May 1976, p. 12; "Excerpts from O.E.C.D. Text on Conduct Code," *New York Times,* 27 May 1976.

4.   "U.S. Ends Duties on Some Products from 'Less Developed' Lands," *New York Times,* 25 November 1975, p. 5; "Venezuelans Assail U.S. Trade Act," *New York Times,* 27 November 1975, p. 59.

5.   "Excerpts from Kissinger's Address to the U.N. Assembly by Moynihan," *New York Times,* 2 September 1975, p. 20.

6.   Michael T. Kaufman, "Kissinger Offers Program to Help Poor Lands Grow," *New York Times,* 7 May 1976, p. 1.

7. Edwin L. Dale, "Poor Lands Raise I.M.F. Borrowing," *New York Times*, 12 April 1976, p. 45.

8. Trilateral Commission, Task Force on Relations with Developing Countries, *OPEC, The Trilateral World, and the Developing Countries: New Arrangements for Cooperation, 1976-1980* (New York: Triangle Papers no. 7, 1975), pp. 11, 13, 15, 19; Trilateral Commission, Task Force on Relations with Developing Countries, *A Turning Point in North-South Economic Relations* (New York: Triangle Papers no. 3, 1974), pp. 9, 13, 16-17.

9. "Preamble and Excerpts from U.N. Summary of Development Text," *New York Times*, 17 September 1975, p. 10.

10. Bernard Weinraub, "Sweden Meets Third World Aid Goal," *New York Times*, 27 October 1975, p. 4.

11. David H. Blake, "Trade Unions and the Challenge of the Multinational Corporations," *The Annals of the American Academy of Political and Social Science* 403 (September 1972): 36-37; U.N., Department of Economic and Social Affairs, *Impact of Multinational Corporations*, pp. 77-79.

12. International Labour Organization, *Multinational Enterprises and Social Policy* (Geneva: International Labour Office, An ILO Publication on Multinational Enterprises, 1973), pp. 90, 146.

13. Christopher Tugendhat, *The Multinationals* (London: Eyre and Spottiswoode, 1971), p. 185.

14. U.N., Department of Economic and Social Affairs, *Multinational Corporations*, p. 79; International Labour Organization, *Multinational Corporations*, pp. 96-99; Blake, "Trade Unions," pp. 34-45; Nat Weinberg, "The Multinational Corporation and Labor," in *The New Sovereigns: Multinational Corporations as World Powers*, ed. Abdul A. Said and Luiz R. Simmons (Englewood Cliffs, N.J.: Prentice-Hall, 1975), pp. 96-99; Richard R. Janssen, "Global Clout—How One Man Helps Unions Match Wits with Multinationals," *Wall Street Journal*, 17 June 1974, p. 1; Ed Townsend, "Unions Hope for World Front in Disputes with Multinationals," *Christian Science Monitor*, 18 November 1975, p. 1.

15. International Labour Organization, *Multinational Enterprises*, pp. 90, 146.

16. Ibid., pp. 67-68.

17. Ibid., p. 103; Weinberg, "Multinational Corporation," pp. 93-95; Blake, "Trade Unions," pp. 44-45; William J. Curtin, "The Multinational Corporation and Transnational Collective Bargaining," in *American Labor and the Multinational Corporation*, ed. Duane Kujawa, with a foreword by Robert G. Hawkins (New York: Praeger, 1971), pp. 203-215.

18. Adolf Sturmthal, "The Changing Role of the International Labour Organization," *Monthly Labor Review* 93 (May 1970): 41-46; International Labour Organization, *Multinational Enterprises*, p. 148; U.N., Department of Economic and Social Affairs, *Impact of Multinational Corporations*, p. 76.

CHAPTER 13: AN ASSESSMENT OF
THE NEW TRANSNATIONAL ORDER

1. Keith Griffin, *Underdevelopment in Spanish America: An Interpretation* (Cambridge: M.I.T. Press, [1969]), pp. 269-270.

2. Robert W. Tucker, "Egalitarianism and International Politics," *Commentary* 60 (July 1975): 86-87.

3. Theodore H. Moran, "Foreign Expansion as an 'Institutional Necessity' for U.S. Corporate Capitalism: The Search for a Radical Model," *World Politics* 2 (April 1973): 386, 284.

4. Thomas E. Weisskopf, "Capitalism, Socialism, and the Sources of Imperialism with a Commentary by Harry Magdoff," in *Testing Theories of Economic Imperialism*

ed. Steven J. Rosen and James R. Kurth (Lexington, Mass.: D.C. Heath, Lexington Books, 1974).

5.   Frantz Fanon, *The Wretched of the Earth,* with a preface by Jean-Paul Sartre, trans. Constance Farrington (New York: Grove Press, 1968), pp. 35–103.

6.   Robert W. Tucker, "Oil: The Issue of American Intervention," *Commentary* 59 (January 1975): 21; Robert W. Tucker, "Further Reflections on Oil and Force," *Commentary* 59 (March 1975): 45; I. F. Stone, "War for Oil?" *New York Review of Books* 51 (6 February 1975): 7–8.

7.   Kwame Nkrumah, *Neo-Colonialism: The Last Stage of Imperialism* (New York: International Publishers, [1966]), p. 256.

CHAPTER 14: TRANSNATIONAL CONFLICT AND THE ORIGINS OF THE I C P

1.   Robert J. Ledogar, *U.S. Food and Drug Multinationals In Latin America: Hungry for Profits,* with an introduction by Ralph Nader (New York: IDOC/North America, 1975).

2.   D. Redlhammer, interview at Hoëchst A. G. in Frankfurt, West Germany, 16 May 1975; J. Rosner, interview at Hoëchst A. G. in Frankfurt, West Germany, 16 May 1975; Ray Vicker, *This Hungry World* (New York: Charles Scribner's Sons, 1975), pp. 224–225.

3.   Abraham Maslow and John J. Honigmann, "Synergy: Some Notes of Ruth Benedict," with an introduction by Margaret Mead, *American Anthropologist* 72 (April 1970): 320–333; Abraham Maslow, *The Further Reaches of Human Nature* (New York: The Viking Press, 1971), ch. 14.

4.   V. E. Gale, interview at ICP in Rome, Italy, 20 May 1976.

5.   United Nations, Food and Agriculture Organization, Industry Cooperative Programme, Secretariat, *Multinational Enterprise and the Developing World: The Role of the Industry Cooperative Programme (I.C.P.)* (WS/E/ 1068), July 1973, p. 2; United Nations, Food and Agriculture Organization, Industry Cooperative Programme, *Regulations of the General Committee* (DDI:G/74/30), 1973, p. 2.

6.   U.N., Food and Agriculture Organization, *Regulations,* pp. 3–6.

CHAPTER 15: ANALYSIS OF GENERAL ACTIVITIES OF THE I C P

1.   J. F. P. Tate, interview at Tate and Lyle, Ltd., in London, United Kingdom, 5 May 1976.

2.   Sir George Bishop, interview in London, United Kingdom, 4 May 1976.

3.   Aaron S. Yohalem, interview at CPC International, Inc., in Englewood Cliffs, New Jersey, 25 May 1976.

4.   Alan J. Maier, interview at Imperial Chemical Industries, Ltd., in Haslemere, United Kingdom, 7 May 1976.

5.   J. I. Hendrie, interview in London, United Kingdom, 6 May 1976; A. Bodmer, interview at Ciba-Geigy A. G. in Basle, Switzerland, 19 May 1976; H. A. R. Powell, interview at Massey-Ferguson Holdings, Ltd., in London, United Kingdom, 4 May 1976.

6.   E. A. Asselbergs, interview at FAO in Rome, Italy, 20 May 1976.

7.   Alan J. Maier, interview; V. E. Gale, interview at ICP in Rome, Italy, 21 May 1976; W. W. Simons, interview at ICP at the United Nations in New York, New York, 23 May 1976.

8.   Alan J. Maier, interview; J. I. Hendrie, interview.

9.   Cooperative Programme of Agro-Allied Industries with FAO and other United Nations Organizations, *Pesticides in the Modern World* (London: Newgate Press, 1972).

10. W. W. Simons, interview.
11. United Nations, World Food Conference, *Consultation with Agro-Industrial Leaders 10-11 September 1974, Toronto, Canada* (E/CONF. 65/NGO/1), 2 November 1974, pp. 4-5, 11-12.
12. W. W. Simons, interview.
13. Ibid.
14. Arnold Robinson, interview at Fisons, Ltd., in London, United Kingdom, 6 May 1976; Edwin Wheeler, interview at the Fertilizer Institute, Washington, D.C., 2 June 1976.
15. Alan J. Maier, interview.
16. W. W. Simons, interview; Alan J. Maier, interview; Brian W. Cox, interview at Imperial Chemical Industries, Ltd., in Haslemere, United Kingdom, 7 May 1976.
17. United Nations, World Food Conference, *Report of the World Food Conference, Rome, 5-16 November 1974* (E/CONF. 65/20), 1975, p. 42.
18. Ibid., p. 12.
19. W. W. Simons, interview; Alan J. Maier, interview; Brian W. Cox, interview.
20. Ibid.,
21. United Nations, Food and Agriculture Organization, *Report of the Ad Hoc Government Consultation on Pesticides in Agriculture and Public Health* (AGP: 1975/M/3), 7-11 April 1975, pp. 10, 19.
22. W. W. Simons, interview.
23. U.N., Food and Agriculture Organization, *Pesticides in Agriculture and Public Health*, p. 86.

CHAPTER 16 : ANALYSIS OF SPECIFIC ACTIVITIES OF THE I C P

1. J. I. Hendrie, "The U.N./Industry Cooperative Programme," *Span: Progress in Agriculture* 15 (1972): 38.
2. J. I. Hendrie, interview in London, United Kingdom, 6 May 1976; A. V. Adam, interview at FAO in Rome, Italy, 21 May 1976; A. Bodmer, interview at Ciba-Geigy A. G. in Basle, Switzerland, 19 May 1976; Alan J. Maier, interview at Imperial Chemical Industries, Ltd., in Haslemere, United Kingdom, 7 May 1976.
3. J. I. Hendrie, interview; A. V. Adam, interview.
4. A. V. Adam, interview; Alan J. Maier, interview; United Nations, Food and Agriculture Organization, Industry Cooperative Programme, *Fourteenth Session of the Pesticides Working Group (PWG)* (DDI:G/76/8), 1976.
5. A. A. Bouwes, interview at Cooperatieve Condensfabriek "Friesland" in Leeuwarden, the Netherlands, 13 May 1976.
6. Ibid.
7. H. A. R. Powell, interview at Massey-Ferguson Holdings, Ltd., in London, United Kingdom, 4 May 1975; V. E. Gale, interview at ICP in Rome, Italy, 20 May 1976.
8. Sir George Bishop, interview in London, United Kingdom, 4 May 1976.
9. E. Bignami, Memorandum to Members of the Working Party on Programme Objectives, Industry Cooperative Programme, 30 July 1971.
10. A. Goedhart, interview at H. V. A. in Amsterdam, the Netherlands, 12 May 1976; A. Bodmer, interview at Ciba-Geigy A. G. in Basle, Switzerland, 19 May 1976.
11. Hector Watts, interview at B. P. Proteins, Ltd., in London, United Kingdom, 6 May 1976.
12. B. Gardner-McTaggart, interview at ICP in Rome, Italy, 20 May 1976.
13. V. A. Jafarey to Lewis D. Solomon, 13 April 1976.
14. United Nations, Food and Agriculture Organization, Industry Cooperative Programme, *ICP Mission to Pakistan* (MR/F9144/E/5175/1/500), 12-22 May 1974, pp. 2-3.

15.   J. I. Hendrie, interview; A. A. Bouwes, interview; U.N. Food and Agriculture Organization, *Mission to Pakistan*, pp. 4–5.
16.   A. A. Bouwes, interview; U.N., Food and Agriculture Organization, *Mission to Pakistan*, p. 8.
17.   J. I. Hendrie, interview.
18.   A. A. Bouwes, interview; J. I. Hendrie, interview.
19.   Syed Sarfraz Ali to Lewis D. Solomon, 17 April 1976.
20.   U.N., Food and Agriculture Organization, *Mission to Pakistan*, pp. 12–22, J. I. Hendrie, interview.
21.   U.N., Food and Agriculture Organization, *Mission to Pakistan*.
22.   Pakistan, "Policy towards Foreign Private Investment," n.d., pp. 1–2.
23.   United Nations, Food and Agriculture Organization, Cooperative Programme of Agro-Allied Industries, Industry Cooperative Programme, Draft Annual Report of the Industry Cooperative Programme (DDI:G/76/15), March 1975 to February 1976.
24.   Syed Sarfraz Ali to Lewis D. Solomon, 17 April 1976.
25.   United Nations, Food and Agriculture Organization, Industry Cooperative Programme, *ICP Mission to Sri Lanka (Ceylon)* (MR/D2825/10.72/E/2/600), 24 September–3 October 1972, pp. 3–5.
26.   W. DeJonge, interview at Philips in Eindhoven, the Netherlands, 12 May 1976.
27.   Kasturi Rangan, "Sri Lanka, Economy Ailing, Pushes Nationalization," *New York Times*, 13 October 1975, p. 41; B. H. S. Jayewardene, "Sri Lanka: Colombo Relents," *Far Eastern Economic Review* 84 (24 June 1974): 65–66.
28.   Leslie Herath to Lewis D. Solomon, 5 April 1976.
29.   Ibid.
30.   United Nations, Food and Agriculture Organization, Industry Cooperative Programme, *ICP Mission to Cameroon* (MR/E2257/E/2.74/2/100), 7–21 June 1973, pp. 1–2.
31.   Jacques Bertrand, interview in Paris, France, 14 May 1976.
32.   Louis Turner, "Multinationals, The United Nations and Development," *Columbia Journal of World Business* 7 (September–October 1972): 16–17.
33.   Ibid.
34.   W. W. Simons to J. A. C. Hugill, 25 October 1973.
35.   F. E. Agnew, telephone interview, 15 April 1976.
36.   Robert B. Norman to Lewis D. Solomon, 14 June 1976.
37.   W. W. Simons to J. A. C. Hugill, 25 October 1973.
38.   C. E. Gillett, interview in London, United Kingdom, 4 May 1976; W. W. Simons to J. A. C. Hugill, 25 October 1973.
39.   John Tate to Lewis D. Solomon, 2 June 1976; W. W. Simons to J. A. C. Hugill, 25 October 1973, J. F. P. Tate, interview at Tate and Lyle, Ltd., in London, United Kingdom, 6 May 1976.
40.   Ibid.
41.   Ibid.; see United Nations Development Programme, *Global Research: Research on Single Cell Proteins from Carob Beans: Toxicological and Nutritional Animal Testing Scheme of Fungal Protein Grown on Carob Bean Extract* (DP/GLO/Final Report/3, GLO/71/003), 1976, pp. 4–5.
42.   U.N. Development Programme, *Global Research*, p. 2.
43.   Alan Berg, *The Nutrition Factor: Its Role in National Development* (Washington: Brookings Institution, 1973), pp. 146–147.
44.   Melvin Bandle, interview at World Food Systems, Inc., in Washington, D.C., 5 June 1976; Martin Forman, "Barriers to Initiating Food Delivery Systems," *The Professional Nutritionist* 7 (Fall 1975): 14–17.
45.   Melvin Bandle, interview; Edwin M. Martin, interview in Washington, D.C., 4 June 1976; A. S. Yohalem, interview at CPC International, Inc., in Englewood Cliffs, New Jersey, 25 May 1976.

46. United Nations, World Food Conference, Industry Cooperative Programme, *Consultation with Agro-Industrial Leaders in Preparation for U.N. World Food Conference*, 10–11 September 1974 (WS/F 2313), 1974.
47. A. S. Yohalem, interview; W. W. Simons, interview; Guy Knapton, interview in Paris, France, 10 May 1976.
48. W. W. Simons, interview; Guy Knapton, interview.

CHAPTER 17: THE FUTURE OF THE ICP

1. George L. Beckford, *Persistent Poverty: Underdevelopment in Plantation Economies of the Third World* (New York: Oxford University Press, 1972).
2. Sir George Bishop, interview in London, United Kingdom, 4 May 1976; J. F. P. Tate, interview in London, United Kingdom. Dr. A. Goedhart, interview in Amsterdam, the Netherlands, 12 May 1976.
3. The World Bank, *Uses of Consultants by the World Bank and Its Borrowers* (Washington, D.C.: World Bank, 1974), pp. 1–2.
4. Donald Pickering, interview at the World Bank in Washington, D.C., March 1976; The World Bank Group, *Policies and Operations* (Washington, D.C.: World Bank, 1974), pp. 53–54.
5. World Bank, *Uses of Consultants*, p. 12.
6. Ibid., p. 4.
7. Donald Pickering, interview.
8. Imprese Italiane All'estro (Impresit), "Note on a New Approach to Agricultural Projects," 30 September 1975; Graham T. Allison, *Essence of Decision Explaining the Cuban Missile Crisis* (Boston: Little, Brown and Co., 1971), pp. 81–87.
9. United Nations, Food and Agriculture Organization, Industry Cooperative Programme, General Committee, *FIAT S.p.A. Delegation Report* (no number), 18 February 1976.
10. U.N., Food and Agriculture Organization, FIAT S.p.A., pp. 3–6; Impresit, "New Approach"; V. Bonisconti, interview at Fiat in Turin, Italy, 15 May 1976.
11. See Harry Magdoff, *The Age of Imperialism: The Economics of U.S. Foreign Policy* (New York: Monthly Review Press, 1969), pp. 122–144; Teresa Hayter, *Aid as Imperialism* (Baltimore: Penguin Books, 1971), pp. 87–98; Marina von Neuman Whitman, *Government Risk-Sharing in Foreign Investment* (Princeton, N.J.: Princeton University Press, 1965).
12. W. A. DeJonge, interview in Eindhoven, the Netherlands, 12 May 1976.
13. Ibid.
14. United Nations, World Food Conference, Industry Cooperative Programme, *Discussion Papers for Consultation with Agro-Industrial Leaders, 9–11 September 1974, Toronto, Canada* (no number), 1974; Paul Cornelson, interview in St. Louis, Missouri, 9 August 1976.
15. Ad Hoc Panel of the Board on Science and Technology for International Development Commission on International Relations, *Systems Analysis and Operations Research: A Tool for Policy and Program Planning for Developing Countries* (Washington, D.C.: National Academy of Sciences, 1976), p. 9.
16. J. I. Hendrie, interview in London, United Kingdom, 6 May 1976.
17. Graham Williams, interview in Washington, D.C., 1 June 1976; Oversea Private Investment Corporation, "Annual Report, 1975," p. 25; R. W. Mist to Lewis D. Solomon, 7 July 1976.
18. John Botts, interview in London, United Kingdom, 3 May 1976.
19. J. I. Hendrie, interview.
20. "Business Brief: How to Feed the Third World," *Economist* 254 (22 March 1975): 72–73.
21. "Text of Resolution," *U.N. Chronicle* 12 (October 1975): 12.
22. United Nations, Food and Agriculture Organization, Industry Cooperative

Programme, *Summary Report of the Third Session of the ICP Task Force on Food Loss Prevention* (DDI:G/76/19); V. E. Gale, interview in Rome, Italy, 20 May 1976.
23.   United Nations, Food and Agriculture Organization, *Reducing Post-Harvest Food Losses in Developing Countries* (AGPP: MISC/21), 1975, pp. 4, 9.
24.   Ibid., p. 4.
25.   United Nations, World Food Conference, *Consultation with Agro-Industrial Leaders: Discussion Paper for Agenda Item 4a, Total Crop Utilisation,* by Tate and Lyle, Ltd. (MPP 74/a), 8 September 1974, pp. 10–12.
26.   Sterling Wortman, interview in New York, New York, 27 May 1976; Sterling Wortman, "Extending the Green Revolution," *World Development* 1 (December 1973) 45; Sterling Wortman, *The World Food Situation: A New Initiative,* prepared for U.S. Congress, House, Subcommittee on Science, Research and Technology and on Domestic and International Scientific Planning and Analysis (New York: Rockefeller Foundation, 1975), pp. 22–24.
27.   Sterling Wortman, "The Technological Basis for Intensified Agriculture," p. 4; Nicholas Wade, "International Agricultural Research," in *Food: Politics, Economics, Nutrition, Research,* ed. Philip A. Abelson (Washington, D.C.: American Association for the Advancement of Science, 1975), pp. 91–95.
28.   United Nations, Food and Agriculture Organization, *Report on the Expert Consultation on Seed Industry Development, Second Meeting* (AGP:SIDP/75/Rep. 2), 1–5 December 1975, pp. 4–5.
29.   Ibid., p. 1.
30.   J. I. Hendrie, interview; United Nations, World Food Conference, Industry Cooperative Programme, *Consultation with Agro-Industrial Leaders in Preparation for UN World Food Conference (WFC): Agenda Item 4(a): Seed Production and Plant Breeders' Rights,* (WS/F2337), 10–11 September 1974, p. 2.
31.   U.N., World Food Conference, *Seed Production and Plant Breeders' Rights.*
32.   U.N., World Food Conference, Organization, *Expert Consultation on Seed Industry,* p. 8.
33.   Conference Board, *Special Report: Food and Population: The Next Crisis* (New York: Conference Board, 1974).
34.   Erik A. Erikson, *Childhood and Society* (New York: W. W. Norton, 1950); Gail Sheehy, *Passages: Predictable Crises of Adult Life* (New York: E. P. Dutton & Co., 1976), ch. 20.

CHAPTER 18: ASSESSMENT OF MULTINATIONAL AGRIBUSINESS CORPORATIONS IN DEVELOPING NATIONS

1.   A. S. Yohalem, interview in Englewood Cliffs, New Jersey, 25 May 1976; Massey-Ferguson, *The Pace and Form Mechanizations in the Developing Countries: A Study* (Toronto: Massey-Ferguson, 1974), p. 15; Sterling Wortman, "Strategy for the Alleviation of World Hunger," speech presented at the University of Rochester, 12 April 1976, pp. 18–19.
2.   Keith Griffin, *The Political Economy of Agrarian Change: An Essay on the Green Revolution* (London: Macmillan, 1974), p. 51–78; Francine R. Frankel, *India's Green Revolution: Economic Gains and Political Costs* (Princeton, N.J.: Princeton University Press, 1971), pp. 191–194, 198; Keith Griffin, *The Green Revolution: An Economic Analysis* (Geneva: United Nations Research Institute for Social Development, 1972); Wolf Ladejinsky, "Ironies of India's Green Revolution," *Foreign Affairs* 48 (July 1970): 758–768; Walter P. Falcon, "The Green Revolution: Second Generation of Problems," *American Journal of Agricultural Economics* 52 (December 1970): 705–707.
3.   Griffin, *Political Economy,* p. 232.
4.   Edgar Owens and Robert Shaw, *Development Reconsidered: Bridging the Gap Between Government and People* (Lexington, Mass.: D. C. Heath, 1972), p. 62.

5.   Continental Bank, International Conference, "Transcript of the Proceedings, Feeding the World's Hungry: The Challenge to Business," an International Conference sponsored by Continental Bank, 20 May 1974, p. 89.
6.   H. A. R. Powell, "Nations in Need: Men Replaced by Mechanization," *The* (London) *Times,* 8 April 1976, p. VII.
7.   A. J. Maier, interview in Haslemere, United Kingdom, 7 May 1976; D. Redlhammer, interview in Frankfurt, West Germany, 17 May 1976; Dr. A. Bodmer, interview in Basle, Switzerland, 19 May 1976.
8.   United Nations, Consultative Group on Food Production and Investment in Developing Countries, *Report on the Second Meeting* (FPI/76/1-1), 10–12 February 1976, p. 6; United Nations, Consultative Group on Food Production and Investment in Developing Countries, *Document E: Regional Planning for Fertilizer Industry Development* (FPI/76/1-6), 3 December 1975.
9.   Barry Commoner, *The Closing Circle: Nature, Man and Technology* (New York: A. Knopf, 1971), chs. 5–6; Lester R. Brown, *By Bread Alone* (New York: Praeger, 1974), pp. 449–53; Paul R. Ehrlich and Anne H. Ehrlich, *Population Resources Environment Issues in Human Ecology* (San Francisco: W. H. Freeman, 2d ed., 1972), pp. 220, 223–225, 229–230.
10.   Daniel H. Janzen, "Tropical Agroecosystems: These Habitats are Misunderstood by the Temperate Zones, Mismanaged by the Tropics," *Science* 182 (21 December 1973): 1212, 1215; Lester R. Brown, "The World Food Prospect," *Science* 190 (12 December 1975): 1053, 1059.
11.   David Pimentel, and others, "Food Production and the Energy Crises," *Science* 182 (2 November 1973): 443, 448.
12.   Dr. V. Bonisconti, interview in Turin, Italy, 15 May 1976.
13.   United Nations, Food and Agriculture Organization, Industry Cooperative Programme, *First Meeting of the Steering Group on Farm Mechanization* (DDI:B/ 74/70), 1974, p. 2.
14.   Marc Parsons to Lewis D. Solomon, 25 June 1976.
15.   E. F. Schumacher, *Small is Beautiful* (New York: Harper & Row, 1973), pt. 3, chs. 2–3; E. F. Schumacher, "The Work of the Intermediate Technology Development Group in Africa," *International Labour Review* 106 (July 1972): 75.
16.   D. J. Greenland, "Bringing the Green Revolution to the Shifting Cultivator," *Science* 190 (28 November 1975): 841–844.
17.   United Nations, World Food Conference, Industry Cooperative Programme, *Consultation with Agro-Industrial Leaders in Preparation for UN World Food Conference (WFC): ICP Mission to Pakistan* (WS/F2426), May 1974, p. 4.
18.   Owens and Shaw, *Development Reconsidered,* pp. 59–61; Brown, *By Bread Alone,* p. 214.
19.   United Nations, World Food Conference, *Consultation with Agro-Industrial Leaders: Attracting International Resources to Developing Country Agriculture,* 9–11 September 1974, p. 2.
20.   Commonwealth Development Corporation, *Report and Accounts 1975* (London, Commonwealth Development Corporation, 1975), p. 8; A. Wadey, interview at Commonwealth Development Corp. in London, United Kingdom, 3 May 1976.
21.   J. David Morrissy, *Agriculture Modernization Through Production Contracting: The Role of the Fruit and Vegetable Processor in Mexico and Central America* (New York: Praeger, 1974), chs. 3–5; Ray A. Goldberg and others, *Agribusiness Management for Developing Countries–Latin America* (Cambridge, Mass.: Ballinger, 1974), p. 144.
22.   U. S. Department of Agriculture, Packers and Stockyards Administration, *The Broiler Industry: An Economic Study of Structure, Practices and Problems* (Packers and Stockyards Administration, August 1967), pp. 47, 55–68.
23.   Ewell P. Roy, *Contract Farming and Economic Integration* (Danville, Ill.: Interstate Printers and Publishers, 2d ed. [1972]), p. 629.

24. Thomas T. Poleman, "World Food: A Perspective," *Science* 188 (9 May 1975): 510–518.

25. Orville L. Freeman, speech presented at Business International Corporation, Conference on "New Structures for Economic Independence," United Nations Headquarters, 15 May 1975.

INDEX